Calcutta

INSIGHT *City* GUIDES

Produced and Edited by Michel Vatin
Editorial Director: Geoffrey Eu

APA
PUBLICATIONS

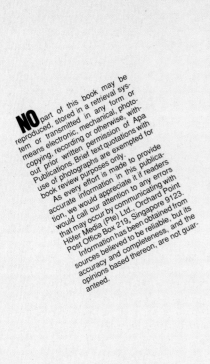

No part of this book may be reproduced, stored in a retrieval system or transmitted in any form or means electronic, mechanical, photocopying, recording or otherwise, without prior written permission of Apa Publications. Brief text quotations with use of photographs are exempted for book review purposes only.
As every effort is made to provide accurate information in this publication, we would appreciate it if readers would call our attention to any errors that may occur by communicating with Höfer Media (Pte) Ltd., Orchard Point Post Office Box 219, Singapore 9123. Information has been obtained from sources believed to be reliable, but its accuracy and completeness, and the opinions based thereon, are not guaranteed.

Calcutta

First Edition
© **1991 APA PUBLICATIONS (HK) LTD**
All Rights Reserved
Printed in Singapore by Höfer Press Pte. Ltd

ABOUT THIS BOOK

Calcutta celebrated her 300 years in 1990. With her splendid decaying palaces, her communities from all over the Subcontinent, her festivals throughout the year and her *joie de vivre*, she is one of the liveliest and warmest cities in India. Few visitors however come to Calcutta. They are discouraged by her much-exaggerated negative image abroad, and when they are in India, non-Calcuttans advise them not to include the city in their itineraries as it is a fact that Calcutta's strong personality and fascinating beauty generates jealousy and resentment in the rest of the country. Put together by a group of Calcuttans and foreigners who have lived in the city and have loved it, *Cityguide: Calcutta* hopes to contribute to the repairing of the injustice done to Calcutta.

The Right Staff

Project Editor **Michel Vatin** has been living in India, China and Southeast Asia for over 10 years and has contributed to the *Insight Guides* to *Indonesia* and *India*. He also took some of the photographs in this book. To produce the guide, Vatin put together a team of leading figures in Calcutta, who are also long-time resident friends.

A former tour operator in Calcutta, **Sumanta Bannerjee** helped as a sub-editor to start the book. He also wrote the article on sports in Calcutta.

A graduate of Calcutta University and of the Chelsea School of Arts, **Ruby Palchoudhuri** is a leading figure in India in the field of folklore and handicrafts. She organized exhibitions of art and traditional handicrafts from Bangal and Eastern India in the United Kingdom, the United States, Germany, France, Japan and the U.S.S.R.. Palchoudhuri is also the author of several books and articles and is the owner of a textile printing and design concern. She contributed to the guide with the texts on the *pujas*, shopping and the performing arts.

The author of the articles on polo and on the tiger of the Sunderbans, **Anne Wright**, the daughter of a member of the defunct Indian Civil Service, was born, raised and married in India. A keen horsewoman and a handicapped polo player, she is a Trustee of the Worldwide Fund for Nature in India. To mark her charity work with the Graham Homes in Kalimpong and on wildlife issues, she was made a member, then an officer, of the Order of the British Empire.

Jit and Bunny Gupta wrote the articles on bazars, and haunted houses and colonial cemeteries. Jit Gupta is a former executive with a major tea house. His wife Bunny is a freelance journalist. Specializing on the history of Calcutta, their prose has appeared in the *Illustrated Weekly of India*, the *Statesman*, the *Telegraph*, *India Traveller*, *Destination India* and *Frontiers*.

The article on the foods of Calcutta is by **Jeannine Siniscal**, a French model turned freelance writer. She contributed articles and photographs to *Insight Guide: India*, various cookbooks and Singapore publications.

Archana Roy, the director of the Birla Academy of Art and Culture, is one of the leading figures on the Calcutta Art scene, organizing numerous exhibitions and art festivals. She is the author of articles on Indian arts and wrote the one on the Birla Art Academy in this guide.

Francoise Imaeda, a longtime resident of

Bannerjee

Palchoudhuri

Jit and Bunny Gupta

Bhutan, is a French Tibetologist who has led tours to Bhutan and Tibet. She works with the Bhutan Tourist Corporation and has published several books and articles on Bhutan and Tibetan religion. She is the author of the text on Bhutan in the present guide. Imaeda is also an editor of *Kuenzel*, Bhutan's weekly newspaper.

Born in Bangladesh, **Puritosh Sen** studied at the Ecole des Beaux-Arts and Ecole in Louvre, Paris. Back in Calcutta, he founded the Calcutta Group in 1947. He is today one of the leading painters of Bengal. He taught at Indore, Calcutta and Baltimore, has published books and articles on art and given talks on the BBC and All-Indian Radio. His works were exhibited in France, the United Kingdom, the United States, Brazil, Cuba, Japan and Australia. He is a member of the Senate of the Vishwa-Bharati University in Santiniketan. He wrote the articles on painting and on graffitti, one of his fascinations in Calcutta.

Sujoy Das, an accountant by profession, is also a free-lance journalist and a photographer. A typical 'Darj Freak', he spends all his free time trekking around Darjeeling and the Himalayas. He has published articles and photographs in the *Statesman*, the *Telegraph*, *Destination India*, *Sawasdee*, and is preparing a book on Sikkim. He is the author of the article on the Eastern Himalayas and of a good number of the photographs appearing in the guide.

R.P. Gupta, a former business executive, has written extensively on Calcutta. He has also published books on such specific subjects as the 'the fish and the Bengalis' or 'the street cries of Calcutta', articles in the *Statesman*, the *Times of India*, as well as an introduction to Raghubir Singh's book of photographs on Calcutta, and the section on the Bengali Babu in this guide.

A painter, a photographer, a journalist and a dancer at the same time, Frenchman **Gilles Massot** contributed to this book with photocollages on the decaying architecture of Calcutta and various photographs. In Asia for over 10 years, Massot has been living in Singapore, Thailand and Calcutta, making frequent and extensive trips all over Asia. He took part in the Fringe Festival of Singapore, has exhibited his works in France, Thailand, Japan, Bangkok and has written in several Asian magazines.

Most of the old prints and postcards for this guide were supplied by **Michael Gélénine**, a French diplomat who has served in Australia, the USSR, Singapore, Calcutta and now lives in China. He also took a number of the photographs appearing in this book.

This book would not have been possible without the *Statesman*, the Victoria Memorial Hall, the Netaji Research Institute, Messrs. J. Thomas and Company, the late **Shirley Rome**, Sheikh Ahmed Siddique, Bob and Anne Wright, the Princely Family of Burdwan, Ranjit Gupta, Christine Renault, Sophie Pastinelli, Tan Guo-pei, Mumtaz Ahmed, Krishna Reddy, Pearson Surita, Sidharta Ghosh, Martine Bannerjee and Yoshiro Imaeda.

– APA Publications

Siniscal

Sen

Das

Massot

CONTENTS

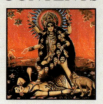

HISTORY AND PEOPLE

- 23 **Decay as an Art Form**
  —by Michel Vatin

- 29 **The History of Calcutta**
  — by Michel Vatin

- 45 **A Mosaic of Communities**
  — by Michel Vatin
  and R.P. Gupta

- 52 **The Chinese of Calcutta**
  — by Michel Vatin

- 61 **The Religions of Calcutta**
  — by Michel Vatin

- 71 **Painting**
  —by Puritosh Sen

- 80 **The Graffitti Capital of the World**
  —by Puritosh Sen

- 86 **Sports**
  —by Sumanta Bannerjee

- 90 **Polo**
  —by Anne Wright

- 97 **Calcutta Non-stop**
  —by Ruby Palchoudhuri
  and Michel Vatin

- 110 **Shopping**
  —by Ruby Palchoudhuri

- 117 **The Foods of Calcutta**
  — by Jeannine Siniscal

PLACES

131 **Introduction to Places**
—by Michel Vatin

137 **The White Town**
—by Michel Vatin

150 **Colonial Cemeteries and Haunted Houses**
—by Jit and Bunny Gupta

155 **Palaces and Bazars**
— by Jit and Bunny Gupta

167 **The Waterfront**
—by Michel Vatin

177 **South Calcutta**
—by Michel Vatin

186 **The Birla Academy of Art and Culture**
—by Archana Roy

193 **Side-trips**
—by Michel Vatin

205 **The Hooghly Heritage**
—by Michel Vatin

215 The Sunderbans and the Delta of the Ganges
—by Michel Vatin

220 The Royal Bengal Tiger of the Sundarbans
—by Anne Wright

225 The Buddhist Sites of Bihar
—by Michel Vatin

231 The Eastern Himalayas
—by Sujoy Das and Francoise Imaeda

MAPS

128 Eastern India
130 Calcutta
136 The Maidan Area
192 Around Calcutta
214 The Western Ganges Delta

TRAVEL TIPS

GETTING THERE
- 242 By Air
- 243 By Rail
- 243 By Road

TRAVEL ESSENTIALS
- 243 Visas & Passports
- 244 Money Matters
- 244 Health
- 245 What to Wear
- 245 What to Bring
- 245 Customs
- 246 Bond Facilities
- 246 Prohibited Articles
- 247 Unaccompanied Baggage
- 247 Export of Articles

GETTING ACQUAINTED
- 247 Time Zones
- 247 Climate
- 248 Culture & Customs
- 248 Weight & Measures
- 248 Electricity
- 248 Business Hours
- 248 Holidays/ Festivals
- 248 Religious Services

COMMUNICATIONS
- 249 Media
- 249 Postal Services/ Telephone & Telex

EMERGENCIES
- 249 Security & Crime
- 250 Medical Services
- 250 24-Hour Medical Shops
- 250 ambulance
- 250 Blood Banks

GETTING AROUND
- 250 Orientation
- 251 Maps
- 251 Public Transport
- 252 Private Transport

WHERE TO STAY
- 252 Hotels
- 253 Youth Hostel

FOOD DIGEST
- 253 Where to Eat

THINGS TO DO
- 256 City
- 256 Country
- 256 Tours Operators
- 257 Tour Guides

CULTURE PLUS
- 257 Museums
- 259 Art Galleries
- 259 Concerts
- 259 Theatres
- 260 Movies

NIGHTLIFE
- 260 Pubs & Bars
- 260 Discos
- 260 Cabarets

SHOPPING
- 260 What to Buy
- 261 Government Emporia

SPORTS
- 262 Clubs

PARKS & RESERVES
- 263 Parks & Gardens

SPECIAL INFORMATION
- 263 Doing Business
- 263 Children
- 264 Pilgrimages
- 264 Photography

LANGUAGE
- 265

FURTHER READING
- 267 General
- 267 People
- 267 Arts
- 268 Culture
- 268 History
- 268 Religions
- 268 Guidebooks
- 269 Outside Calcutta

USEFUL ADDRESSES
- 269 Tourist Information

DECAY AS AN ART FORM

"The most wicked place in the universe" according to one visitor. A city "where the cholera, the cyclone, and the crow come and go, by the sewerage rendered fetid, by the sewer made impure", wrote Kipling. "I shall always be glad to have seen it for the reason that it will be unnecessary for me to see it again," confided Sir Winston Churchill. Negative descriptions of Calcutta abound.

It is true that Calcutta has suffered and the city lets it show. Built for a downtown population of one million, inhabited by over 10 millions, with a floating population of 2 maybe 3 millions, heavily congested with only 6% of its area covered by roads, "chance-erected, chance-directed" as Kipling puts it, flooded by millions of refugees over three occasions in 1947, 1951 and 1971, Calcutta is in an advanced state of decay. Telephones do not work – a memorial to the Dead Telephone has even been erected in the city centre. There are traffic jams, power cuts tactfully called "load-sheddings", floods in the Monsoon. Surprisingly there are less slums than in other cities. The "slum ratio" in Calcutta is 33% of the population against 45% in Bombay, and many slums have actually evolved into groups of brick houses, without proper amenities though.

Against this background of decay and material problems, what strikes is the resilience shown by the city, and its intense life: notwithstanding apocalyptic clichés, Calcutta remains the City of Palaces, the intellectual and cultural capital of India as well as an important centre of economic activity.

Above all Calcutta is the City of Palaces, as it has been known since the 18th century. The trend was set by Lord Wellesley, who had Government House built on the grounds that "India is a country of splendour, of extravagance and of outward appearances: the head of a mighty empire ought to conform himself to the prejudices of the country it rules over. The result is a most impressive display of architecture, the grandest city ever built by Europeans outside Europe. "We felt that we were approaching a great capital", wrote one traveller as early as in the 18th century. "On landing, I was struck with the general appearance of grandeur in all the buildings; not that any of them are according to the strict rules of art, but groups of columns, particoes, domes and fine gateways, interspersed with trees and the broad river crowded with shipping, made the whole picture magnificent."

Calcutta is a standing museum of 300 years of architecture. There is great variety of styles: Bengali Ek-Bangla and Ratna, Palladian, neo-Gothic, Serascenic, neo-Moghul, Art Nouveau, Art Deco, Barocco, neo-Renaissance, Romantic, Medieval, even Bauhaus. The buildings have been more or less well-preserved. Some are

Preceding pages: The Royal Bengal Tiger, in the logo of the Calcutta Transaport Corporation; the ever-busy Sealdah Station flyover; a rickshaw wallah and his calling bell; Calcutta — the capital of graffitti art; chandeliers are rented out for garden parties. **Left**: an example of Calcutta's stunning architecture.

empty, feared haunted, squatted, overgrown with weed, even small trees, others have been restored. All have retained their grandeur and decay only added to it. The variety of colours on is richer, for instance. Fresh layers of ochre, orange, blue, brick-red, yellow, white and off-white paint are washed off by the Mansoon, the bleeding colours combining with layers from previous years to form a wide range of hues and nuances that remind of water colours , the density of buildings, like in Cairo or Shanghai reinforces the impression of beauty created by the decaying monuments. Calcutta is the city where one realises that decay is an art form, a place where one comes to terms, or even falls in love with decay.

Calcutta is also the intellectual capital of India. The main actor, the Bengali, who has been in contact with Western culture for 300 years absorbing many European customs and behaviors. "The last Englishman left in India is the Bengali," wrote Ashoke Mitra, a leading political figure in Calcutta. Western culture, indeed, entered India through Calcutta. The Serampore Press was established by Baptists in 1799, Fort William College in 1800; Macaulay' "Minutes of Education" opened the English system of education to Indians as early as 1835. The Calcutta University was founded in 1857. Eastern cultures came later, in the first quarter of the 20th century. Chinese studies were promoted by Rabindranath Tagore and his friend Tan Yun-Shan, and under the form of a Buddhist revival. This interaction of cultures, gave birth to an elite that first introduced changes in literature, then religion, finally in political life. Thinkers like Bankim Chandra Chatterjee, Michael Madhusudan Dutt, Henry de Rozio, added new genres in Bengali literature and poetry. Rejecting rituals and the cult of the Gods, they launched religious movements, Brahmajism, then the Ramakrishna Math. In the late 19th century the elite became nationalists and pioneered the Independence movement. The Indian Association was founded in 1876, nine years the Indian Congress in Bombay. At the turn of the century the intellectual leadership of calcutta was such that Gopal Krishna Gokhole, the Indian statesman wrote: "What Bengal does today, the rest of India will do tomorrow." In the 20th century, the political leadership was taken away from Calcutta by the Hindi Belt, that is North and Central India. Calcutta remains the cultural and intellectual capital of India. There are non-stop exhibitions, concerts, talks, a book-fair drawing over a million visitors.

In addition, Calcutta is a cosmopolitan city. Communities from all over the subcontinent brought their own cultures, and festivals. Combining with the Bengali Durga and Kali Pujas they make of Calcutta one of the liveliest cities in India.

Decay above all, allied to but intense intellectual and cultural life, non-stop celebrations, a warm population welcoming the visitor – such is Calcutta. The only problem with Calcutta is that it grows on you to an extent that other cities in India seems dull.

Right: a collage of some of Calcutta's buildings, displaying a fascinating variety of architectural styles.

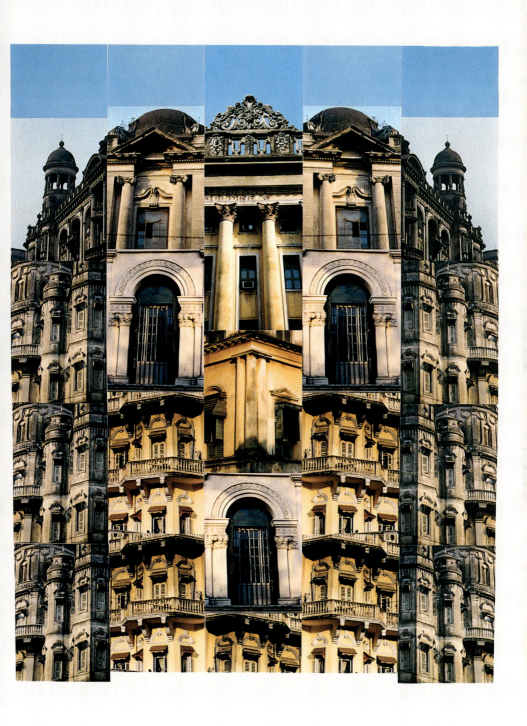

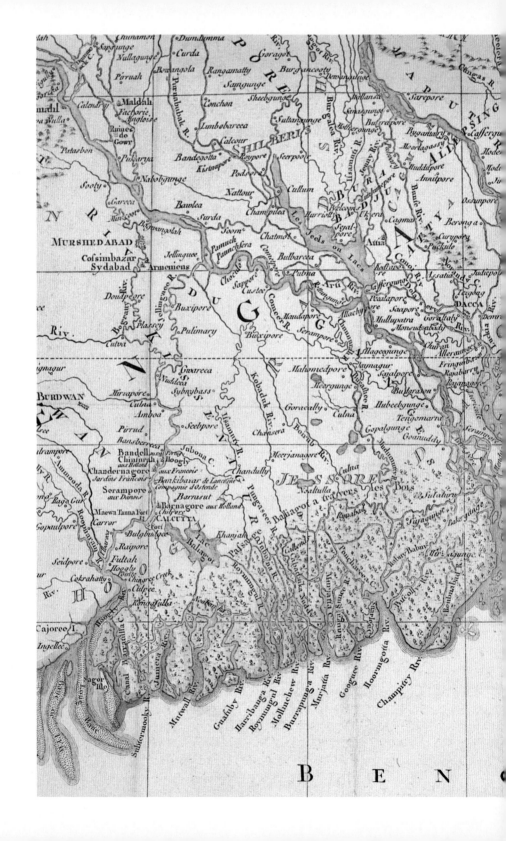

HISTORY OF CALCUTTA

The Early Days: In 1990 Calcutta celebrated its 300th Anniversary. Before 1690, there had been a trading centre known as Sutanuti. It was an active market for textiles, wares and spices. Many of the present big family names in Calcutta were then already prosperous traders or bazar owners Armenian and Portuguese merchants were staying there.

European traders started to establish 'factories' in Bengal at the end of the 16th century. The Portuguese at Bandel and Chittagong, the Danes at Serampore, the Dutch at Chinsurah, the Greeks at Rishra, the Prussians at Bhadeshwar, the Oostende Company at Bankibazar, the Armenians at Saidabad and Chinsurah, the East Indian Company at Hooghly, Cassimbazar and English Bazar. As the East India Company's factories were rendered progressively inaccessible to shipping by the accumulation of silt, a new site was requested from the Nawab. In 1687, the Company was offered Uluberia. Job Charnock inspected the location, found it too prone to silting and proposed instead the site of Sutanuti on the eastern bank of the Hooghly slightly upstream from Uluberia, a site he knew, that he had previously visited on several occasions. The Nawab accepted.

On August 24th 1690, a factory was established at Sutanuti. It prospered and in 1692 its agency was moved there from Hooghly. In 1696, the Company received the right to build fortications. In 1698, financed by Armenians, it purchased the Zamindari land rights from the Sabarna Roy Chowdhury family for Sutanuti, and the neighbouring villages of Kolikata and Gobindapur. In 1699, the construction of the first fort William was completed.

In 1707, Calcutta, as the union of the three villages became known, had grown large enough to become a separate presidency of the East India Company answerable directly to the Directors in London. The origin of the

Preceding pages: a view of Calcutta in the first part of the 19th century. <u>Left</u>: an early map of Bengal.

name 'Calcutta' is subject to controversy — the Klikata village, Kalikshetra, the field of Kali, or Kalighat, after the temple that stood where Fort William is today.

In 1715, the Company needing more space, an embassy was sent to the Moghul Emperor, Farruck Siyar, in Delhi. Luckily, it was headed by a surgeon, Dr Hamilton, who managed to cure the Emperor of an illness and received in thanks the confirmation of the Company's rights to trade in Bengal, as well as 37 townships, altogether including Howrah, across the river, forming a stretch about 15 kilometres long (9 miles) on both banks of the Hooghly. The reinforcement of Calcutta went on. In 1742, the company further reinforced Calcutta, erecting additional structures and placing cannons on walls when Siraj-ud-Daula ordered the unauthorised structures removed, and asked for the surrender of the son of the Begum's advisor, a refugee in Company territory. Having met with a flat refusal, Siraj marched on Calcutta on June 16th, 1757. Governor Drake and some of the Company's top officers and management fled the city by boat and took refuge downstream at Falta, Dutch-held. Surrounded by the maze of narrow lanes of the native town spreading up to its walls, Fort William could not make use of its cannons and surrendered on June 20th.

English prisoners were hastily rounded up

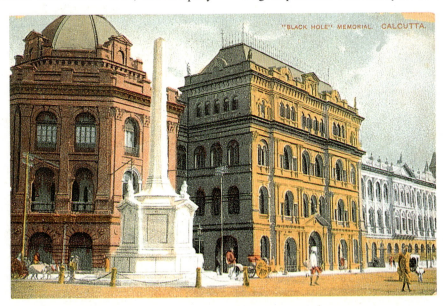

received the right to build a moat around the settlement against possible attacks by Marathas. The moat, called Maratha Ditch and dug out the same year, still exists in North Calcutta but has become Circular Road in the south.

As its power grew, the company became aggressive. It embarked upon the dangerous game of the Nawab making. When Ali Vardi Khan, the Nawab of Bengal, died in 1756, the Company was convinced that his grandson Siraj-ud-Daula, aged 18, would not last long and backed Ghasiti Begum, Ali Vardi Khan's widow instead. The Company had by the Nawab's troops and squeezed into a tiny room in the Fort with only a small window for ventilation, Indian summer temperatures of over 35°C (95°F) and almost 100 percent of humidity. By the next morning, 123 out of 146 had died in what is known as the incident of the Black Hole of Calcutta. A monument to the victims erected opposite Writers' Building, the seat of the Government of West Bengal, was shifted to St John's Church in 1940 under pressure from the Bengali Nationalists, officially to make way for traffic.

Learning of the fall of Calcutta, the Madras Headquarters of the Company at Fort St George sent relief troops, led by Robert Clive, an old India hand, and Admiral Charles Watson to take the city back. They did so on January, 2nd. Calcutta became the first territorial possession of the Company. The force continued north, stormed the French settlement of Chandernagore and beat Siraj-ud-Daula on June 23rd at the Battle of Plassey. Siraj-ud-Daula was assassinated soon after in his capital of Murshidabad. The Company installed on the throne Mir Jafar, the husband of Ali Vardi Khan's half-sister, and received from him as a gesture of appreciation the land rights for the Twenty-Four Parganas, a rice-growing area on the east

organised a party at his house, inviting Robert Clive and his top staff on the occasion of the *Durga* festival. Clive's success at Plassey against Siraj-ud-Daula was equated with Durga's victory over the demon. Overnight, the tradition of public celebrations of *Durga Puja* was born.

Living conditions were difficult in the early days. "Calcutta was located near a salt water lake that overflows in September and October, in November and December, when the floods are dissipated, those fishes are left dry, and with their putrefication affect the air with thick stinking vapours which the northeast winds bring with them to Fort William, that they cause a yearly mortality." A third of

bank of the Hooghly.

The Company immediately built a second Fort William, more to the south, clearing a large tracts of jungle, the present Maidan, to make sure the guns could fire from the Fort in all directions without obstruction.

Incidentally, the Battle of Plassey is at the origin of Calcutta's famous public festival of *Durga Puja*. In 1757 Raja Naba Kissen Deb, one of the financial backers of the Company

Left: location of the infamous Black Hole of Calcutta. **Above**: opium was a chief export in the 19th century.

the European population would in those days die of malaria, cholera or heat strokes. Company staff in the early days lived in thatched mud houses and ate at common tables. Some years later a "Writers' Building" was erected to house them. In later days, groups of bachelors would jointly rent out a bungalow as a 'mess' or a 'chummery'. Distractions were limited. Most writers, as Company servants were called, were bachelors in their 20s and 30s who spend much of their free time at punch houses or brothels. Brawls and duels were common. The richest would organise parties in their homes where

History of Calcutta 31

the *hookah* was smoked and dances performed by 'nauch girls', usually courtesans. There were few European women. Company's servants lived with local mistresses, their 'sleeping dictionaries' or with *cheeschees*, as half-caste women were called. The *linguae francae* were Persian and Portuguese.

The Rise Of Calcutta: In 1765, Calcutta became the administrative centre of a large territory: the East India Company which had abstained from seizing too much land during its recent campaigns was rewarded with the Dewani rights of civil and revenue administration for Bengal, Bihar and Orissa. Its new role in Calcutta was acknowledged by Parliament in the Regulating Act of 1773. The Company's Charter was renewed. The capital of Bengal was shifted from Murshidabad to Calcutta. Madras and Bombay became subordinates to a council headed by a Governor-General of Fort William in Bengal. A mint was set up. The Company already had the monopoly of the India trade consisting chiefly of indigo, salpetre, muslin, silk and spices, Clive having abolished private trade in 1767. In addition, it received the monopoly of the China trade. The opium trade is another factor of development. During the American Independence War, Spain, supporting the British Colonies in North America fighting for their Independence, stopped supplying the Company with South American silver used to pay in China. The Company resorted to pushing more actively exports of opium from Calcutta to China. Opium was in demand. A first shipment of 1,400 chests in 1773 had sold well, having been found superior to opium from Yunnan or Sechuan. In 1789, 4,000 chests were exported to China. By 1850, with over 40,000 chests, opium represented a third of Calcutta's exports. For a good 100 years thus, growth of Calcutta depended largely on the opium exports.

This is about when pressure started on

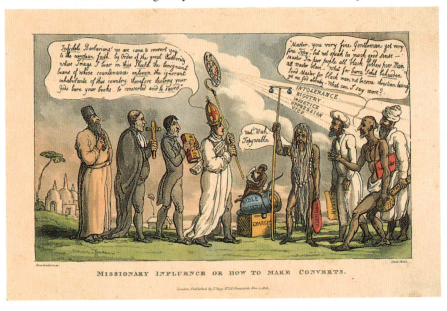

MISSIONARY INFLUENCE OR HOW TO MAKE CONVERTS.

London to let individuals trade. Two groups were especially vocal. The new local landed aristocracy, the Zamindaris, a group created by introducing in 1793 a land revenue system conferring ownership of land to those previously in charge of simply collecting taxes, had amassed fortunes they reinvested chiefly in the Company's opium ventures, becoming its "partner in Empire". They now wanted trading rights for themselves. Similar demands came from employees of the Company, mostly Scots. At that time, individuals were only allowed to ship a limited number of goods on Company clippers and had to resort to illegal trade under the pavilions of the other nations settled in Bengal. In London too, businessmen were lobbying to abolish the Company's monopoly on China and India trades. Finally, in 1813, Parliament renewed the Company's Charter but threw open the India trade.

The powers of the Company were further reduced by Parliament in 1833, barring it from trading in India and abolishing its monopoly in China. However, it gave the Company more administrative powers, entrusting it with the government of India under the authority of a Governor-General, assisted by a Council. In 1854, all properties of the Company were vested in the Crown, the Company retaining their management against 10 percent on profits. These measures boosted trade in Calcutta. Companies were formed, some, joint-ventures between powerful business groups, mostly Bengali and Parsee, and Scots.

The city was not much affected by the 1857 Mutiny and continued to grow. Its links with the rest of the country were improved with the introduction of the telegraph in 1853 and the building of a railway network allowing the flow of goods to and from the hinterland. The prosperity of Calcutta attracted more Armenians, Jews from Iraq and Afghanistan, Parsees, Gurajatis and the Marwaris from Rajasthan, soon the dominant trading community in Calcutta, almost totally wiping out the Bengali merchant class.

The Mutiny prompted the complete takeover of India by the crown. On November 1st, 1858, a royal proclamation at the Allahabad Grand Durbar announced that the Queen Victoria had assumed the Government of India. Calcutta became the Royal Capital of India ruled by a Governor-General and Viceroy under the Indian Council Act of 1858. On January, 1st, 1877, a Grand Durbar in Delhi proclaimed Queen Victoria the Empress of India. Calcutta became the Imperial Capital.

By the middle of the 19th century, Calcutta was a City of Palaces, "all white, their roofs invariably flat, surrounded by light colonnades, and their fronts relieved by lofty columns supporting deep verandahs. The Supreme Court, the High Court, Old, then New, Court House, St John's, Government House, Writers' Building, St Andrew's, the Indian Museum and St Paul's were built at

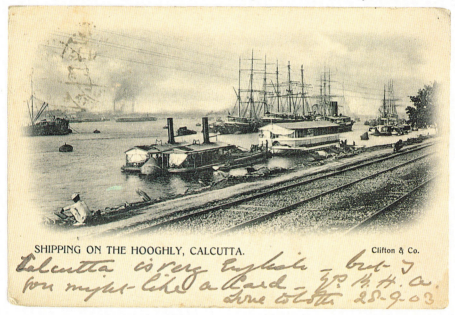

SHIPPING ON THE HOOGHLY, CALCUTTA.   Clifton & Co.

Left: the aggressiveness of the missionaries was one of the causes of the Mutiny in 1857. **Above**: at the turn of the 20th century, Calcutta was the second city of the British Empire.

that time. In 1852, Calcutta became a Municipality. Technological progress came early: public sewerage system in 1859, filtered water network in 1860, horse-drawn tramway line in 1873, the modern Stuart Hogg Market in 1874, electricity in 1899.

By then, life had become socially organised. More clubs were formed: the Cricket Club, the Turf Club, the Royal Calcutta Golf Club. Calcutta became at that time the intellectual and cultural capital of India.

Western ideas were funnelled through newly installed printing presses and the first English language newspapers. Thomas Bubington Macaulay's minutes on education in 1835 gave Indians access to European culture. Learned societies were founded, like the Asiatic Society formed in 1784 by Sir William Jones and a group of orientalists. A group of Baptist missionaries, headed by William Carey, established the Serampore Press in Danish territory in 1799 and started printing Bibles and books on theology in Oriental languages. Later in 1819, they set up a college in Serampore that became a Danish University in 1827 incorporated by the Royal Charter at par with Copenhagen and Kiel. The Fort William College was opened in 1800. In 1835, the Jesuits opened a college and in 1836 La Martiniere School was set up with the money left by the late Major General Claude Martin, a Frenchman at the service of the Company. In 1857, the Calcutta university was founded. Several figures dominate this 'Bengal Renaissance' period: Ram Mohan Roy (1774-1833), born into an orthodox Hindu family, a businessman, a philosopher, and above all, whose followers founded the Brahmo movement; Louis Vivian Derozio (1809-1831), a Eurasian, the pioneer of the Young Bengal Movement, a poet and a thinker; Rai Bahadur Bankim Chandra Chatterjee (1838-1899), a companion of the Order of British India, a top civil servant, known as Bankim Babu, the father of modern Bangla literature

Clive St, Calcutta

whose books based on his observations of everyday life in the smaller towns and the countryside, are written in the style of western novels; and Michael Madhusudan Dutt (1829-1873) who introduced Western genres into Bengali poetry. All were advocating modernism, benevolent government, free trade. Orthodox Hindu traditions, castes, the cult of idols were criticised as preventing people from reaching the Supreme and Unique God.

The Decline: Paradoxically, at the time Calcutta became the imperial capital of India, its decline was starting. The opening of the Suez Canal in 1869 gave more importance to Bombay and the West Coast on India. An anti-opium movement was growing after the two opium wars in China. The indigo, salpetre markets had collapsed. New centres of growth had appeared in the rest of the country.

Intellectually, a change had taken place too. Although the Mutiny did not affect Calcutta directly, it created a rift. The British became more aloof and kept their distance from local society. The Bengali intellectuals dropped their advocacy of Western values to launch an Independence Movement.

The first Nationalists appeared: Rashbihari Ghosh (1845-1901), Surendranath Banerjee (1848-1925), founder of the Indian Association in 1876. The fact the Indian National Congress appeared in Bombay only in 1885 shows the leadership of Calcutta at that time. Religious movements were launched, with spiritual leaders like Ramakrishna (1836-1886), his disciple Vivekananda (1862-1902) and Sri Aurobindo (1872-1950), first a terrorist, later a preacher, advocating a return to the purity of the Hindu religion, less focus on rites and deities, and more on God. The figure of Rabindranath Tagore (1861-1941) dominated the spiritual and nationalist movement. Universally acclaimed, a poet, the author of dramas, choreograhies, novels, of the lyrics fo the present national athem, he was also a prominent Brahmo thinker and an inspirer of the Independence Movement. In 1913, he was awarded the Nobel Prize for Literature.

Tension rose in 1903 when Lord Curzon, then the Governor-General and Viceroy, announced the imminent partition of Bengal, a measure officially meant to better manage the province, too large and administratively starved, but actually to break Bengal into smaller territorial entities to better control the emerging nationalist movements.

A first proposal incorporating the districts of Chittagong, Dhaka and Mymensigh to Assam met with too much opposition and was dropped. A second proposal creating two provinces, Bengal — incorporating Bihar and Orissa, with Bengalis as a minority, and Eastern Bengal, with a majority of Muslims received the Royal Assent and was enforced on October 16th, 1905. Ironically, instead of eliminating potential dissent, the First Partition of Bengal reinforced nationalistic feelings and triggered a wave of terror-

Left: Clive Road, with the office gharees. **Above, left**: Lord Curzon; **right**: Rabindranath Tagore.

ism in Calcutta using as a slogan *Bande Mataram* (Hail thee, Motherland), taken from Bankim Babu's poem 'Anandamath', with British officials as prime targets. A campaign to boycott British goods was launched. Tension reached its peak when three men were hanged for a raid on Writers' Building. Finally in 1911, George V, at the Royal Durbar of Delhi, announced that the decision of Partition had been rescinded. A Presidency of Bengal was set up with Calcutta as the capital. At the same time the capital of India was transferred to Delhi, far, it was hoped, from the Bengali terrorists and the Independence Movement, and closer to the new centres of economic activity in India. Ten years later, the politicians from the Hindi Belt (Northern and Central India) took the leadership of the Independence Movement from Calcutta in the early 1920's, putting stress on Hindu values and non-cooperation while Calcuttan politicians favoured 'council entry' to fight the British within the system and refused to be drawn along communal lines. Several names stand out. Chittaranjan Das (1870-19250), the Mayor of Calcutta, resigned as the Congress president over the boycott issue and formed the Swaraj Party; Rash Behari Bose (1886-1945) escaped arrest and fled from India to Japan and set up the Indian Independence League in exile; Subhas Chandra Bose (1897-1945), a follower of Chittaranjan Das, and chief executive officer of the Calcutta Corporation, resigned too as Congress President and founded the Forward Bloc, before escaping from Calcutta — where he was under house-arrest — to Afghanistan, the USSR, Germany, before reaching Japan by submarine. He set up in Singapore the provisional government of Azad Hind during World War II and the India National Army, and died in a plane crash in Taiwan in 1945. Many believe in Calcutta that 'Netaji', the leader, is still alive and will come back.

Despite the National Movement, the Partition issue, the growing anti-opium movement in Britain and the United States, and the opening of the Suez Canal, Calcutta showed its resilience, managing to sustain a remarkable growth during this turbulent era. It was the point of entry to a hinterland which kept growing through territorial conquests. The first plane landed in 1920 on the Maidan and an airport was established two years later on the grass fields of Dum Dum. The province began to diversify its economy. The first jute mill opened in 1853. Tea was introduced in 1836 in Assam, and in the early 1840s it became a major export.

During World War I, Indian groups entered sectors traditionally the monopoly of the British. The war had little effect on the economy, except in the first months of the war, when a German cruiser, the *Emden*, rampaged through the Bay of Bengal, blocking tea exports and forcing the port of Calcutta to close for a month, before she ran aground on reefs off the Coco Islands. In 1918, the Birlas, an enterprising Marwari family from Rajasthan, opened a jute mill and they were followed soon by other Marwaris. In 1942, the Birlas set up Hindustan Motors, the first car factory in India.

Up to World War II, Calcutta remained a lively city. More clubs appeared: the Tollygunge Club, Bengal Club, and Calcutta Club. In 1936, Boris Lissanevitch, a White Russian emigré, set up the '300 Club', which remained, until after World War II, as the place for the jetset of Calcutta to meet and be seen. The War saw the Japanese drop bombs over the city and the docks area. Calcutta became headquarters of the Southeast Asian Command, the base for the War Effort against the Japanese, dispatching US troops or weapons by rail to Assam from where they were flown to Burma and over the 'Hump' to Kunming in the part of China that the Japanese had not managed to occupy. The War Effort rationing, successive bad crops and the interruption of rice supplies from Burma in Japanese hands, brought famine to Bengal in 1943. An average of 700 people died in the streets of Calcutta every day from July to December; over 1.5 million in the whole of the Presidency of Bengal.

As Independence approached, tension mounted. Calcutta woke up to the famous Great Calcutta Killings of February and August, 1946 where members of the Muslim League and Indian Congress fought in the streets, leaving thousands dead. Communal riots took place again on September 1st, 1947. The Mahatma Gandhi had to come to Calcutta and start a fast until death which he ended when the killings stopped.

After Independence: Soon after Independence and Partition, Calcutta saw a massive influx of refugees from Eastern Pakistan as East Bengal was called, although there had been not much violence against Hindus there. The population of Calcutta swelled in several months. A second wave of refugees came in 1951 when riots took place in Dacca and Narayangunge. The Bengali is not communalist. The riots were directed not so

Left: the Japanese bombed Calcutta several times during WWII. **Above**: a Naxalite slogan.

much against the Hindus as such but were fuelled by the regime against the East Pakistan Communists that yielded considerable support from the middle-class and white-collar workers in the cities, most of whom were Hindus. More refugees came in 1971 after the Bangladesh War.

This influx of landless peasants and left-wing potential voters' resentment at the treatment of Calcutta by Delhi tilted the balance from the Congress Party to the Left. Already in 1948 Calcutta had become an important centre of the Communist Movement. In February and March, 1948, the Conference of the Youth and Students of Southeast Asia and the Second Congress of the Communist Party of India were held in Calcutta. Those two meetings actually discussed the future communist uprisings in China, Malaya, the Philippines, Burma and Indochina. The first government to go was Dr B.C. Roy's, then P.C. Sen's, then, little by little, the Left Parties allied to Ajoy Mukherjee and his dissident Bangla Congress, then without him gained control of the Government of West Bengal since 1967 and has remained in power since then, not withstanding two President's Rules of 371 days in 1968, again of 19 months in 1975-77 Emergency to fight the Maoist Naxalite urban guerilla insurgency, and an Emergency. The present Chief Minister, Jyoti Basul, Ajoy Murkerjee's deputy, has thus on and off been in power for over 20 years.

Present Day Calcutta: Having lost the poilitical power, suffered from obselete infrastructures, sunset industries, penalised by unjust taxation such as the "equalisation scheme" that took from Calcutta the adventages of having cheap energy sources nearby, the city shows remarkable resilience. With a population of over 10 million and a floating population of over 2 million, poor infrasturctures, a telephone network performing badly, regular power cuts, Calcutta is, nevertheless, far from being a dying

city as Rajiv Gandhi, then the Prime Minister of India, suggested in the 1980s. A good number of the country's large business groups are headquartered here. A third of India's foreign trade and most tea exports pass through Calcutta. A new town has been built at Salt Lake, a metro, a new port at Haldia, an export zone at Falta. Calcutta remains the intellectual and cultural capital of India. Will Calcutta finally really die in the long run? The city has shown enough resilience in the past to prove that it can continue as it is, stabilised at its level of decay while other cities of India are now experiencing.

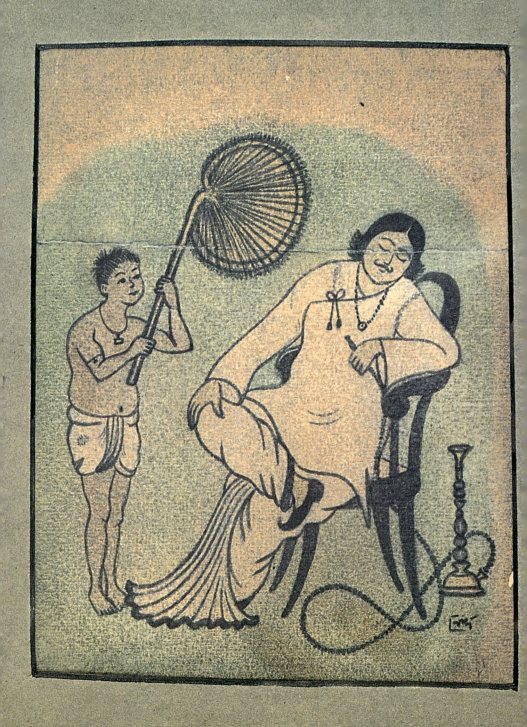

A Mosaic of Communities

As the main point of penetration by foreign powers, as the capital of British India until 1911, and being the only large city in this part of the Indian Subcontinent, Calcutta has since the 16th century been a magnet for colonialists, traders, invaders, intellectuals, peasants looking for jobs, and refugees. Some communities in the city come from as far as Kerala in the south, or Kabul in Afghanistan. There are groups of all races and creeds but little friction because no community has ever been dominant and because Western liberal ideas, including Marxism, have attenuated caste consciousness and communalism.

The largest group are the **Bengalis**. They constitute about 40 percent of the city's population. Bengalis are basically Aryans and Bangla, the language of Bengal, is highly sanskritised. However, Mon-Khmer and Tibeto-Burmese strains can be clearly seen in the east of Bengal and towards the tribal Chhotanagpur Plateau. The Bengali society is characterised by its blend of tradition and Western influences that have progressively eroded caste distinctions still felt nowadays in other Indian communities. There are few **Bengali Harijans**, as untouchables are called. Most of them, taking advantage of the social changes brought in by the flow of Western ideas, have altered their family names and upgraded themselves socially without much resistance from the rest of the society. The tolerance is also due to the fact that there is no leading caste in Bengal: the Brahmins are offset by the *kaesthos*, a caste of scribes, doctors and professors, all being functions normally the privilege of the conservative Brahmins.

There are actually two groups of Bengalis. The **Gothi** Bengali is the real Calcuttan. There are good chances that his family was living here before Charnock. Gothis are generally doctors, judges, skilled workers, diamond cutters, civil servants and intellectuals. The **Bangal** comes from Eastern Bengal. Arriving as a refugee after the India-Pakistan and Bangladesh wars, or fleeing poverty and communal strife, the Bangal is hard-working as his roots are in the rural delta where the terrain is difficult. Bangals can be found in the top management of companies and in high government posts. Many are engineers, some are entrepreneurs. The poorer are menial workers or taxi drivers. North Calcutta is Gothi. South Calcutta is Bangal.

The archetype of the Bengali is the **Babu**. According to the 'Hobson-Jobson, a Glos-

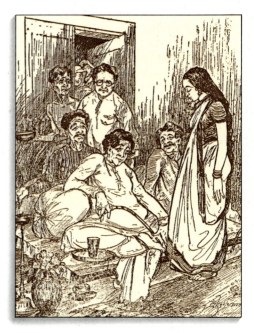

sary of Colloquial Anglo-Indian Words', the Babu is a term of respect attached to a name, like Master, and formerly in some parts of Hindustan applied to certain persons of distinction. It has come to mean much more. In the days of Clive the word acquired a first connotation. The Babu represented that class of Bengalis who financed or worked, as tax-collectors, *dewans*, *zamindars*, *munshees*,

<u>Preceding pages</u>: Political rallies are common in Calcutta; Vivekananda, 'Netaji' S.C. Bose, Chitteranjan Das, B.I. Birla; a Bengali family; the synagogue. <u>Left</u>: "Babu" by Nandalal Bose. <u>Above</u>: "Babu" being introduced to future wife.

A Mosaic of Communities 45

and *gomasthas*, for the East India Company. They became a rich and powerful class, the leaders of the old Calcutta society. Owning land in many cases, some families were even raised by the British to the status of raja and maharaja.

Rivalry amongst prominent Babu families was strife. They would make a great show of their riches in various ways through conspicuous consumption or by building many-pillared neo-palladian mansions chiefly in North Calcutta. Their homes had battalions of servants, imported furniture, chandeliers from Bohemia, floors made of rare wood, and European *objets d'art*. Many Babus had several wives and a number of mistresses. Outside Calcutta, they had Garden Houses and would travel there in silver palanquins, ornate carriages or peacock boats. At first, the Babus, despite their closeness to the Westerners remained genuinely devout Hindus performing faithfully all religious rites, establishing temples and undertaking philanthropic work. A few were even scholars and patrons of arts, such as Nobo Kissen Deb, a sanskrit scholar and the author of a famous dictionary; Raja Man Mohun Roy who founded a religious movement, the Brahmo Samaj; and the Tagore family.

The 19th century saw a degenerescence of the Babu society. Many scions of well-established families started to lead idle lives, squandering away the family wealth surrounded by psychophants devising such ridiculous past-times as weddings of pets and bets over bird-fights. Wild parties with dancing girls were held in the garden houses or on boats cruising on the Hooghly. At Baghbazar smoking sessions were held where a *hookah*, the traditional water-pipe, was passed among participants. It was filled with a mixture of opium and *charrass*, and Scotch whisky was substituted for water. The winner, that is the last one to collapse, would preside the next session sitting on a sterling silver brick. Simultaneously, they would continue to spend on religious and social functions to maintain their social status.

This way of life, known as the 'Babu culture' has been satirised in numerous plays, books and works of art such as the famous Kalighat *pats*. Progressively, with the flow of Western ideas, a third type of Babu emerged in the late 19th century, educated, mixing European and traditional influences, universal in his thinking, rejecting religious rituals and worshipping one supreme God. Many members of well-to-do Bengali families played an active and militant role in the Independence movement, the archetype of the Bengali Babu being figures such as Chittaranjan Das, the Mayor of Calcutta and Netaji Subhas Chandra Bose, the hero of Indian Independence.

Few Babu families have retained their wealth and power, the only tangible relics of their wealth being the ruined palaces of North Calcutta. Far from the past image of

RICKSHAW WALLAH — JULY 21, 1945. 8 ANNAS

degenerescence, the archetype of the present-day Babu is altogether a different character. He is a Government official or an intellectual, a man often of limited financial means, not ashamed of wearing *khadi* and *dhoti* instead of Western clothes, more interested in intellectual pursuits than in money and physical pleasure.

The largest exogenous community are the Hindi-speaking **Biharis,** usually economic migrants from the neighbouring state of Bihar. They work as manual workers, servants, *darwans* (door-keepers), *coolies*, and beggars. Most of the rickshaws-pullers are Biharis. The majority of Biharis are Hindus; a large minority are Sunni Muslims. The most colourful Bihari festival is the Hindu Sun Festival of *Chhat Puja*, held three days after *Kali Puja* in November. On that day, the lower castes carry cart loads of fruits and vegetables to the ghats accompanied by dancing *hijras* as eunuchs are called.

Trading communities in Calcutta are chiefly from Western India. They have virtually wiped out the Bengali merchant families. The **Marwaris** are considered to be the richest. The first families came fleeing Rajasthan plagued by drought and desertification in the 19th century, following the Valley of the Ganges, east down to Calcutta. Some families settled in towns on the way, in Benares or Patna, thus establishing the bases of a network that allowed them later to relay business intelligence and organise money flows from one end of the country to the other. The Marwaris first made their fortune in opium, cotton, money-lending. At first, they financed and supported the British, then progressively started competing with British companies, ending up buying them, especially after Independence. The Marwaris were active in the Independence Movement which they partly financed. The Birlas, for instance, were close to the Mahatma Gandhi. It was while he was staying at their house in Delhi that he was assasinated in 1948.

Since Independence, the Marwaris have diversified into new sectors and have become with the Parsees, the leading industrialists in India. Many of the largest business houses in India belong to Marwaris from Calcutta: Birlas, Singhanias, Bangurs, Goenkas. The richer Marwaris live in posh bungalows in the residential areas of Ballygunge or south of Park Street. The less prosperous ones, the **Barabazar Marwaris**, draw their name precisely from the area in North Calcutta where they live. Marwaris are known not only for their shrewdness but also for their philanthropy. They have set up several cultural institutions to help the performing arts, built museums, hospitals, schools and temples. Marwaris are orthodox Hindus. A minority of them are Jains. Celebrations of the *Divali* festival by the Marwaris in Barabazar, and Marwari weddings in Alipore during the cool season are famous for their pomp.

Jains in Calcutta are also traders. They originate from Rajasthan although the Jain

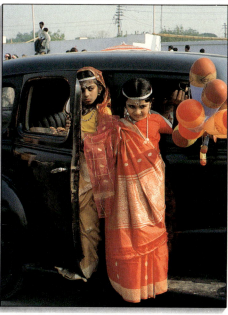

<u>Left</u>: old print of a Bihari rickshaw wallah. <u>Above, left</u>: Bengali girls decked out in traditional finery; <u>Above, right</u>: Jain girls in elegant saris.

A Mosaic of Communities 47

religion, like Buddhism was born in Eastern India. Their supreme prophet, Lord Mahavira was born and died in Bihar. Altogether 20 out of 24 Jain prophets attained nirvana in Bihar, on Parasnath Hill, near the border with West Bengal. Many Jains are jewellers or businessmen. They live in North Calcutta. The **Digamber Jains**, the strictest sect has a temple on Kalakar Street.

Most Jains belong to the **Svetamber** sect. They have a complex of four temples, the famous Jain Temples, in the east of the city and a smaller one in Barabazar (96 Canning Street). Their main festival *Mahavira Jayanti* in April, marks the birth of Lord Mahavira. On that day, a procession starts on Harrison Road and proceeds north along Chitpore Road.

The **Parsee** community is even smaller, numbering about 1,500. Parsees came to Calcutta to participate in the opium trade. At the turn of the century they were pioneers in industry. In 1911, Jameshed Tata built the first Indian steel mill, 350 kilometres (217 miles) west of Calcutta. The Tatas still maintain a strong presence in Calcutta with their Eastern headquarters the tallest building on Chowringhee. Parsees have always been involved in the social life of Calcutta, many being theatre actors, professionals, doctors, consultants, journalists or philanthropists. They introduced cinema to Calcutta. The Tata group has financed the sound-and-light system of the Victoria Memorial Hall. The Parsees have an agiary temple on Ezra Street and a tower of silence on Beliaghata Road, both off-limits to non-Parsees.

The **Sikhs** arrived mostly at the turn of the century, fleeing the overpopulated rural areas of the Punjab. They live in Bhowanipore, south of the Maidan, at Jadu Babu Bazar in Barabazar and Dunlop Bridge in North Calcutta, forming a community 200,000 strong. Their main celebrations are on *Dusserah*, when a huge *Ravan* is set on fire on the Maidan, the *Holi* colour festival at Punjab Bhawan in March, and Guru Nanak's Birthday in November, marked by a large procession from Barabazar to Belgachia.

Most **Muslims** in Calcutta are **Sunnis**. The low-caste Muslims are chiefly Biharis from Bihar Sharif the former capital of Bihar, Bengalis from Murshidabad and Eastern Bengal, Cuttackis from Orissa. Traders are from Punjab, Peshawar, Lucknow and Rajasthan. The money-lenders of Chandni Chowk are Pathans from Afghanistan. Sunni Muslims live around Zakaria Street in Barabazar, at Machuabazar and Rajabazar in North Calcutta, Park Cir-

cus, Manicktola, Ultadanga and Narikeldanga in the East, in Howrah, across the Hooghly and in the port area of Kidderpore. On the main festivals of *Idulfitr* and *Bakraid*, as well as on *Muharram*, fairs are held around mosques, while the Otcherlony Monument on the Maidan is used as a minaret for mass prayer meetings.

Shiites are a minority. Mostly Bihari and Gujarati, they concentrate around Metiaburuz, an outskirt of Calcutta and in areas of Barabazar. Amongst the Shiites, the richest are the **Bohras**, a community of traders around Canning Street and Brabourne Road. The main Shiite festival of *Ashura* is marked by processions on Chitpore Road and at Metiaburuz where devotees carry on their shoulders tazias, miniature replicas of Hussain's grave, while others flagellate themselves as a sign of extreme penitence. The main Shiite mosque is on Garden Reach Road in Metiaburruz. Bohras have their own mosque on Landsdowne Road.

Calcutta has a large community of **Christians**, comprising Anglo-Indians, Goanese, Tamils, Armenians as well as some Ben-galis. Most are Catholics. Their main churches are the Our Lady of the Rosary Cathedral of Murgihatta on Brabourne Road and the Sacred Heart Church on Dharamtola Street. The others follow the United Church of Northern India, a merger between the Anglican Church and Protestant denominations, is second in strength. The bishop sits at St John's Cathedral on Chowringhee. The Armenians have their own distinct autocephalous church.

The **Anglo-Indians,** formerly called Eurasians before the term was found derogatory, are the descendants of marriages between Europeans and the local population. The best-known Calcutta Anglo-Indian figure is probably the actress Merle Oberon. The community is some 35,000 large. Traditionally the Anglo-Indians held postings in the Civil Service, Railways, Customs, Port, Excise and the Police. After 1947, many left for Australia. The remaining ones work as teachers, nurses, jockeys, office secretaries and supervisors. Most of the Anglo-Indians have low income and live in mixed, Muslim dominated neighbourhoods such as Wellesley Road, Ripon Street, Chowringhee Lane, Sudder Street or Mominpur.

The **Armenians** are the oldest foreign community in Bengal. They came in the 16th

<u>Left</u>: the Parsee Theatre of Calcutta had only male actors. <u>Above</u>: On Muslim festivals, Red Road is used for prayers.

A Mosaic of Communities

century from Armenia, as well as Khorasan and Ispahan in Persia, and managed to gain an influential position at the Nawab's Court as bankers, generals or ministers. When the British came, the Armenians lent the East India Company the money to purchase the Zamindari rights in Bengal in 1698. Later, they pioneered jute in Bengal.

From Calcutta the Armenians spread to Burma, China and Southeast Asia. Arathoon Stephen, who owed the Grand Hotel in Calcutta, set up the Raffles in Singapore and the Eastern and Oriental in Penang. Paul Chater migrated to Hong Kong where he rose to the rank of Governor. After 1947 most of the families emigrated to Australia and New Zealand and only 200 Armenians remain in Calcutta. The Armenians have their own autocephalous church. The Armenian Holy Church of Nazareth is the oldest Christian church in Calcutta. The Armenian religious festival of St John the Baptist is celebrated in January at the Armenian church in the northern suburbs of Chinsurah while the Christmas and Easter masses are held in the two Calcutta churches.

The **Jews** were once a thriving community with five active synagogues in town. Most of them were Shepharads from Baghdad. They were joined by Ashkenaz Jews from Rumania fleeing persecutions during World War II. Most of the Calcutta Jews have left for Singapore and Australia. Few are left nowadays and, of the three remaining ones, only the Maghen David Synagogue, at the corner of Canning Street and Brabourne Road, is used regularly.

Basically, every community in India is represented in Calcutta. Among the smaller groups, some have monopolised a specific job: **Oriyas** from Orissa are gardeners; **Nepalese** are door-keepers; the best cooks used to be **Moghs** from Chittagong; money-lenders are **Kabulis**. The **Gypsies** set up camp north of the race-course under the access driveway to the second Hooghly Bridge. They are mainly fortune-tellers or sell sundry objects. Two tribes are represented in Calcutta, the **Bhanjaras** from Hyderabad and the **Khana Buddos** of West Bengal.

There are also non-racial communities. The **Hijras** are eunuchs, mostly Untouchable Hindus. They form a community of about 500,000 across the country, taking in some 50,000 new members every year. Hijras stay in different parts of the city in small groups of five to 20 individuals, under the guidance of a *guru*. Hijras are associated with black magic and are said to bring bad luck if antagonised: no household with a new-born male child would refuse them a donation. Hijras are also invited to sing and dance on weddings and religious festivals to fend off the Evil Eye.

Beggars in Calcutta also form an interesting community. The visitor to Calcutta cannot escape them as they congregate near the main hotels, at traffic lights in the centre, at markets, and in front of some churches, mosques and temples. The rest of the city is free of them. According to the Beggars Research Bureau, the majority do not live on the streets, but in rented rooms in slum areas, have a concubine and children, but hardly ever marry. Most beggars are retrenched workers, not peasants, and consider begging as a form of employment. They have their cooperatives, in which they take turns at begging, rent children and pool their earnings. Beggars are lobbying the government to be recognised as a profession. The richest ones can earn up to Rs 2,000 a month.

Street Beggars.

THE CHINESE OF CALCUTTA

Calcutta is the only city in India with a sizeable Chinese population. Of the 25,000 Chinese living in India, 20,000 reside in Calcutta. The intercourse between India and China goes back to the end of the Gupta period in the 7th century AD if not before. The first Chinese to come to India were traders, Buddhist pilgrims and students. The most famous was Huen Tsang, in the 7th century, who spent several years in India and left a rare description of India at that time. Chinese trade was carried on land through Himalayan passes and along the southwestern Silk Road (Yunnan-Burma-Assam-Bengal). By sea, traders would call at Tamralipti, now Tamluk, a port at present heavily silted on the Damodar River not far from the Hooghly, some 120 kilometres (75 miles) downstream from Calcutta. Admiral Zheng He's fleet, sent by Ming Emperor Yongle, called there in the 15th century. The first settler was a tea-trader Yong Tai-Chew, known as Ah-Chi, in the early 19th century. He was given land at a village now called Achipur to grow sugar-cane, with 500 *coolies* imported from China, but failed. During a local uprising, all the coolies were murdered by the population. Only Ah-Chi was spared, thanks to his marriage to a local woman. He died here later peacefully and his ghost is now said to be haunting the village.

The Chinese community grew with the arrival of Shanghainese merchants, tailors, launderers, Fujianese tea cultivation experts, Hakka tanners and shoemakers, smugglers from Yunnan, dentists from Hubei,

teachers, opium den operators, *coolies* and rickshaw *wallahs*. By World War II, the Chinese community had prospered and was estimated to have reached 200,000. In the 1930s, a large section of Barabazar was an impressive Chinatown with its clubs, trading businesses, shops, restaurants, temples and opium dens. People would dress the traditional way, some even wearing pigtails long gone in mainland China. The wars with China after Independence brought the number of Chinese down to 20,000 through emigration to Canada, Australia and the USA, or to fast developing new cities in

India such as Bangalore.

The remaining Chinese can be found at Tiretti Bazar in a small part of what used to be Chinatown. There is a Chinese grocery shop on Sun Yat-Sen Street. Nearby, starting every morning before six, a Chinese market sells pork sausages, herbs, rice and flour noodles, magazines from the mainland and Taiwan, incense and traditional calendars. On Chata Wallah Gully stands the Taoist Sea Ip Temple decorated with Swatow gilted wood and Dutch tiles. The Nanking Restaurant now hardly operates but remains the meeting place for the elders of the Chinese community. On Metcalfe Street operates Chinatown has grown up in Tangra, to the east, on the way to Dum Dum Airport. Most of the Chinese there are Hakkas from the Guangdong province in South China, who made their fortune in leather, a trade that Hindus and orthodox Buddhist Chinese would not touch as it included contact with dead animals, especially cows. The Hakkas control most of the Calcutta leather and shoe-business. Each family lives in a compound enclosed by high walls reminiscent of the fortified Hakka villages of China and the New Territories of Hong Kong. Behind the walls is the factory. The clan lives on the higher floors. Some buildings even feature a

The Chinese Journal of India. Founded in 1935, it is the oldest Chinese publication in the country. Each issue is hand-written in old characters, then litho-printed. In the neighbouring lanes are some smaller Taoist temples. Most of the Chinese in town run restaurants, beauty-parlours, carpentry businesses, shoe-shops or are dry-cleaners and dentists. The largest concentration of Chinese shops is on Bentinck Street. A second

Preceding pages: old prints of street beggars. Left: the Jade Emperor Wong Tai Tai. Above: children form a mixed lion dance group.

Chinese rooftop garden. Between those fortified compounds there are Chinese restaurants, Kuomingtang schools and clubs.

Chinese festivals are actively celebrated in Calcutta. For the Chinese New Year there are lion dances in both Chinatowns, as well as all over the city in front of every Chinese-owned shop, and Tangra is illuminated for a whole week. At Achipur, the village near the surburb of Budge-Budge, where Ah-Chi, the first settler died, the Chinese of Calcutta gather on the 15th day of the Chinese New Year to offer prayers to his grave, facing the Hooghly, and the nearby Taoist temple.

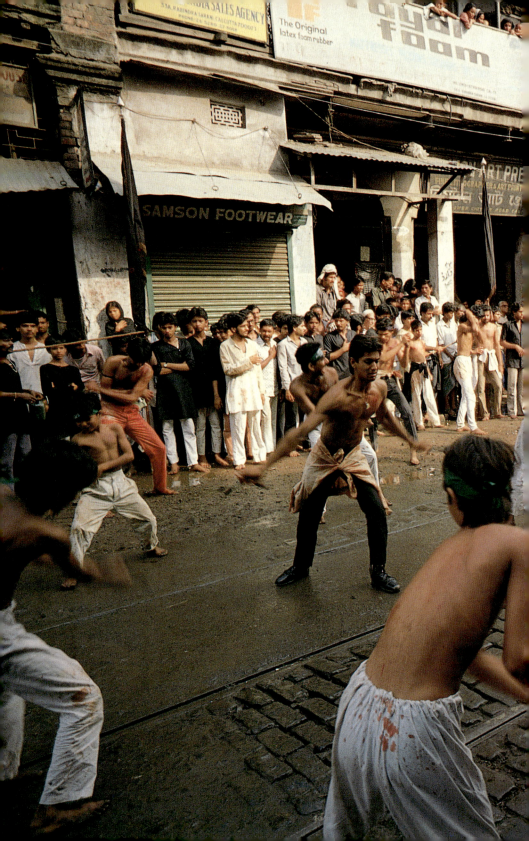

THE RELIGIONS OF CALCUTTA

The Aryans entered India around the 16th century BC but the Aryanisation of Bengal that started much later under the Gupta dynasty in the 4th century AD could not be carried thoroughly as Bengal became Buddhist in the 8th century and remained so under the Palas for 400 years. In the 12th century, for a short period, Bengal came again under a Hindu dynasty, the Senas, but in the 13th century, the process of Hinduisation and Aryanisation was once more disrupted by the arrival of Muslims rulers. Then Westerners started coming in the 16th century, progressively introducing Christianity and Western philosophies. Because of so many mixed influences, Hinduism as practised in Bengal and Calcutta is different from the rest of the country and several religious movements were born in Bengal, some of them in Calcutta itself.

Shaktism is the main cult followed in Calcutta. It is the result of the absorption by Hinduism, a religion dominated by male gods, of the Mother Goddess cults that prevailed over most of the Subcontinent before Aryanisation. Shaktism worships Shaktis, the wives of the male gods of Hinduism: Sarasvati, the Goddess of Learning is the consort of Brahma the Creator; Lakshmi, the Goddess of Fortune, the consort of Vishnu the Preserver; Parvati, the consort of Shiva the Destroyer and the source of his energy. Shaktism has retained the use of sacrifices. Human sacrifices have stopped and those of buffaloes have become rare but the offering of goats remains common. Cows protected by Aryan taboos, however, cannot be touched. Many Shakti temples are former Mother Goddess shrines taken over by Hinduism by establishing a linkage between the local goddess and the wife of an Aryan god.

One of the most popular deities is **Durga**, the symbol of Prosperity and of Victory over Evil. According to the main legend about

Preceding pages: a cow worshipped at the Ganga Sagar Mela; Krishna devotees; Shiite Ashoura festival. <u>Left</u>: Kali, Calcutta's resident deity.

her, a demon, Mahisasura, was threatening the Gods. He had chased them away from Heaven and was preventing priests to perform the rituals. The Gods turned to Shiva the Destroyer for protection and Shiva, in turn, asked his wife Parvati to do battle. She went as Durga, an avatar shaped and armed jointly by all Gods. After a fierce battle she killed Mahisasura, using the trident given to her by Vishnu. Durga is generally represented in her *dashabhuja* 10-armed form with three eyes and black flowing hair, killing Mahisasura coming out of the body of a slain buffalo, one of the forms he had taken to fight Durga. Often she is riding a lion or has a lion at her side. As the symbol of Victory over Evil and of Female Energy, Durga, although not an indigenous deity, is worshipped all over Bengal and in Calcutta for protection. She is also venerated as the mother of Ganesh, the God of Wealth, of Saraswati, the Goddess of Learning, of Kartikeya, the God of War and of Lakshami, the Goddess of Fortune. Traditionally, Durga is worshipped at home. There is only one Durga temple in Calcutta, on S.N. Bannerjee Road. In 1757, however, Raja Nobo Kissen Deb, a rich Bengali who had financially backed the East India Company at the Battle of Plassey, decided to make a social event out of the *Durga Puja*, the yearly Durga festival celebrated at the end of the monsoon. In 1757, he held in his North Calcutta palace celebrations assimilating Durga's victory over Mahisasura to Siraj-ud-Daula's defeat at Plassey, and invited to his home British dignitaries on that occasion, including Clive himself. Raja Deb thus set a trend. Since then, *Durga Puja* has become an open festival, with rich families competing over which had celebrated it the most brilliantly, while poorer neighbourhoods or associations organise celebrations on the streets.

Kali, or Rakshaya Kali, the protecting Kali, is a form of Durga, the consort of Shiva. She is the symbol of female energy, of destruction, creation and preservation and, as such, the deity through which most local Mother cults have been incorporated into the Hindu pantheon. Kali worship has retained many pre-Aryan rituals and most Kali temples stand on the sites of former Mother Goddess shrines. As in Durga, sacrifices are still performed. According to the *Kalika Puranas*, the flesh of an antelope or a rhinoceros will satisfy Kali for 500 years, a human sacrifice for 1,000, and the sacrifice of three men for 100,000 years. Up to the 19th cen-

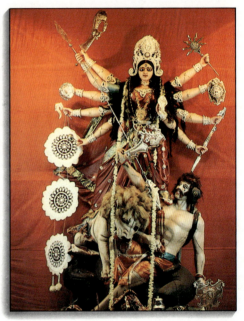

tury, the mystic robber community of the Thugs would kill their victims in the name of Kali. There are no more human sacrifices. Only goats, and sometimes buffaloes, are sacrificed.

Kali is represented as a terrible-looking black, sometimes blue, woman, naked except for a girdle of hands and a necklace of skulls. Her face and breasts are smeared with blood. She has four arms. The upper-left one holds a sword, the *khorgho*, the lower one the severed head, dripping with blood, of Raktaviya, one of the demons she has killed. Her upper-right arm is raised in sign of protection, her lower one extended as to show the extent of her victory and to bestow blessings. Kali is generally shown standing on her husband: after killing Raktaviya she went into trance and danced so furiously that the Earth began to tremble. To save the world, Shiva lay down across her path to block her. As she stepped on her husband, she came out of her trance and thrust out her tongue in shame. Kali is the resident deity of Calcutta. There were already active Kali temples here when Job Charnock came in 1690. At the turn of the 20th century the Bengali revolutionaries adopted a slogan, *Bande Mataram*, 'Hail to the Mother', and launched a Kali cult revival encouraging worship of the Goddess for courage and strength to fight the British. It is at the Kali Temple during the *Kali Puja* festival of 1905 that the Swadeshi Movement took the pledge to boycott British goods. Even now Kali remains the most popular deity in Calcutta. *Kali Puja* is the most intense festival in the city with about 2,000 altars erected thoughout Calcutta in her honour.

Several other Shaktis and rural female rural deites are also popular in Calcutta. Lakshmi, the Goddess of Love, Beauty and Prosperity, is worshipped by the trading castes in their houses. She is usually represented as a beautiful woman with a bright golden or yellow face, standing on a lotus. Her festival falls in autumn. Sarasvati, the Goddess of Wisdom, Music, Poetry, Science and Learning, is prayed to by artists, intellectuals and students. She appears as a fair woman sitting on a lotus playing the sitar. Her festival falls in late January or early February. Shitola, 'the Cooling One', is the Goddess of the Monsoon and Small-pox, a

Opposite, left: a sola pith statue of Kali; right: Durga overcomes the Evil. Above: devotees immerse the deity on the last day of a puja.

disease that errupts in the torrid weeks before the monsoon. People ask her for to bring a cool monsoon at the end of the hot Indian summer. She is represented dressed in red, riding a donkey.

Of the male gods, the most popular in Calcutta are Shiva, Durga's husband, called Thakur, 'the Lord', worshipped by women for fertility especially at the *Shivarati* festival in February; Ganesh, Durga's son, the God of Property, worshipped by traders; and Vishvakarma, the architect of the universe. As Calcutta is an industrialised city with workshops and factories *Vishvakarma Puja* is widely cele-

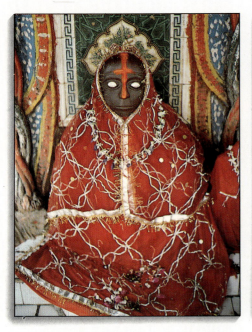

brated. Workers clean their tools, repaint their machines, and erect small altars with clay statues of Vishvakarma, often holding pliers and a hammer.

The other Hindu cult followed in Calcutta is **Vaishnabism** also known as the **Bhakti Movement**, born in the early 16th century as a reaction against the violence, the sex rituals and the decadence of Shaktism at that time. The main prophet was Chaitanya who lived, mostly in Bengal, in the 16th century. Vaishnabs worship Vishnu, the supreme god, through avatars like Krishna and Jagannath, or Chaitanya himself now considered as an incarnation of Vishnu. They are strict vegetarians, forbid violence, reject the caste system and refuse to worship idols to which sacrifices are made. There is a Vaishnab temple, Sri Saraswata Gondiya Asan and Mission at 29B Hazra Road. The **International Society for Krishna Consciousness**, ISKON, known in many countries for its local devotees chanting *Hare Krishna* on the streets, is a Vaishnab sect that developed when a *guru* told his pupil to go and preach abroad. His follower took a new name Swami Prabhupada and left for the United States in 1965, a time when the country was fighting a war in Vietnam and was going

through a deep moral crisis. When he returned to India five years later, the ISKON movement was a structured organisation with members all over the world. ISKON has a centre in Calcutta at 3A Albert Road. Ceremonies are held there every evening. In the afternoon, the centre runs a Veda Vision Positive Alternative Video Show that explains the Vaishnab philosophy. It also organises bus excursions to its headquarters some 125 kilometres (78 miles) north of Calcutta at Mayapur, the village where Chaitanya was born. The ISKON compound houses a temple, a guest house, gardens with lotus-shaped fountains and a museum in the house where Swami Prabhupada lived. A 'Vedic City' is under construction there. The central building will be a flower-shaped stupa in memory of Prabhupada who died in 1977, with a Vedic planetarium inside. Like any Hindu temple, Sri Mayapur charges for ceremonies. For 1,001 rupees one can have a *Shova Jatra*, an elephant procession with two fully-decorated elephants bearing a statue of Radha, Krishna's mistress, 24 lamp-bearers, umbrellas, flags, peacock fans, mantras and gongs. Every year, on the day of the *Jagannath* festival, in late June or early July, depending on the lunar calendar,

founded in 1828 by a group of progressive followers of Raja Ram Mohan Roy, a Bengali businessman who was also a religious thinker. Born into a family of rajas, courtiers of the Nawab of Bengal, Raja Ram Mohan Roy studied the Hindu philosophy in Benares, then travelled in Tibet for three years before joining the East India Company. He learnt Persian, Arabic, read the Bible, and met European traders, writers and missionaries. In 1828, with a few followers, he founded the **Brahmo Sabha**, an association worshipping one God and aiming at the purification of Hinduism by casting off rituals not described by the scriptures, such as

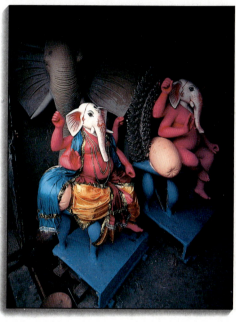

an ISKON *Rathayatra* (chariot festival) crosses Calcutta. The main chariot carries images of gods Jagannath, Balaram and Subhadra, Krishna's brother and sister, and is followed by floats representing scenes from the lives of Krishna and Chaitanya.

Christian and Western ideas are at the origins of two religious movements indigenous to Calcutta.

The **Brahmo Samaj** is a movement

idol worship and by discarding the caste system. The movement split in 1866 over the reference to the Hindu scriptures and the necessity of reforms. The progressive Brahmo Samaj of India opened its ranks to women and managed to push some reforms through, like the right of widows to remarry, inter-caste marriages, or the right to join the movement for those who do not profess Hinduism. The Brahmo Sabha, meanwhile, fell into oblivion. A second split took place around the issue of the emancipation of women, the personality cult that had grown around the leader of the movement and his

Across, left: Sitola, the goddess of coolness and measles; **across, right**: Lakshmi. **Above, left**: a Vishnu devotee; **above, right**: statues of Ganesh.

The Religions in Calcutta

decision to give his 14-year-old daughter in marriage to the Maharaja of Cooch Behar. In 1878 the progressives formed the Sadharan Brahmo Samaj, that has remained up to now the mainstream of the movement. Later Brahmo Samaj was joined by Debendranath Tagore of the powerful Tagore family. His son Rabindranath thus summed up the movement's philosophy in his book, *The Religion of Man*: "the God of Humanity has arrived at the gates of the ruined temple of the Tribe". Tagore also composed hymns for the meetings of the movement. The Brahmo Samaj draws nowadays a large following among middle and upper-class Bengalis.

Rashmoni did not belong to the Brahmin caste. First a follower of Shaktism, he later turned to Vaishnabism, then studied with Muslim and Christian masters before evolving, under his new name of Ramakrishna, his own distinct philosophy based on equal validity of all religions, on the oneness of God, the potential divinity of Man, and service to Mankind as a way of worshipping God. Ramakrishna's charisma brought him many followers. The chief one was Swami Vivekananda, a law graduate influenced first by the Brahmo Samaj, before joining Ramakrisna in 1881. He went to the United States in 1893 to speak on Ramakrishna's

However, Intellectuals are split between Samajists and followers of the Shakti cult. The main Brahmo meeting hall is at 11, Cornwallis Street.

The **Ramakrishna Math** order follows the teachings of Ramakrishna (1836-1896) and his chief disciple Vivekananda (1862-1902). Born Gadadhara Chattopadhyaya, he came with his brother to officiate at the new Dakshineshwar temple that Rani Rashmoni, a rich Calcutta widow, had built. By accepting the posting, the young Gadadhara and his brother had broken with tradition. All other priests had refused on the grounds that Rani

philosophy at the Parliament of Religions in Chicago, then went to Europe, before returning to India where, in 1897, one year after Ramakrishna's death, he founded the Ramakrishna Math, a non-proselytising religious organisation following a monotheistic philosophy striving to promote education and charitable work.

The order nowadays runs two monasteries at Belur Math, North of Calcutta and Mayawati, in the Himalayas near Nainital. It also has schools, colleges, hospitals, charity organisations and relief centres all over India, in several cities of Asia as well as in the rest of the world. It is now seeking from the Indian authorities its recognition as a religion separate from Hinduism.

Bauls are a religious sect indigenous to Bengal with representatives living and performing in Calcutta. They are nomad singers of either Hindu or Muslim background that follow a common religious philosophy mixing elements of Vaishnabism, Sufism and Shakti eroticism, travelling alone or in small groups and singing their religious philosophy in villages or at social gatherings. They have no written tradition, and collections of their songs have only recently been published, including a translation in English by

copulating continuously in a jungle of lust and love". Bauls from all over Bengal congregate every year on January 14th, for three nights of devotional singing at the *Baul Mela*, in Bolpur some 200 kilometres (124 miles) northwest of Calcutta. One of the leaders of the movement, Purna Das Baul, lives in the city and performs regularly at gatherings in North Calcutta.

'Never be afraid of giving, but don't give from your abundance, give until it hurts' sums up the philosophy of another order, Christian this time, born in Calcutta. Its founder, a Yugoslav of Albanian stock, Agnes Gonzha Bojaxhin, joined the mis-

the Bengali poet Deben Bhattacharga of some of the most revealing of their philosophy: "God is deserting your temple as you amuse yourself by blowing conch-shells and ringing bells"; "the road to you is blocked by temples and mosques. I hear your call, my Lord, but I cannot advance, masters and teachers bar my way"; or "the blood is white, and on the lake of blood float a pair of swans

Across, left: a performing Baul; **across, right**: statue of M.N. Roy, the founder of the Brahmo movement. **Above, left**: Mother Theresa; **above, right**: Father Christmas ā-la-Bengali.

sionary Sisters of Loretto at the age of 18, taking the name of Theresa and was sent to Bengal. A year later, in 1948, she became an Indian citizen and founded her own order, the **Missionaries of Charity**, after having received the Pope's approval. In 1952, she opened Hridoy Manzil, a home for the dying. The order has since grown considerably. It now has 3,000 nuns and runs more than 500 homes in five continents.

The order caters not only to dying destitute people, restoring them to health or giving them the opportunity to spend their last moments in dignity but also runs homes for

PAINTING

The art heritage of Calcutta, a city founded by the British in 1690, falls broadly into two categories: the British and the Indian.

The British heritage or the Western style of paintings, a vast body of which is preserved in foreign and Indian museums, (notably the Victoria Memorial Hall in Calcutta), comprise the works of a large band of British and European painters, who came to Calcutta between the 1760s and the 1850s. The "magnet that drew so many to India," said Sir William Foster in his essay, *British Artists in India 1760-1820*, "was the same as attracted thither a large number of their compatriots, namely that in the land of the Pagoda tree, Fortune might prove kinder than over-crowded markets at home." While money was the main spur, the lure of the exotic, the cult of the picturesque and a spirit of adventure also combined to draw them to India. Landscapists, portraitists, miniaturists, etchers, wood engravers, lithographers and others, found their patrons among the rich British residents of Calcutta, and also among the native princes, rulers, traders and Bengali landlords.

The first British painter, **Tilly Kettle**, reached Calcutta in 1769. Basically a portraitist, he also painted large heroic scenes. Tilly Kettle was followed by **William Hodges** who lived in Calcutta from 1778 to 1783. Essentially a landscapist, he travelled across the country and drew superb views of India. To him possibly goes the credit of painting the first landscape of Calcutta, a view seen from Fort William.

John Zoffany, possibly the most well-known painter to come to India, reached Calcutta in 1783 during Warren Hastings' regime, when the city was a kind of miniature London, and the political and cultural capital of British India. Zoffany was sought after by all those who could afford his stiff fees for portraits and conversation-pieces.

Preceding pages: Company School — 'European child on a pony'. **Left:** 'The Saint, the Carcass', by Ganesh Pyne.

He also drew scenes from Indian life. Some of his liveliest paintings were done for Nawab Asaf-Ud-Daula of Lucknow. Zoffany also found in Lucknow a generous patron in Claude Martin, a rich French mercenary. Two famous pictures he painted for Martin were Col. Mordaunt's *Cockfight* and a conversation-piece called *Col. Polier and his friends*, now a rare treasure of the Victoria Memorial. Zoffany's last famous work in India, *The Last Supper*, an altar-piece, adorns St John's Church.

The two painters who still remain in the public eye as most celebrated of all British and European painters in India were the uncle-and-nephew team of **Thomas** and **William Daniell**. Through their vast oeuvre, they helped to bring India to fireside travellers in Britain. The Daniells came to Calcutta in 1786 via China. Two years after their arrival in Calcutta, they produced an album of 12 views of Calcutta in the newly-invented technique of acquatint. It was later reprinted in London. The Daniells, with the help of a *camera obscura* and spot sketches, made a vast body of drawings and paintings during their travels all over India. Returning to England in 1794 via Macao, the Daniells got down to the immense task of transforming their Indian sketches in paintings into engravings. The result was *Oriental Scenery*, a series of 144 coloured plates in six parts, the first of which appeared in 1795 and the last in 1808. The most extensive collection of the Daniells paintings — 47 oils and 97 water colours — are to be found in the **Victoria Memorial Hall**, Calcutta.

The next great documenter of Calcutta in the 1790's was the Belgian painter, **Balthazar Solvyns**, who arrived in Calcutta in 1791. The main difference between Solvyns and the principal British depictors of Calcutta lies in the fact that while hardly any of the latter ventured into the dark, dingy "black town" of Calcutta, Solvyns concentrated on the black town and its life. His *Les Hindous* (The Hindus), with its 278 engravings, published from Paris between 1808 and 1812, remains possibly the only comprehensive documentation of Indian life in Bengal in the last years of the 18th century. The subjects covered by Solvyns include characters from all walks of life, scenes of ceremonies and festivals, market and river scenes, architecture, modes of transport, including carriages, palanquins, bullock carts and boats of numerous types. *Les Hindous*, now a collector's item, did not sell and Solvyns died in Amsterdam in 1824, a penniless man.

Coming to the 19th century, mention should first be made of **George Chinnery**, the celebrated portrait painter and landscapist who reached Calcutta in 1807. He died in Macao in 1852. **James Fraser**, an amateur resident artist in Calcutta, also deserves mention. He, with the Daniells, Capt. Bellew, Sir Charles Doyly and William

Wood, remains one of the noted documenters of Calcutta. His 12 engravings vividly evoke European Calcutta of the early 19th century: Wellesley's new Government House, its neo-Palladian architecture, its street scenes and its busy waterfront. With his brother William, he explored the Himalayas to the sources of the Jamuna and the Ganga. The result was the famous album *Views in the Himal Mountains*.

Sir Charles Doyly, was a gifted and prolific amateur who lived in India from 1797 to 1838. He died in Italy in 1845. Doyly's engravings are noted for their lively colours and human interest. His range was vast: architecture, natural scenes, human characters, scenes of daily life of the Europeans and Indians, costumes, festivals, market scenes, animals and birds. He was a stimulator of the *Patna Qalam* paintings through his *Bihar Amateur Lithographic Scrap Book*. His famous *Calcutta and its Environs* was published posthumously in 1848.

Finally from the long list of British and European painters, **Madam S.C. Belnos** deserves special mention. Of her two lithographic albums, *Sandhya* and *Hindu and European Manners in Bengal,* the latter is more famous. They contain 28 lithographs following: **The Company School**, **Kalighat Paintings**, **Bengal Oils** and the graphic arts of **lithograph** and **woodcuts**.

The Company School of artists was composed of those Indian painters who executed paintings of various Indian subjects and scenes from Anglo-Indian life, drawn to suit the tastes of European patrons. The Company painter's repertoire, executed in western fashion, was gradually extended to cover a wide variety of subjects such as human characters, portraits, and scenes of daily life. The best among the Company painters were **Ghulam Ali Khan** and the better known **Shaik Mohammad Amir** of

of surpassing beauty, mostly devoted to Indian life.

The enormous corpus of British paintings on India that are still existent remain the richest among all colonial arts in the world. They present an accurate view of India, its people and their way of life, in the late 18th and the early 19th centuries.

The Indian paintings and graphics that came into existence through an interaction of British and Indian influences, were the

<u>Left:</u> detail of a painting by Thomas and William Daniell. <u>Above:</u> Calcutta woodblock prints.

Karaya. The latter's drawings of horses, done around the 1840s, can stand comparison with the celebrated British horse painter, George Stubbs. Similarly, his painting, *Dogs in a Landscape*, demonstrates his mastery of western technique and perspective. A large collection of Company paintings forms an asset of the **Victoria Memorial Hall** in Calcutta as well as at the Victoria and Albert Museum in London. The Company painters declined largely because of the emergence of photography. Though they took to painting on glass, ivory and mica, these innovations did not save them.

Just as the Company artists were painting for the British public in India in western technique, a school of painting making a fusion of western and Indian influences arose at Kalighat in the 1820s. Reference is made to Kalighat paintings which derived their name from their place of origin, the famous Kali Temple at Kalighat in South Calcutta. The present Kali Temple was built in 1809. From the beginning of the 19th century, Kalighat drew an increasing number of pilgrims from all over India, and became a thriving centre for trade and commerce. Along with other traders it attracted the traditional scroll painters from various

Without minimising the beauty and the technical virtuosity of religious and mythological Kalighat *pats,* one can say that, to the world today, the secular Kalighats hold a far greater appeal. These Kalighat paintings include a marvellous satirization of manners and morals, particularly of the rich Bengalis (called the Babus) of the second half of the 19th century; a gallery of beautiful women, the mistresses of the Babus; documentary pictures of sensational events such as *crimes passionels*, and events that created unprecedented excitement in Calcutta. It is indeed sad that, out of literally hundreds of thousands of 'Kalighats' that were turned out in

parts of Bengal. To meet the growing demand, Kalighat *patuas* or painters adopted certain foreign techniques for speedy execution of their paintings, such as the use of paper and the medium of water instead of the traditional *tempera*. Kalighat *pats* began with religious and mythological themes. By the 1850s, however, the Kalighat *patuas* took to secular subjects. Many causes have been advanced by experts for this novel development in an essentially religious school of painting. One such explanation is the secularisation of all aspects of life (and hence the arts), in Bengal in the 19th century.

the 19th century, only a few hundreds survive in museums in India and abroad. The largest collection of them is in the Victoria and Albert Museum in London, while in India a sizeable number is presented in the **Gurusaday Museum**, a few miles to the south of Calcutta.

The graphic arts, woodcuts and lithographs of old Calcutta were, again, the result of a combination of western and eastern influences. The first book containing woodcuts was published as early as 1816. Till the 1860s, the art was confined to illustrate inexpensive books. It then found its flowering in loose rectangular prints, coloured in hand. They were inspired both in their subject matter and in style by the 'Kalighats', and sometimes copied them almost wholly.

Lithographic prints were successfully executed by two Frenchmen, Belnos and Savignac, for the first time in India, at Calcutta, around 1822. By 1825, the Bengalis had started a lithographic press to print pictures of gods and goddesses, maps and other similar material, mainly to illustrate books. Calcutta's lithographic art reached its high point with the establishment of the Calcutta Art Studio which, in 1778, introduced the art of chromolithography to India.

draughtsmanship was superb, and reflected a happy assimilation of Western technique with an essentially Indian spirit. In fact, these works were singularly free of the hybrid elements that characterised the paintings of Ravi Varma, India's first painter in oils.

With the rise of nationalism at the turn of this century, Indian artists faced an enormously difficult question. The question was, "where does one pick up the thread that snapped as a result of colonial rule which ushered in a period of barrenness lasting nearly 200 years?". In other words, it was a question of starting all over again. For inspiration, artists looked back not only to their

The lithographs of the Calcutta Art Studio and those that followed it, are now preserved in museums both in India and abroad.

While these innovations were taking place, the art of painting on canvas in oils developed in Calcutta around 1850. Hitherto unknown local painters began executing large paintings in oils of gods and goddesses and diverse mythological scenes. The

recent artistic past in the *Rajput* and *Mughal* schools of miniatures but also to the art of *Ajanta* of two millenia ago.

To a great extent, the prevailing spirit was to revive the glory of India's artistic heritage. This spirit was tinged with a deliberate aversion for all that contemporary European art represented. No one ever doubted the Indian artists' noble intentions even though their search demanded the adoption of the principles of a dead past. What is to be noted here is that the sweeping patriotic upsurge called, first and foremost, for an immediate deliverance of Indian art from the imitative burdens

Opposite page: Examples of work by Abanindranath and Gaganendranath Tagore. <u>Above, left</u>: 'Head of a Woman', by Rabindranath Tagore; <u>right</u>: 'The Tailor', by Nandalal Bose.

of Western academicism.

The answer that Indian artists found, led by **Abanindranath Tagore**, nephew of the poet and Nobel Laureate, Rabindranath Tagore, was, probably, not an ideal one. They, perhaps, wrongly believed that, to be truly Indian, their art had to be religious, mythological and lyrical. Japanese water colour wash technique was borrowed to give art works an overall Oriental look, and to create mystery. All this seemed to belong to a more cherished world than the present one. This criticism apart, those who have had a chance of seeing a sizeable body of Abanindranath Tagore's later works, the illustra-

by Picasso and Braque. These works represented a fantasy world. They were built around a strong geometric structure through which light and shade filtered in highly dramatic patterns, curiously resembling the attempts of some German stage productions and films of the 1930s. Gaganendranath's oeuvre projected a personal vision that belonged more to the realm of dreams.

Abanindranath Tagore's chief disciple was **Nandalal Bose**. He was initially influenced by the aesthetics of his *guru*, but soon branched out to develop a style of his own based on the direct observation of nature. He had a more exploratory mind than his con-

tions from the *Arabian Nights* and a series of mask-like faces, would ungrudgingly admit that he was a man of extraordinary sensitivity and imagination. Thus the history of contemporary Indian art began with him. His elder brother, **Gaganendranath Tagore**, after a brief and hesitant start with lyricism in the wash technique, successfully developed a personal style for which he became famous. He did a series of paintings, mainly in Chinese ink, in a style that borrowed certain Cubistic values such as breaking up the picture surface into small cubes and cones, different from the analytical cubism evolved

temporaries and freely experimented in different media. He learnt much from Indian classical and folk traditions and imbibed a great deal of the traditions of China and Japan. From them he adopted the two-dimensionality of the picture surface, the arbitrary division of space and the use of colour, the predominance of the line and the ability to see things at different levels. The countryside in and around Santiniketan and its tribal inhabitants were depicted by him with great feeling and a sureness of touch uniquely his own. His finest work was the series of inspired paintings, which came to be known as the *Haripura Posters*, done at the request of Mahatma Gandhi.

Jamini Roy was as much in search of a national identity as his contemporaries. He found his sensibilities echoed in bazar paintings of Kalighat, in woodcut prints of North Calcutta, in scroll printings of rural Bengal, in traditional terracotta clay figures and in the famous terracotta temple reliefs of Bankura and Bishnupur. Even *kantha* quilts, traditionally embroidered by grandmothers, drew his serious attention. The initial spark, born of a genuine desire for formal innovation, was, however, dimmed by a tendency to repeat himself endlessly in order to capitalise on the growing demand for his very colourful and decorative works.

One of the major events on the art scene in Calcutta was the appearance as a painter of the poet **Rabindranath Tagore**, when he was about 70 years old. He became aware of his enormous potential as a painter almost by accident. The dark and ugly erasures on his manuscripts offended his sensitive mind so much that he felt an irresistible impulse to bind them with rhythmic lines and to give them some shape, however abstract, rather than leave them like black gaping wounds on the white surface of the paper.

This playful urge led him to ever newer discoveries, frequently ending with some startling results. All kinds of figurative forms sprang up from the depths of his unconscious: strange birds and animals, mysterious portraits of women, funny male faces, landscapes, flowers and the like. Altogether a world halfway between the real, the half-known and the completely unknown where the line between whimsicality and fantasy seemed hardly distinguishable. This mysterious manifestation of a very private world is suffused with a life that only a high degree of aesthetic validity can bestow. And this validity is not limited to the forms alone, but extends equally to colour, texture and other plastic qualities that characterise contemporary sensibilities. Admittedly, they are the works of an amateur *par excellence,* but they are also the fruit of an unique vision that encompasses the totality of human experience. Unquestionably, Rabindranath remains modern India's most original painter.

Many visitors to Calcutta make it a point to go to **Santiniketan** to view the works not

<u>Opposite</u>: Paintings by Jamini Roy, 'Jesus Christ' (left) and 'Woman' (right). <u>Above, left</u>: Nirode Majumdar's 'Kali'; <u>right</u>: Mica painting, Company School.

Painting 77

only of Rabindranath and Nandalal but also the sculptures of **Ramkinker Baij** and the murals of **Binode Behari Mukhopadhyay**. Ramkinker's daring formal innovations were made at a time when there was hardly any contemporary sculpture worth the name. Looking at his works, one gets the feeling that he experienced the exhilaration of ploughing a virgin soil. The monumental, open-air sculptures and his other smaller works would nowadays earn him a place among the great sculptors of any country. Besides these, he also left behind a body of drawings, water-colour sketches and paintings in oils, that are no less important than his creations in the round.

Binode Behari is equally known for his *Magnum Opus,* the large mural on the walls of the Cheena Bhavan. This enormous work was executed when he was more than half blind. He had earlier done another large mural on the ceiling of the Kala Bhavan hostel. These, in addition to his numerous paintings in opaque water-colour and Chinese ink, have won him an important place in the history of contemporary Indian art. Common everyday scenes in many of his works are rescued, tilted up and invested with extraordinary importance by the evocation of volume, suggested by swift brush strokes (that delineate the forms) and then made sharper by lightning black lines, thus giving them the solidity of a *bas-relief* in stone. **K.G. Subramanyan,** Benode Behari's worthy disciple who has recently made Santiniketan his home, is an unique artist. His brilliant series of glass paintings and terracotta *bas-reliefs* have made him one of the most original artists of the country.

Four events of great import took place in the early 1940s, and left their indelible mark on the cultural scene, not only of Bengal but of the entire country: World War II, Subhas Chandra Bose's initial success in pushing back the British (with the Indian National Army), the man-made famine launched by the ruling authority (in which over five million people died in rural and metropolitan Bengal), and Mahatma Gandhi's historic "Quit India" call to the British. These earth-shaking events came in such quick succession that the world never looked the same again afterwards.

In this unprecedented situation, artists felt that a new language and a new expression were called for, forcefully portraying the crisis. Some young painters formed a group and christened themselves **'The Calcutta Group'.** They tried to evolve a language that synthesised classical Indian values with those of the new values propounded by contemporary European artists, especially in France. Originally, the members of this group were Prodosh Das Gupta, Kamala Das Gupta, Nirode Majumdar, Prankrishna Paul, Suboho Tagore, Gopal Ghosh, Paritosh Sen and Rathin Maitra. Later, other names were added to the list. The new upsurge was not limited to the field of art alone. Cinema, theatre, literature, music and dance responded with equal enthusiasm as if a whole new era had dawned. In order to experience the modern revolutionary art of Europe at first hand, a few front-ranking young artists like **Nirode Majumdar** and **Paritosh Sen** felt the need to go and work in Paris, then the Mecca of world art. They came back with a greater understanding and love of their traditional art.

Prodosh Das Gupta, **Chintamoni Kar** and **Meera Mukherjee**, after their return from Europe, not only did some outstanding works but inspired a whole lot of young students, some of whom — like Ajit Chakravarty, Sharbari Roy Chowdhury, Bepin Goswamy, Niranjan Pradhan and Manik Burman — have been doing excellent work over the past two or three decades. **Somenath Hore**, senior to them, and now given mostly to sculpture, has made some simple but startling statements in metal.

In the 1970s, a whole new generation of talented artists appeared on the Calcutta art scene. Those who have drawn wide attention are Bikash Bhattacharya, Jogen Chowdhury, Ganesh Pyne, Veena Bhargava, Shyamal Dutta Roy, Sunil Das, Dharmanarayan Das Gupta, Amitabha Banerjee, Shubhaprasanna and others. Still younger artists like Chitrabhanu Majumdar, Shekhar Roy and Shyamal Roy, among others, have, of late, made the local art scene appear bursting with new energy. This energy is also to be seen in the street graffitti art of the city.

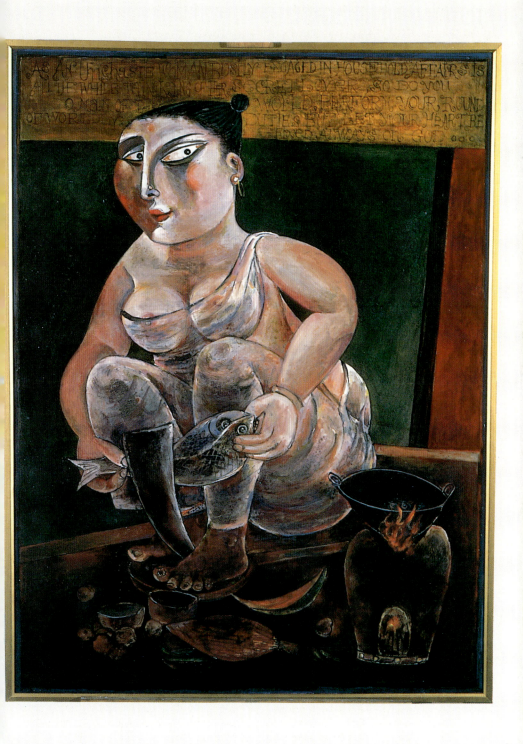

THE GRAFFITTI CAPITAL OF THE WORLD

Even more than New York with her 'bombers', Calcutta can be considered as the real graffitti capital of the world. Calcutta's burgeoning graffitti art is a post-Independence phenomenon. That is, it gained its popularity as an effective means of expression against the establishment after 1947. Before this historic date, it was inconceivable that the then colonial rulers would have permitted any political slogan on private or public walls. Yet it is a fact that when Mahatma Gandhi asked the British to "Quit India", the slogan appeared on many walls, in bold letters written in coal-tar.

Scratching letters recounting some satirical or erotic joke or drawing in chalk on empty boundary walls, are universal activities indulged in by adults as well as by children. The point to be noted here is man's irrepressible urge to express himself. And Calcutta's people are no exception.

Jawaharlal Nehru called it the "City of Processions". Indeed, not a day passes when a few of them, mainly in support of economic demands and led by one political party or the other, wind through the city centre causing enormous traffic jams. It is a fact of life everywhere that the media are not generally available to the oppressed and the rebellious. Because of this, graffitti has fast developed into an important means of communication to bring about social change. Although it has been used elsewhere in recent times, the popularity of "walling" in Calcutta is undeniable. A drive around the city will prove it.

Most walls in and around the city, private or public, are constantly being covered with new political slogans in support of or against current issues, by leftists, centrists and rightists in equal measure. Any newly painted wall is immediately appropriated by a flexing of muscles by the stronger party in the locality, and righteous objections are met with force especially if parliamentary, State Legislative Assembly, or municipal elections are imminent. During such periods, one sees bands of young men with buckets of cheap paint, fat brushes and ladders frenziedly dashing off huge, bold letters on walls at strategic locations.

Depending on the skill of the budding artist, he may well include appropriate images such as portraits of popular leaders, a political poem, or a scene depicting a fresh scandal or just something plainly satirical or comical. Sometimes mythological or folkloric episodes which have relevance to present day events are also used. These visuals are not always of a very high aesthetic standard. Sometimes, however, the amateurs or the half-baked creators of these images do achieve a naive or child-like quality in their portrayal — which eminently succeeds in drawing the attention of passers-by. Which is precisely what they are meant to do.

able pictorial impact, permitting the viewer quite an aesthetic experience. Someone familiar with the nuances of contemporary abstract art can sometimes be impressed by the varied and rich textural and tonal effects caused by rain and sun. The strong colours, the heavy lettering, partially washed away, create unusual accidental results which could be the envy of many a first-rate professional. Some works can appear a trifle pretentious though, especially those done by local art students.

Now to consider their calligraphic aspect. Much of these writings on the wall, although based on printing types, are not without

The unconscious departure from academic realism and the resultant stylisation or distortion, the flat treatment of a subject, the integration of lettering into the overall design (Gothic letters can be used) and the utter spontaneity of execution, nonetheless, often make these works fairly good examples of forceful expression. The division of space in parallel panels and the unconscious sophistication of drip-painting can make consider-

Preceding page: 'The Bengali Woman' by Puritosh Sen. **Opposite, left**: graffitti painters can strike anywhere; **right**: Rajiv Gandhi. **Above**: Tintin is as popular as politicians in Calcutta.

spontaneous flourishes. Others can be amazingly innovative and can manifest an excellent sense of form and design. The calligraphy, in general, is strong and betrays a good sense of proportion of the ascending and descending strokes in their thinness and thickness, a characteristic of quill-pen writing which is quite successfully adapted by the brush. The overall effect, although decorative, is apt to bring out the message clearly and is pleasing to the eye. At their best they are reminiscent of the works of the Abstract Expressionists as exemplified by the powerful brush-strokes in black on stark, lime-washed walls.

In predominantly Bengali neighbourhoods most of the writing is done in Bengali, whereas in mixed or cosmopolitan areas, the Roman alphabet, rather the English language, is commonly used. In the predominantly Hindi-speaking areas in the north of the city and in the industrial areas on the periphery, the *Devanagari* script which resembles Bengali is omnipresent.

Can graffiti take the form of murals? The answer lies in the positive. After all, they are painted on large wall surfaces and are viewed from a distance. At election time one occasionally witnesses such attempts by students who study mural painting at the local art college and who might be motivated because of their political commitment. Such works can sometimes be aesthetically very pleasing. An element of comic-strip art can also be added, thus giving the murals a more popular appeal by the use of strong and vivid colours by the disposition of the figures, by their literary content, and by the manner in which they are executed.

Considering that this form of street art in Calcutta is a round-the-year phenomenon, though limited in scope, it does offer some opportunities to develop one's artistic talents. But it does not offer much financially. It is, however, a known fact that many potential artists waste their talents in doing commercial or advertising art. Or in painting huge cinema boards. The extraordinary competence with which this is done, is nothing short of a small wonder. In a society which offered greater opportunities for mass creativity, such talent would have flowered into fine, painterly qualities. The magnitude of such flowering in a city with a population of more than 11 million is almost unimaginable. Though not strictly the kind of street art under discussion here, a great opportunity did arise when the newly built Calcutta Metro decided to have its station walls both underground and overground, decorated with panels of drawings, paintings and mosaics. What has gone up on the walls remains a subject of controversy. But the truth is that these works, together with political graffiti, are manifestations of a city which has traditionally been art-conscious.

SPORTS

Calcutta has been widely acknowledged as the 'Sports Capital of India', a reputation based on two related facts: sports infrastructure is well developed, and spectator support is boundless. The city boasts of one modern indoor and two open air stadiums of international standards, numerous public and private grounds, two 18-hole golf courses, polo grounds, and a number of venerable sporting clubs. The average Bengali sports fan is aware of the latest international develop-

through May. Individual sports such as **golf**, **tennis** and **squash**, are played throughout the year. Quite naturally, the winter months are preferred for all major tournaments.

True to its colonial past, Calcutta has kept its love of **rugby** alive and witnesses an active season in June-August every year. **Equestrian sports** are fairly popular too. Events are held between November and February. The **polo** season is generally in December. There is rowing all year round on

ments in his preferred game, a theoretician, a connoisseur of tactical nuances and, above all, a fun-loving and passionate admirer of great sport.

The main sporting seasons correspond inevitably to the climatic conditions. **Soccer** is traditionally played from mid-May through September, during the monsoons, when ground conditions do not permit the practice of other outdoor games. **Cricket** takes over from mid-October and continues through February, when the relatively drier and cooler winter months allow long hours in the sun. **Field hockey** is played from March

the Dhakuria Lakes.

The origins of most major sports now popular in Calcutta can be traced to the presence of a large British community in the city through the 18th and 19th centuries — officers and gentlemen otherwise engaged in the pursuit of Trade and Empire.

The Calcutta Cricket Club was founded in 1792, under the name of Ballygunge Cricket Club, becoming the first and today, the oldest Cricket Club outside the British Isles. The first match played in the city took place on the Maidan opposite the south gate of Government House. Much later, and thanks to the patronage of rich Bengali landowning families from Cooch Behar, Nator and Santosh, the game was adopted by local enthusiasts. It spread to central, northern and western India under the patronage of the Holkar of Gwalior, and the Maharajas of Patiala, Baroda and Nawanagar. The relatively milder Indian winter here attracted a number of English professionals who participated in local tournaments on a regular basis. Thus, Alec Hosie and C.H. Skinner played in Calcutta in the 1930s. Tom Longfield, the Kent professional, led Bengal to its only victory in the interstate tournament for the Ranji Trophy in 1938-39. Local cricketers of repute include Shute Banerjee, a fast bowler who figures in the record books as one of the only two end-of-order batsmen to have both scored centuries in a First Class match (for India versus Surrey, in 1946). Pankaj Roy, a distinguished opening batsman for India, also holds a world record for the highest opening partnership in a Test Match (413 runs for India versus New Zealand, in 1954-55). Endowed as it is with the Eden Gardens, a magnificent cricket stadium that accommodates about 100,000 spectators, Calcutta has witnessed many great matches between India and some of the best teams in the world. In November 1987, the final of the Reliance World Cup was played at the Eden Gardens. A visit to the stadium during a Test Match or a One-Day International can be a memorable experience. A measure of the enthusiasm amongst young cricketers in Calcutta can be had by taking a stroll on the Maidan on a Sunday morning in December: at least 100 games are in progress simultaneously. This enthusiasm is also visible in other areas of the city, where streets and lanes are temporarily converted into impromptu cricket pitches by younger residents. Weekend cricketers passing through the city can contact the Calcutta Cricket and Football Club at Ballygunge in order to join in a friendly game. A word of caution: the Cricket Club "hill" can be as boisterous as its now-defunct analogue at the Sydney Cricket Ground.

The Calcutta Football Club was founded in 1872, following exhibition matches on the Maidan between sailors of the British ship *Galatea*. Initially, teams were constituted from amongst the British, but local players soon got involved. Nagendra Sarbadhikary,

Preceding pages: Maoist nostalgia in Bengal; during a chukka. <u>Opposite</u>: rowing on the Lakes. <u>Above</u>: riding on the Maidan.

Sports 87

a resident of North Calcutta, collected a group of boys in his area and built the first team. Gradually the game grew in popularity among Bengalis, and the first important football club, Mohun Bagan, was founded in 1889, followed soon by the Mohammedan Sporting and the Aryan Sports Club. Local teams played barefoot. Their first breakthrough came in 1911 when the 'Barefoot Babus' of Mohun Bagan defeated a well-shod British team in the Indian Football Association (IFA) shield final. The progress of the team had been avidly followed throughout the country, and its victory was hailed in Bengal and by many Indians as a significant breeding ground of players. The 1948 and 1952 Olympic teams were composed mainly of Calcutta players such as Sailen Manna, Taj Mohammad and Mewalal. In 1962, led by their star forward Chuni Goswami, India beat South Korea in the final of the Asian Games to win the gold medal. Since this victory, Calcutta soccer has been in decline, despite players like Jarnail Singh, Pradip Banerjee, Balaram, Arun Ghosh and S. Nayeemuddin. Football remains, however, a passion in Calcutta where life slows down everytime an important match is played in the city or broacast, be it a national, or an internaitonal one. The Calcutta Football

step forward in the struggle for Independence. An Indian team was among the 16 teams invited to the first ever World Cup, but could not take part in the tournament as they did not play in boots! At home, football fever gripped Calcutta every monsoon. The major clubs nurtured local talent, and attracted players from other regions to make the Calcutta Football League the most prestigious in the country. The keen competition against superior British Army teams, suitable ground conditions and generous spectator interest provided a good nursery for local soccer. Calcutta assumed the role of a fertile Club (CFC) was admitted to membership of the Rugby Football Union in 1874, and presented them with the Calcutta Cup in 1878. This Cup is played for annually between England and Scotland (alternatively at Murrayfield and Twickenham), and remains an integral part of the British rugby calendar. In 1890, a new Calcutta Cup was presented and won by the CFC. There are currently six teams in the city, but with rugby pratically having died out at school level, the future of the sport is no longer assured. Nonetheless, a number of tournaments are held during the monsoons at the Calcutta Cricket and Football club grounds where the All Indian and South Asia Tournament is hosted every alternate year.

Field hockey has been a very popular sport in India since the 1920s, and Calcutta has produced its share of Olympic hockey stars such as Carl Tapsell, R. Allen and Brendish. This sport is ideally suited to the Asian physique, as it demands suppleness, quick reflexes and a great deal of skill rather than sheer power. It was not surprising therefore to see India's total domination of world hockey through the 1920s and 1930s. The Beighton Cup, the oldest hockey tournament in the country, was played annually in Calcutta. Calcutta teams often won this tournament, since there existed a large hockey playing population amongst officers, and men of organisations headquartered in the city. Teams of the Bengal-Nagpur Railway, the Port Commissioners and the Calcutta Customs deserve mention. The local Anglo-Indian community produced numerous stars. One name stands out among the rest. Leslie Claudius, a specialist centre-half who represented and led India to four Olympic finals in 1948, 1952, 1956 and 1960, winning gold in the first three and silver in the last.

After 1947, with the emigration of numbers of Anglo-Indians, the hockey scene in Calcutta lost its lustre. Moreover, the growing popularity of cricket and soccer in the city has reduced the availability of cricket players and playing grounds. Nevertheless, a number of tournaments are played every year, such as the Beighton Cup and the Merchants' Cup Five-a-side tournament held at the Calcutta Cricket and Football Cup each April.

There is a strong golf tradition in Calcutta. The Dum Dum Golfing Club was founded in 1829, later shifting its promises to its present location in Tollygunge in south Calcutta where it became the Royal Calcutta Golf Club, the oldest golf club outside the British Isles. The course was designed by Peter Thomson, the Australian professional, and is

Opposite: a mural honouring the 'Gods of Cricket'. **Above**: an almost deified Maradonna standing next to the Goddess Durga during a festival.

among the best in Asia, through rather natural and therefore old-fashioned, like courses along the British coast. There are two 18-hole courses, the Royal Calcutta Golf Club and the Tollygunge Club. There are two nine-hole courses on the Maidan: Fort William's Officers' Club and the Ladies' Golf Club. Tournaments are played all year round, in all clubs, even during the monsoon.

Tennis has been very popular in Calcutta since the late 19th century, and has found a suitable home at the Calcutta South Club, in Woodburn Park, in the heart of the city. With its 10 grass courts and eight clay courts, the South Club has spawned a host of tennis

players of Asian and internatinal repute — Dilip Bose, Sumant Misra, Naresh Kumar, Akhtar All, Premijit Lall, Jaidip Mukerjea, Gaurav Misra, Enrico Piperno and Zeeshan Ali. Tennis is also played in most clubs of Calcutta.

Traditional sports continue to be practised. *Kushtia*, a form of wrestling imported from the northwest of the country, along the north side of the race course, traditional gymkhana gymnastics performed every morning on Armenian Ghat, and Kabbadi, on the Maidan opposite the Mahatma Gandhi Statue.

POLO

Polo, in its international form, originates in Calcutta. The Calcutta Polo Club is now the oldest in existence and its red-and-white colours are used to decorate the goal poles of polo grounds all over the world.

It seems that polo was born in the Central Asian steppe somewhere between Mongolia and the Caspian Sea. Indeed, most known polo games are played along invasion or horse-trade routes originating from Mongolia. One variety, *Chaugan*, developed in

mese onslaught on Manipur. They soon joined the game and in 1863 formed the first polo club in the world, in Silchar, the distict capital. They called it the Silchar Kanjai Club after the name of the game in Meithei, *Sagol Kangjei* (*sagol*, horse; *kang*, ball; *jei*, stick). Their enthusiasm spread quickly to other locations. In 1861, teams were formed in Calcutta at Barrackpore as well as in Kanpur, then known as Cownpore. In 1863, the game spread to Tongboo in Burma. In the

Iran; another one born in Northern China, later entered Japan where it became a court game called *Daiku*; other varieties developed in Northern Kashmir and in Manipur, at one time a powerful state neighbouring Burma, where horses and polo seem to have been introduced by the Kublai Khan Army of Yunnan.

The first British tea planters stationed in the remote district of Cachar, in Assam, had little to do to amuse themselves. They became fascinated by a game of 'hockey on poney' played by the Meithei refugees from Manipur that had settled here after the Bur-

same year 1863, a lieutenant in the Indian Army, Joe Shearer, posted as Assistant Commissioner of Cachar, and a keen player of *Kangjei*, drew the rules of what would become modern polo as it is now played world-wide. Finally, in March 1863, the Calcutta Polo Club was founded under the auspices of the same Shearer who, a year later, brought a team of Manipuris to Calcutta after a voyage by boat that took them two weeks. The Calcutta players were beaten flat.

The late 19th and the early 20th centuries saw great competition among the British Cavalry teams and in those days matches were regular social events. The rulers of the Princely States too became enthusiasts and teams from Jodhpur, Mysore and Hyderabad began to win cups.

Little is known, however, about the Calcutta Polo Club itself for several decades except for the famous names which are listed on the historic Indian Polo Association Trophy, and the Ezra, Darbhanga and Carmichael Cups, still played to this day during the Calcutta polo season. One incident worth noting from that period: during the 1934 earthquake that occurred while a polo match was under way, the ground opened under the horses, forcing an interruption of the *chukka*.

After World War II, in 1951, a group of polo fanatics, the Maharajas of Jaipur, Cooch Behar and Burdwan, the Birla family and a bunch of Britishers, the Wrights, the Haywards, tea-planter Pat Williamson and others, managed to get ponies and a polo ground and started practice on the Ellenborough Grounds. In 1956, the Indian Polo Championship was played again.

**Opposite: Manipuri players at the first international polo meet in Calcutta in 1863.
Above: a crack in the ground during the 1934 earthquake.**

The 1960s saw a revival of polo in Calcutta with crowds of over 40,000 coming to watch the Maharaja of Cooch Behar and the great Rao Raja Hanut Singh of Jaipur with his sons, Kanwar Hari and Kanwar Bijay Singh. In 1961, a Centenary Tournament was played to celebrate 100 years of polo in Calcutta and, in 1988, the Calcutta Polo Club celebrated another jubilee, its 125 years of existence.

Since its revival, the club has seen play, such famous players as Sinclair Hill, James Ashton, Eduardo Moore, Julian Hipwood, Hesky Baig, Yvan Guillemin, the Lucas Brothers and H.R.H. Prince Philip, the Patron of the Club; and, on the Indian side, several hard-hitting generals, namely Habibullah, Wadiala, Kumaramangalam and Verma, and in the recent years, Rupi Brar, V.P. Singh, Jolly Ahluwalia, Kuldip Garcha and Prem Sirohi.

Polo is played on the Pat Williamson and Bahadur Singh Polo Grounds in the middle of the Race Course. The Calcutta polo season lasts from November to early March. Tournaments take place from the first week of December till the first of January, culminating in the Indian Polo Association Cup played generally on Christmas Day.

CALCUTTA NON-STOP

Life never stops in Calcutta. At any time of the year there is something going on — a festival, a wedding, a match, a demonstration, a concert, a vernissage or a party.

Festivals non-stop: *Boro mosh, tero purbo*, 12 months, 13 festivals. The Bengali saying, in fact, underestimates the number of festivals, civil and religious, celebrated in Calcutta, where communities belonging to all religions and from all over the subcontinent have brought along their own local cults which even within the Hindu religion vary from area to area.

If there is an activity which can be said to be typical of Calcutta, it is **Puja**. Basically, *puja* is an offering to the presiding deity, performed by an individual, a family, a community, a group of people or a locality. The offering may be of flowers, incense, fire, or, in some cases, animal sacrifices.

The community *puja* is one of the most spectacular events in Calcutta. It starts with the ordering of the *murthi*, a clay image of the deity at Kumartuli or Baghbazar in North Calcutta, or Patuapara at Kalighat. The *murthi* is fashioned from a straw armature coated with clay and modelled to the image of the deity, then mounted on a structure embellished with sola pith or tinsel, a vegetal material similar to white plastic foam, and installed in the *Puja Pandal*, a dais made of bamboo and pleated cloth, decorated with chandeliers and neon lights. Musical and cultural shows, exhibitions and fairs are held around the *pandal*.

A festival lasts several days, 10 in the case of *Durga Puja*. Offerings, prayers, animal sacrifices of goats and even buffaloes are made to the deity. On the occasion of *Kali* and *Durga Pujas*, special drummers, the Dhakis, using huge powerful drums made of a hollow mango tree branch and goat skin, arrive from all over Bengal to play during the festival. Besides Hindi and pop music lasting

<u>Preceding pages</u>: the Royal Calcutta Golf Club; all-male Jatra actors; a Natch girl performing in the 18th century (by Sir Charles Doyly). <u>Opposite</u>: Fireworks on Dussehra.

all night from loudspeakers, the rumble of their drums can be constantly heard all over the city on these occasions. On the last day, the *murthi* is carried by cheering devotees in festive processions, sometimes preceded by bagpipes playing Scottish tunes, to the Hooghly where it is immersed. The main Hindu festivals in Calcutta are **Durga Puja** (*Dussehra* for Northern Hindus), **Lakshmi Puja**, **Kali Puja** (*Divali* in the North) and **Sarasvati Puja**.

The first festival of the year in Calcutta is **New Year's Day**. Although most communities follow their own calendar, the first day of the Christian year is celebrated by all. Buses are garlanded. The city is in a festive mood, with decorations from Christmas past still very much in evidence.

The **Makar Sankranti** festival in mid-January marks the winter solstice. Over 500,000 pilgrims gather on Sagar Dwip, an island some 150 kilometres (93 miles) south of Calcutta, for the three-day **Ganga Sagar Mela**. The city in the second week of January is full of pilgrims on the way to the *mela*, sleeping in make-shift tents erected on the Maidan. The festival lasts from January 12th to 14th.

On the day the *Ganga Sagar Mela* ends, the **Baul Mela** begins. Hindu Vaishnab and Sufi Muslim Bauls from all over Bengal, from West Bengal as well as from Bangladesh, gather at Bolpur, 150 kilometres (93 miles) west of Calcutta to sing for three nights devotional songs.

Vivekanda's Birth Anniversary on January 12th, which is marked by ceremonies at the philosopher's house on Gaur Mohan Mukherjee Lane and processions from Maddox Square to the Ramakrishna Mission on Gul Park. **Netaji's Birthday**, on January 23rd, is a major civil festival in Calcutta. Speeches and gatherings take place at his house and around statues of the leader on the Maidan near Raj Bhavan and at the Shaymbazar Five-Point Crossing.

Republic Day, on January 26th, another civil festival, marks the day in 1948 when

India proclaimed herself a Republic. A parade takes place along Red Road, with Gurkhas, the Assam Rifles and the Tibetan Border Security Force, Sikhs from the Punjabi Regiment, the Bengal Mounted Police, followed by floats.

Late in January or in early Fabruary, *Saraswati Puja*, the festival of the Goddess of Learning, is celebrated by students, artists and professors. **Chinese New Year**, also in late January or early February, is noisily celebrated with dragon dances and firecrackers in front of every Chinese shop or business. The Tangra suburb, where the Chinese tanners live, is illuminated at night for

Holi, as it is called by Northern Hindus, heralds the short **spring** season. People from all walks of life celebrate the coming of spring by drinking *bhang*, a mildmilk beverage laced with marijuana, by smearing each other with powdered colours, red especially, and spraying coloured water at passers-by. Social barriers are broken. It is a time when poor may touch rich, lower-cast touch uppercast. *Ching Ming*, the Chinese festival of the dead, is marked with prayers, offerings and the loud sound of firecrackers at the Cantonese and Hakka Si Yu, Tsong Fa, Tong Oon and Tchung Lai Shan Tong cemeteries of Tangra.

a week. Some two weeks after Chinese New Year, all the Chinese of Calcutta gather at Achipur, 50 kilometres (31 miles) west of Calcutta for prayers at the local Chinese temple and at the grave of Ah Chi, the first Chinese to settle in India.

On February 21st, **Ramakrishna's Birth Anniversary**, ceremonies are held at the Ramakrishna Mission on Gul Park and at the Belur Math headquarters of the movement. In late February, on *Shivarati*, the festival of Shiva, women flock to the Ghats to take a dip in the Ganges and pray for fertility.

In March, the festival of **Dol Purnima**, or

On **Charak Puja**, the eve of the Bengali New Year, devotees at Chatu Babu Bazar attach themselves to giant rotating swings symbolising the cycles of life. In the past, they hanged from sharp hooks passing through their flesh.

Noboborsho, on April 14th, marks the beginning of Bengali New Year and also the beginning of **Summer**. Businessmen carry their new *halkata* account books, statues of Ganesh and Lakshmi to the Kali temple for blessings. In the evening, customers make token payments to their favourite shops while owners offer them sweets. Shops are decorated with garlands, auspicious mango leaves, sala pith ornaments and young banana. A few days later, on **Mahavira Jayanti**, the birth anniversary of the last and greatest Jain prophets, there are processions of the Svetamber Sect from Harrison Raod to Kalakar Street, and of the Digambar Sect from Belgachia to Baisakh Lane.

May Day, another civil festival, is celebrated by a huge meeting on the Maidan, then by songs and dances throughout the town. **Buddha Jayanti**, in the first week of the month, marks the Buddha's Birth Anniversary. Prayers are held in the Buddhist temples of the city. Also in May, on **Shitola** organised on the streets, on makeshift stages. The main celebrations are held at his palace in Jorasanko.

The first festival of the **Monsoon** is **Rath Yatra**, in late June or early July, in honour of Jagannath, an avatar of Vishnu. Processions are organised in Calcutta by the ISKON movement in the downtown area and in Serampore, north of Calcutta. There are prayers at the Vaishnab temple on Hazra Road. Replicas of Jagannath's chariot are sold at Kalighat. Children decorate the chariots with flowers and place in them clay images of Jagannath, his brother Balaram and sister Subhadra.

Puja, the festival of the Goddess of Cool Weather and of Measles, a disease that errupts during the Monsoon, people pray for coolness and protection against the disease at street altars where Shitola is represented riding a donkey or in a bust form, with a dark-brown face, silver hallucinated eyes and draped in red. On May 9th, **Rabindra Jayanti**, a festival marking Tagore's Birth Anniversary, song and dance shows are

Opposite: blessing new account books on Bengali New Year's Day. Above: videoshow during Kali Puja.

On **Manasha Puja**, or **Naag Panchami**, the festival of the Goddess of the Snakes in August, prayers are offered to her to protect farmers from getting bitten by snakes when harvesting the monsoon paddy crop at the Manasha Temple by the bridge of the Alipore Jail.

On **Independence Day**, August 15th, another civil festival, the Indian Tricolour is hoisted on the Maidan at Shahid Minar and prayers offered at Gandhi Ghat in Barrackpore at 8.30 am. **Janmashtami**, in late August, Lord Krishna's Brithday, is celebrated at midnight in the Krishna temples. On **Ma-**

hatma Jayanti, on October 2nd, Gandhi's Anniversary, an all-faith meeting is held at Gandhi Ghat. The end of the Monsoon is marked by several festivals. ***Ganesh Charthurthi***, in early September, is celebrated by traders from northern and southern India who worship the elephant-headed God of Fortune.

In the same month, ***Vishna Karma Puja***, the festival of the God of Creation, is marked by all industrial houses, artists, craftsmen and weavers. The tools of production are cleaned, machines repainted, statues of Vishwakarma holding a hammer and pliers are erected in workshops.

up virtually at every street corner. The *puja* climaxes on ***Mahadashami***, the 10th day when the image is carried in decorated carts or trucks in festive processions to be immersed in the Hooghly.

Northern Indian communities celebrate the festival of ***Dussehra*** on that day commemorating Rama's victory over the Ravana devil, symbolising the triumph of good over evil. At sunset, huge effigies of Ravana, his son and his brother are burned on the Maidan. ***Laxmi Puja***, five days later, on full moon, is the festival of the Goddess of Prosperity who is worshipped daily in most Hindu households for the family's well-

The start of **winter** coincides with ***Durga Puja*** in October, the most important festival in Bengal. According to Hindu mythology, all gods and goddesses of the Hindu pantheon endowed Durga with a portion of their own energy to give her strength, or *shakti*, to destroy evil forces. Some 2,000 *pandals* are erected throughout the city. The image of Durga shows her slaying the most powerful demon, Mahisasur.

This is the season for gifts. New clothes are purchased. Shops overflow with the latest goods. People take to the streets to visit the thousands of *puja pandals* which spring

being. Public *pujas* are performed in the same premises as for *Durga Puja*.

Kali Puja, two weeks later, is another popular festival. Kali is the Goddess of Destruction. According to Hindu mythology, having rid the earth of demons, Kali went on a rampage of destruction. Her husband Lord Shiva was sent to stop this carnage. When he finally succeeded, and when Kali saw that her husband was on the ground and that she had her foot on his chest, it shocked her back to her senses. Again Calcutta has *pandals* at every street corner. The image of Kali usually shows her with her foot on Lord Shiva's chest, a severed head in one hand, her sword in the other, and wearing a garland of skulls. Kali is worshipped as the Mother Goddess who protects from evil. She also epitomises strength or *shakti* and the darker side of life. She is the presiding deity of the Tantric cult. The actual *puja* takes place at midnight on the day of the new moon.

Kali Puja coincides with **Divali**, the North Indian New Year, the festival of lights that marks Rama's return from exile. Households clean their houses, put on new clothes and light up candles all over their houses. Traders go to the temples to pray to Ganesh and Lakshmi and bring new account books into the Ganga at sunset. *Jagadhatri Puja*, the festival of another image of Durga, is held in Chandernagore nine days later. Two days after that is Brothers' Days, **Bhai Phonta** or **Bhratri Dvitiya**. Elder sisters dip their little fingers into *kajol*, a mixture of *ghee*, rice-paste and almond paste, and put a mark on their brothers' foreheads.

Indira Jayanti, on October 31st, the day of the assassination of Indira Gandhi, is celebrated with the fervour of a religious festival. Shrines, makeshift altars, with a statue of the former Prime Minister of India.

Christmas is widely celebrated in Calcutta, not only by the Christian community.

for blessing. To attract good luck, people gamble all night playing *teenpatta*, rummy, poker or *mahjong*. Children and adults set off firecrackers all night. No one sleeps on that night.

On **Chhat Puja**, two days later, a Bihari festival in celebration of the sun, Untouchables, with transvestite dancers accompanying them, come to the ghats to make offerings of fruit and vegetables by dipping them

<u>Opposite</u>: most marriages take place in winter.
<u>Above</u>: Live bands are available for weddings or parties.

Streets are illuminated. There are parties in clubs and hotels. The best masses are at St Paul's Cathedral, candle-lit on this occasion, at St Andrew's Kirk and at the Murgihatta Catholic Cathedral. A *pandal* with a Nativity erected on Dharantala Street (Lenin Sarani) in front of the St Thomas Church.

On **New Year's Eve**, parties are organised in clubs, hotels, restaurants and private homes. The city is illuminated. People go to bed late. Those who manage will go to the races the next day in the afternoon — a hangover 'must' in Calcutta.

The **Muslim festivals** are celebrated with

intensity in Calcutta. During **Bakraid**, marking the end of *Ramazan* and **Idulfitr** in celebration of the *hajis*, the pilgrims to the Holy Mecca, the northern part of the Maidan becomes the prayer grounds for Muslims who gather around the Saheed Minar while the *muezzin* leads the sessions from the top of the monument.

The Shiite processions on Ashoura along Chitpore Road and, in Metiaburuz, Kidderpore, Rajabazar, Narkeldanga, Beliaghata and Manicktola, are an impressive spectacle. They are led by a white horse, Hussain's mount, followed by tazias, preciously handicrafted replicas of Hussain's grave, and flagellants who alternatively pound their chests singing "*Hassan, ya Hussain*" and flagellate themselves with razor blades attached to the end of a multi-tailed whip.

Performing Arts Non-stop: As the seat of British power, Calcutta experienced an influx of Asian and European cultures that combined to give Calcutta a unique cultural landscape where European and Asian cultures, traditional and modern, at times coexist, at times interact or combine.

As far as **music** is concerned, Calcutta is a responsive city. It offers throughout the year a spectrum of festivals, ranging from private evening concerts to all-night public sessions in a park or week-long festivals.

The peak season is winter. The grand maestros of **Indian Classical Music** such as Ravi Shankar, spend the winter in Calcutta, teaching, playing, and staging performances during that period. Most concerts are arranged by private associations. The best halls are Rabindra Sadan, Kala Mandir, Birla Sabhaghar, the Netaji Stadium, the Ramakrishna Mission and Mahajati Sadan, but there are also concerts in the open, in parks, or on the street on a stage erected for the duration of the performance. Both the Hindustani and Carnatic schools are represented in Calcutta.

Western Classical Music is not popular in Calcutta nowadays. The Calcutta School of Music, the only testimony of consequence remaining, was founded in 1915. Others, like the Gonzales Brothers, the Calcutta Symphony Orchestra and the Calcutta Light Orchestra Group, have disappeared. As far as **Western Modern Music** is concerned, Calcutta saw the world's most famous bands such as Duke Ellington and his orchestra. Today Calcutta is shunned by most performers. Local rock, blues and jazz musicians and bands can usually be seen at fucntions and the open-air concerts organised every year in the Open-Air Theatre at the Lakes or in the yard of the St Xavier College.

All the styles of **Indian Classical Dance** can be found in Calcutta: Bharatnayam, Kuchipudi, Kathakali, Kathak, Odissi and Manipuri. **Odissi**, a classical dance of Orissa based on Vaishnab themes and local folklore was considered as courtesan dancing until recently. It was purified and revived in the 1920s by Guru Kelucharan Mahapratra.

Manipuri originates in Northeast India, in Manipur. Based on Vaishnab themes too, but also on tribal folklore, the Manipuri style was introduced to Calcutta by Rabindranath Art Academy.

As a later development, semi-choreographed performances of **Manipuri Martial Arts** are now held regularly in the city.

Besides traditional Indian and Western Modern forms, there is a distinct category of semi-classical, semi-modern music, lavishly represented and enjoyed in Calcutta. The most popular are the Bengali musical drama, *Gitinitya*, and the dance drama, *Natyanatga*. Drawing from the Manipuri School, and from European choreography, the players sing, while recitation is

Tagore in his choreographical pieces. It is quite different from other forms of Indian classical dance. Women wear a hooped skirt, sequined in bright colours, movements are flowing, reminding of Burmese or Thai dancers. The Manipuri style is also characterized by its vigorous footwork and drum background. One of the leading masters of Manipur dancing, Guru Bipin Sieng, teaches in Calcutta. There is also a school at the Birla

Opposite: Manipuri martial arts are rarely performed outside Eastern India. **Above**: The former facade of the Bengal Club.

used as a backdrop for professional dancers and actors enacting the drama. Shows generally take place at Rabindra Sadan or Mahajati Sadan. Poetry and song recitals are also popular. There are several styles: **Rabindra Sangeet**, a category apart, representing all the songs and poems written by Tagore; **Puratani**, sessions devoted to a composer (Atul Prosad, Nurul Islam) or a theme; and **Kirtan**, based on Vaisnab themes, especially **Padabali Kirtan**, an almost absurd mixture of melodrama, simple narration, repartee, combining prose, poetry, Sanskrit, old Brajboli and Bangla. The folk tradition of Bengal is perpetuated by the **Bauls**, usually found in the countryside. Several of them, however, live and perform in Calcutta in the streets on the occasion of Rabindra Jayanti in May. Fusion of tradition with **modern dance**, accomplished by Uday Shankar, is now carried on by his son, wife and daughter, with three companies, Ananda Shankar, Amala Shankar and Mamata Shankar. Performances are held every year at Rabindra Sadan.

Jatra is a traditional form of street theatre. Actors are all male. Often transvestites play the role of women. Jatra has been extensively used by the Communist Party for propaganda in the countryside. Jatra groups from West Bengal and Orissa come to Calcutta after the Monsoon and leave at the end of summer. **Modern Theatre** was introduced to Calcutta by a Russian, Lebedeff, at the end of the 18th century. Nowadays, most plays are in Bengali and performed in North Calcutta. They are either original creations or translations of foreign plays.

Cinema is nowadays the most popular form of entertainment in Calcutta. The first movies were shot here in 1901 by a Hiralal Sen staging excerpts from traditional Bengali plays. The film industry developed in the 1920s and 1930s with directors such as J.F. Madan, Amar Chowdhury, Saratchandra Chatterjee, Pramathes Barna and Sir B.N. Sarkar, and the first stars Kananbala, Suchitra Sen, Supriya Devi. After the War, it took several years before the big screen made a come-back. New directors appeared, and among them were the late Ritwick Ghatak, Satyajit Ray, Gautam Ghosh, Tapan Sinha, and Aparna Sen. Operating from the Indrapuri Studios at Tollygunge, they gave Bengali cinema its international aura.

Nowadays, the Calcutta film industry is ridden with problems. Movies are now expensive to shoot, the VCR and a diarrhoea of low-grade Hindi movies draw away the public. Nandan, a modern complex on a Lower Circular Road, and the Calcutta Film Society at the Skating Rink, show, however, Bengali movies on a regular basis.

Social life non-stop: The social life of Calcutta revolves around parties, clubs, social events and associations of all sorts. Most parties take place in winter. Wedding parties, an occasion for women to display their best saris and jewellery, private concerts of Indian classical music or *ghazal*, and garden

parties held under a huge dais, the *Shamyana*, where glass chandeliers are hung, are the most popular forms. The season starts at *Durga Puja* and ends with *Holi*. Other major social events are the horse races, the polo season and the vintage car rally organized by *The Statesman*, Calcutta's oldest English language daily. The rally starts at the Eastern Command Stadium on the Maidan and ends up at the Tollygunge Club. Over a hundred vehicles take part, Rolls-Royces, Lord Mountbatten's White Packard, the oldest car being a 1901 Renault. There are also associations: learned societies (the Asiatic Society, the Indian National Trust for the Architectural Cultural Heritage), charitable organisations (the Rotary Club, the Lion's Club, the Worldwide Fund for Nature).

Club life has been introduced in Calcutta at an early stage by the servants of the East India Company who needed a place to let their hair down. Sports clubs appeared first. Then came the social clubs, designed, according to Sir Owen Jenkins, the head of a former British company, "by scheming mamas to keep the eligible bachelors out of the clutches of pretty Anglo-Indian girls and away from the attraction of the red-light district".

The apex of club life was in the late 1930s and through WW II with the 300 Club, a club on Theatre Road, founded in 1936 by a White Russian Boris Lissanovitch. Members were the jet-set of British and Princely India. There was jazz, gypsy music, caviar, vodka.

The **Bengal Club** on Russell Street, the oldest social club in Calcutta, founded in 1827 had as members the cream of the Calcutta Society. Traders, lower ranking civil and military officers were not admitted. Until 1962, the club refused to accept Indians. As a gesture of protest, Lord Mountbatten never visited it. The club has lost its front part and its impressive facade on Chowringhee and the Maidan as the result of a controversial real estate transaction. The unaesthetic Chatterjee International Centre now stands in its place. The Bengal Club is chiefly a lunch club where anyone that counts must be seen regularly. The main features of the club are the Reynolds Room

Opposite: Unexpected winners of the best fancy-dress competition at the Statesman's Vintage Car Rally. Above: January 1st at the races — a social must.

with a real Reynolds, bound 19th-century collections of the *Calcutta Gazette* and *Punch*, and the bar with its silver cobra, the symbol of the club.

The **Calcutta Club** on Lower Circular Road was founded in 1907 by a group of Indians belonging to the elite — Lord Sinha, the Maharajadhiraj of Burdwan, Sir R.N. Mukherjee and the Maharaja of Santosh — and European friends, who would not accept the 'Whites Only' policy of the Bengal Club. Under the rules of the Calcutta Club, a British and an Indian would alternate as Club President. The club has grass and clay courts; a rich library; and the men-only Naughty Bar, still off-limits to women. It is frequented mostly by the Bengali high-society, mostly professionals. The club is famous for its smoked hilsa fish, probably the best in Calcutta.

Horse racing in Calcutta started in 1798. The present race course opened in 1819 adn the **Royal Calcutta Turf Club** in 1897. The race course on the Maidan has a special members' enclosure where members can have drinks or lunch while watching the whole race 'live' on a television screen, through a closed circuit system.

The **Saturday Club**, on Wood Street, founded in 1878, was the *boxwallah's* club. Members would be businessmen and lower civil ranking officers. It is known for its Light Horse bar from where during World War II, members of the Calcutta Light Horse, found unfit for armed service devised and carried out a raid on German ships anchored at the other end of the country, in the harbour of Goa, then a neutral Portuguese enclave. Members still belong chiefly to the business community.

Two new lunch clubs have appeared, the **Chambers** of the Bengal Chamber of Commerce, at the top of the Royal Exchange building and the **Conclave**, on Lower Circular Road, frequented chiefly by the North Indian business community.

The **Tollygunge Club**, founded in 1825, is the only country club in Calcutta. Built in 1797, the club house is one of the few surviving *neel kothis*, as indigo planters' bungalows were called. It was sold by its first owners to Prince Ghulam Muhammad, the son of Tippu Sultan, before being purchased by the club.

The Tollygunge Club offers a wide variety of activities: horse-riding, polo practice, tent-pegging, clay-shooting, tennis, squash, swimming and golf. Horse-races used to be held at the club in winter until the late 1970s when part of the race course was taken away by the Government to be used as the site of the Tollygunge Metro Station. The Tollygunge Club has the best pink gin in town, served at the Tippu Sultan Bar. It is the venue for a number of tennis, horse, golf and squash championships and challenges. It is also the venue known for its traditional yearly functions such as the Monsoon, Christmas and New Year balls. The main attraction on New Year's Eve is the night tent-pegging competition where riders try to pick up flaming peat-coated tent-pegs at full gallop with a pig-stick in the dark.

The **Royal Calcutta Golf Club**, the oldest outside the British Isles, founded in 1829, was allowed to use the adjective 'Royal' in 1912 by King George V. In addition to an 18-hole course, it offers clay-tennis courts, a century-old bowling-green on the Maidan and an excellent open-air *tandoori* lunch buffet on Saturdays in winter.

Sporting clubs in Calcutta include the **Calcutta Cricket and Football Club**, the oldest too outside of Britain, an amalgamation of the cricket clubs at Barrackpore, Calcutta and Dum Dum, mentioned as early as 1792 in the local English press; the **Calcutta Swimming Club**, near the High Court, the **Calcutta Rowing Club** on the Dhakuria Lakes; the **Calcutta Polo Club**, the oldest in the world; the **South Club** at Ballygunge, a tennis club with eight clay- and 10 grass-courts; the **Fort William Club**; and the **Ladies' Golf Club**, a unique feminine institution, on the Maidan.

The club culture has caught up with the poorer sections of the city and many neighbourhoods in the bazar area or even the outskirts have their own club, sometimes nothing more than a simple thatched hut, but bearing unexpected names such as the Pickwick Club, where the local youth assemble to play cards, as well as football or cricket on the adjoining road or vacant lot.

NATIVE SHOPS & SIGNS
E CITY

SHOPPING

If one is equipped with a discerning eye, a taste for the unusual, and time, Calcutta is a shopper's delight, with a mind-boggling number and variety of shopping districts.

New Market, or Sir Stuart Hogg Market, stretching along the entire length of Lindsay Street, is an antiquated supermarket by contemporary standards, but a source of great pride to Calcuttans. Established in the last century, it was one of the first and finest shopping plazas of its time. Within the imposing brick structure, parallel lines of shops house an amazing array of merchandise — gold jewellery, electronics, kitchen-ware, leather, dry fruit, meat, pastries, Tibetan stones and copperware, made-to-order leather shoes and bags, carefully crafted silverware, costume jewellery, and a wide range of traditional sarees and textiles — can be bought here at affordable prices.

New Market is flanked at its rear by a fresh foods market and grocery strips, while on its approach, there are independent retail outlets selling famous brands of sarees, handloom material and readymade garments. An extension of the New Market on to the Free School Street area offers an unique collection of secondhand records, books and magazines. A must for collectors of original singles by the Beatles.

Most merchants in the New Market area are conversant in English and if a good rapport is struck, prices can come down considerably. Porters, with wicker baskets to carry your shopping to the car, are available for hire. An interesting feature of the New

Market is its band of mobile shops. You will often find a "shop on two legs" following you around the market, carrying a variety of merchandise on its head, arms, shoulders and neck, beckoning you to make a purchase.

The **Vardaan Market** on Camac Street, the **Air-conditioned Market** on Shakespeare Sarani, the **Treasure Island** on Lindsay Street, and the **Vaibhan Shopping Complex** on Lee Road are all recently built, modern, air-conditioned shopping complexes, that offer all sorts of merchandise, both Indian and imported, ranging from regular utility durables to fine handicraft items. Prices are fixed here. Amongst other things of interest, an intriguing range of special *masala* is also available. These are usually chewed by an Indian after a meal, to freshen his breath and to aid digestion. Intricately crafted anklets and toe-rings made in silver and sometimes dipped in gold are a speciality at these markets, as well.

The **Dakshinapan**, off Dhakuria Bridge in South Calcutta, is a newly built shopping enclave that has, within its spacious portals, representations of every major state in India. Though it offers both modern and utility merchandise, the predominant accent is on the traditional and the ethnic. **Gurjari**, the unique to Gujarat.

The Bengal State Emporia include **Manjusha**, **Tantushri** and **Tantuja**. A wide range of sarees, from the cheap Dhanekhalis, Tangail cottons and silks to the exotic Jamdanis and Baluchars, are available in the most gorgeous colours and patterns. Men's *dhotis*, raw silk, shirting and trouser lengths are also available.

The Tamil Nadu Emporium, **Poompuhar**, has a display of wood-carved and bronze figurines of mythological origin (Ganesh, Siva), grass mats, baskets, costume jewellery in semi-precious stones, South Indian cotton and silk sarees.

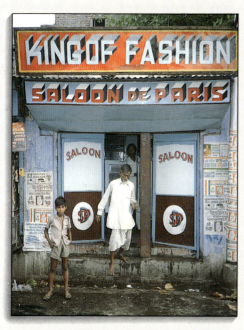

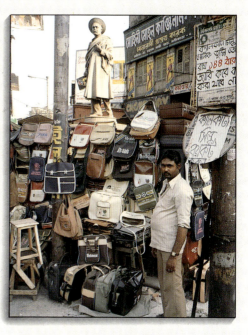

Gujarat State Emporium sells Gujrati handicrafts such as tie-and-dye files, notelets, handbags and purses, leather- and wool-embroidered shoes, mirror-work appliqué, embroidered *salwar kameez*, cushion covers, bed linen and floor mats. Traditional *patola*, vegetable dye prints, tie-and-dye sarees and dress materials are usually available in cotton or silk. Carved wood and thick rope combine to form exquisite furniture

Preceding pages: On Divali, candles are lit everywhere; shop signs of Calcutta. <u>Opposite</u>: ethnic chic is making a strong comeback. <u>Above</u>: hairdo? Want a bag?

The Haryana Emporia, **Weaver** and **Partridge**, specialise in furnishing material, wood work of Saharanpur, readymade cotton *kurtas* and pajamas, cheaply available in different pastel shades.

Rajasthali, the Rajasthan State Emporium, has bedspreads and table linen in miniature prints, eye-catching *durries* woven with intricate geometric patterns, enamelled china in turquoise blue, green and white, a large selection of semi-precious stones, silver jewellery, tie-and-dye light quilts typical of Jaipur and assorted chiffons, cottons and silks for dresses and sarees

Shopping 111

(either printed or in tie-and-dye).

Phulkari, the Punjab Emporium, offers wooden kitchen-ware, leather shoes, furniture, typically Punjabi *phulkari* embroidery on bedcovers and cushion covers, as well as cotton and silk readymade garments.

The Kashmir State Emporium, **Pumposh**, is in a class apart, with intricately embroidered *namdas*, shawls, *phirans*, table linen and exquisitely carved and painted containers and furniture.

The Orissa State Emporium, **Utkalika**, has a collection of the vividly coloured and woven Katki, Vichitrapuri, Sambalpuri and Bamkai sarees and matching blouse pieces

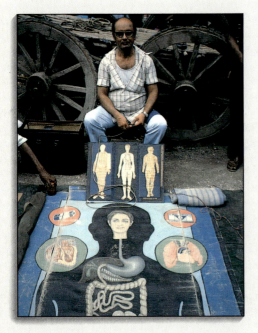

and dress materials. These sarees are not only durable but also eternally fashionable. Another striking form of handicraft, *Patachitra*, an intricate style of painting on mythological themes, practised by village craftsmen of Raghuajpour, is represented here.

Besides the above, the **Tripura State Emporium** offers a large variety of cane crafts while the **Assam State Emporium** sells all sorts of Assamese silks (*muga*, *eri* shawls).

Outside these formal shopping zones, there exists a roadside phenomenon unique to Calcutta. Hawkers, who originally came from Orissa to set up shop for the *Puja* season in October, installed themselves permanently in certain areas of the city. **Gariahat** is one such hub, where the south of Calcutta conducts its business. It's a veritable bargainer's paradise, catering mainly to Bengali middle-class tastes. Clothes, sarees, toys, undergarments, books, shoes, costume jewellery, stick-on bindies, bags, terracotta, crockery, electronics and readymade *cholis* are available in all shapes, sizes and variety. The Gariahat stretch extends on the one hand into the Lansdowne Road Hawkers' Corner and the Lake Market, and on the other into the Ballygunge New Market. Most shops here provide a similar mix to that of the Gariahat Market together with steel utensils and grocery stores.

The **Kalighat Market**, established around the Kali Temple, offers a wide range of ritualistic accessories in brass, copper and stone. An unique shopping zone, almost legendary in stature, is the Burrabazar area. A wholesale purchase zone for most of Calcutta's retail outlets, this market, nestled in perhaps the city's busiest commercial district, is thickly populated. Groups of tiny rooms, aligned in an almost never-ending stream, are divided into sectors according to the kind of merchandise sold. Unending metres of cloth, yards of wool, truckloads of fresh foods, exotic spices, steel and plastic kitchen-ware, footwear in plastic, rubber or leather, and a host of other commodities find their way from Burrabazar into the city every day.

Besides Burrabazar, Chandni Chawk (off Dharamtala Street) and the Bagri Market are similar wholesale outlets.

Calcutta's shopping does not stop at its plazas. If one has a taste for the exclusive and the new 'Ethnic Chic', there are a number of fashionable boutiques that are spread in and around central Calcutta. For a pick of carefully crafted *salwar-kameez*, exquisite sarees, shoes or handbags, Ananda on Russel Street, Ritu's Boutique on Rafi Ahmed Kidwal Road, Razz Matazz, Nekita or Take & Talk are good hunting grounds.

A Calcutta speciality that shoppers might find of paricular interest are the makers of

Indian musical instruments. Readymade tablas, tanpuras and harmoniums are of the highest quality in Calcutta. Sharat Sardar in Chitpur and Pakrashi's, Hemen Babu's and Bimal Babu's units in South Calcutta are of exceptional repute.

For ethnic handicrafts, cloths and materials, a convenient one stop is the Cottage Industries Emporium at Esplanade. Sasha, on Free School Street, also has a large variety crafted with modern utility in mind. The Bengal Home Industries on Lower Circular Road offers a similar range with a specialisation in Bengal-based crafts.

Exclusive, made-to-order pieces of craftsers, plastic pens, innovative toys, cheap clothing, shoes and a myriad of other items, laid out in neat piles along the pavements or displayed in little sheds that serve as shops.

Tea is available at the Dakshinapan Shopping Complex, or at private retail stores in the Chowringhee area. The Firpo's Market, the New Market and Jadu Babu's Bazar are other such markets where a similar range of merchandise can be bought. The Jaggu Bazar area, off Bhowanipur, has a special chain of shops called Lakshmi Babu's Asli Chandi Ki Dukan, where only the purest of silver ornaments are claimed to be sold, for over a century. Custom-made silverware has

manship like *dhokra*, terracotta, *pat* paintings, wood, conch shell and stone carvings, exotic Baluchari sarees, and embroidered Bengal *kantha* can be procured from the Crafts Council of West Bengal, on Southern Avenue.

A walk along College Street or the Esplanade will expose the browser to a wide number of out-of-print journals, magazines and books, a variety of gaily coloured post-

Opposite: Any tension? **Above:** Poster art with a political flavour — an unusual souvenir to bring home.

a distinctive quality crafted by the Bengali silversmith.

Less than 100-year-old Indian jewellery and Anglo-Indiana can be purchased from the 'auction houses' of Park Street, from Saroj's, from Oriental Antique House at the Oberoi or Khazanna at the Taj. Old books on India can be found at the annual Calcutta Book Fair, around College Street and at Punthi Pushtak on Rabindra Sarani. Cassettes of Indian music are sold opposite New Market while second-hand singles and LPs of Western pop music can be found on Free School Street.

CATERERS BY APPOINTMENT
TO HIS EXCELLENCY THE LORD IRWIN,
VICEROY and GOVERNOR-GENERAL OF INDIA

FIRPO'S

GOLD MEDAL AWARDS AT LONDON, MANCHESTER & CALCUTTA EXHIBITIONS.

CALCUTTA :: INDIA

Firpo's Louis XVI Restaurant and Ball-room.

PERFECT CUISINE
Renowned
LONDON and ITALIAN ORCHESTRAS
SPECIALLY SPRUNG DANCE FLOOR

FIRPOS, CALCUTTA.

Nos 1402 and 902.

FOODS OF CALCUTTA

Being a cosmopolitan city, Calcutta is the home to a variety of foods. The main ones are the Bengali and the Anglo-Indian cuisines.

There are actually two sorts of **Bengali foods** in Calcutta. **Gothi food**, indigenous to Calcutta, is eaten chiefly in the north of the city, the home of the old Calcuttan families. Gothis do not take chillies and love sweets. **Bangal food**, on the other hand, is eaten by Bengalis originating from Eastern Bengal. Bangals eat about the same dishes but add little green chillies and hardly put any sugar in their sweetmeat and desserts.

Bengali food is based on fish and a variety of sweetmeats. Strict vegetarian taboos are generally not followed. Fish is not considered as meat and many Bengalis have no objections to eating chicken, mutton, buffalo meat, and even beef in some cases. In Bengal, fish is a symbol of fertility that appears in many rituals. It is touched by the groom and sent to the bride's home before the wedding ceremony. A meal is not considered complete without fish and it is the head of the family who shops for fish. Bengalis living around the delta of the Ganges prefer fresh river fish whereas those inland love salt water fish. The reason most Bengalis prefer fresh water fish is because, according to them, the salt water kind lacks in sweetness. Every neighbourhood has its own market but Gariahat and Lake markets are considered to be the best Bengali markets. They open before 7.00 am and offer a good selection of fish and prawns from the Ganges delta and the Bay of Bengal.

The most prized of all fish is hilish or hilsa, a silvery fish unique to the Bay of Bengal, which spends the winter months in the deep open sea. In late February, it swims up the delta to spawn. Hilsa can be served fried with tamarind sauce, cooked in mustard gravy, steamed in yogurt or smoked in banana leaves with a paste of mustard oil, mustard seeds, green and red chillies, turmeric and salt. Traditionally, hilsa is not eaten during winter between *Durga* and *Saraswati puja*, a period of about four months. Other fishes include the cat fish, tangra, the smaller singhi, sold live swimming in buckets of water, leta, an eel-like fish, rui, a sort of carp full of roe, and koi or climbing perch.

Bengalis also eat *pabda kakkra* (hard-shelled crabs), *bagda chingri* (tiger prawns), from the sea, as well as smaller prawns and crayfishes that abound in the surrounding lakes and rivers, and are available all year round. River fish is generally prepared with mustard oil as it is believed to be the best way to bring out the taste of the fish. The only exception the Bengalis make to sea fish is the betki (beckti in English), which is very versatile and can be served baked, fried or curried.

In Calcutta, one can enjoy vegetable varieties not found in the rest of India, but used in countries east of India, such as Burma, Thailand or Vietnam. The bitter gourd — stuffed with minced pork in a soup or sag, a local variety of spinach — is eaten to cool down the body.

Bengalis also use the banana tree quite extensively. No part of this versatile plant will go to waste, from the delicate heart, not unlike the heart of palm, to the flower (*moccha*) that will go into dishes like fish smoked in banana leaf or curried banana flower koftas. Bananas judged not good enough to be eaten ripe are used to make chips, not unlike potato chips. There is also a green banana cutlet dish. The leaves of the tree are used as plates.

A meal for the Bengali is a ritual itself. Stress is laid down on how food is served and the order followed. Contrary to Mughlai food, Bengalis eat each item separately with a little rice so that the flavours are not mixed. Traditionally, the meal is served on a big round silver or aluminium plate, the *thali*. The various items of food are placed in bowls around the top of the *thali*. Rice is mounted in the middle with a little salt,

Preceding pages: Midday at New Market; **Left**: Firpo was once the Mecca of dining in Calcutta.

chillies and lime placed at the right. First, a little *ghee* may be poured over a small portion of rice and eaten with a pinch of salt. After this some lentils or *dal*, followed by vegetable dishes; the lightly spiced ones first, then the more heavily spiced ones. Then come the fish preparations and again, the lightly spiced dishes are served first, followed by either prawn or crayfish and occasionally, chicken or mutton and chutney with its sweet and sour taste to clear the palate, together with crisp wafers like *papadum*. Dessert is usually sweet yogurt, *misti doi*. The meal concludes with *paan*, areca nut wrapped in betel leaves, and considered as good for digestion. A glass of with milk and sugar. A lunch time favourite is *sukto*, a mixture of diced and fried vegetables, some bitter like bitter gourd, some starchy like potato, some pungent like white radish, some stiff like hard-skinned flat bean. To this is added ground split peas, cooked with milk and water and flavoured with ground ginger, ground mustard seeds, cumin and tumeric. It is usually served with *dal*, fried vegetable, chutney, may be *rui maccher jhol*, carp cooked in cumin, coriander, turmeric, chillies and water. *Mishti doi* or thick sweetened yogurt usually follows. The evening meal, taken at around 10pm, starts with rice, *dal*, pumpkin flowers dipped in chick pea flour and deep fried. Next, come

water is always placed on the corner. Food is eaten with the right hand. For normal, everyday meals *batis* or bowls are not used and the food is placed in ceramics or earthern bowls in the middle for everyone to share from.

A Bengali will start the day with a cup of tea and *moori*, puffed rice tossed with mustard oil and green chillies or mixed with milk and freshly mashed fruit like mangoes or jackfruit. The mid-morning meal, *Jalkabar*, consist often of *singhara*, a Bengali *samosa* such as potatoes and cauliflowers, wrapped in a triangular-shaped pastry and deep fried sweets like *sandesh* or *rossogolla*, and tea

fish or prawns and vegetables, followed by meat, chutney with *loochis* bread and, to finish, *bhapa doi* (steamed yogurt) and sweets made of *chhana* (curded milk).

Finding a Bengali restaurant in Calcutta is difficult as Bengali food is usually home-cooked. There are exceptions: Suruchi, a women-operated cooperative, on Elliott Road, J's Shop, on Rashbehari, the Somargaon at the Taj Bengal Hotel, the Wednesday buffet-lunch at the Bengal Club and the Bengali New Year buffet at the Park Hotel.

Bengali love sweets. In the past, most homes made their own sweets. Nowadays, they are mostly produced by shops. *Chhana*, the main ingredient for Bengali sweets, is obtained by adding lime juice to boiling milk. The curd is then separated from the whey by filtering through a muslin cloth. *Rossogolla* served at most festive gatherings is *chhana* formed into balls and dropped in boiling syrup. *Sondesh* is *chhana* mixed with sugar syrup and cooked over a low fire until the moisture evaporates. It is a delicacy served throughout the year, but in the spring instead of syrup, the season's *jaggery* , or *gur*, a variety of brown sugar obtained from date trees, is added instead. There is also *pantua*, a fried sweetened *chhana* ball. Best known sweet shops are Ganguram's on Elgin Road or Chowringhee, K.C. Das on the Esplanade, and Bhim Nag at Shobha Bazar.

With a larger European presence, an **Anglo-Indian food** has evolved in Calcutta. A typical Anglo-Indian meal will start with smoked hilsa, the substitute found for smoked salmon, or honey-cured ham, followed by a bekti fish, cooked in a sauce or fried, and for dessert mango *phool*, a green mango mousse. A typical Anglo-Indian drink is the pink gin, an aperitif made of gin with a dash of angustura and served with an olive. Ice is not compulsory. For smoked hilsa, the best places in town are the Calcutta Club and the Skyroom Restaurant on Park Street. A number of Western restaurants serve Anglo-Indian food for lunch. The mecca of pink gin is the Tollygunge Club.

Other cuisines are available in Calcutta. **Mughlai food**, chiefly *tandoor*, curries, *masala* and *biryani*, is popular. The best-known restaurants are the Amber on Waterloo Street, and the Kebab-e-Que at the Astor Hotel on Shakespeare Sarani. The Royal Hotel opposite the Nakhoda Mosque and Kabir's at Chandni Chowk serve excellent chicken or mutton *byriani* and *firni*, a dessert made of semolina and rose water. Calcutta has several vegetarian communities. The Marwaris are the strictest as some of them will not even eat vegetables with a smell such as onions or garlic. That does not mean that **Marwari food** is dull. Some of of the Marwari restaurants even feature Mexican or Italian vegetarian food promotions! The Tamils are also vegetarians. **Tamil food** is usually served on *thalis*, steel round dishes with compartments. A typical Tamil meal is based on rice or *dosa*, a rice flour pancake which comes plain, with onions or potato curry filling. Several varieties of vegetable curry are spooned out in small piles on the edges of a steel *thali*.

Calcutta is famous for its **hawker food**. Hawkers, known as *puchkawallas*, are found near offices, markets, along commercial streets, on the Maidan, near every bus stop, railway station, and religious, social or

sports meetings. The largest concentration of *puchkawallas* is probably around B.B.D. Bay near Writers' Building and the Stock Exchange. This is because, unlike in Bombay, in Calcutta there is no organised lunch industry with swarms of carriers bringing lunch-boxes to people at their working place.

Many office workers in Calcutta have lunch in the streets. They congregate around hawkers to eat a quick *kobiraj*, (cutlet covered with an egg), breast cutlet (a distorted name for braised cutlet), eggs, *samosas*, *sukto*, fruit salad, and drink fresh coconut

Left: At the fish market. Above: hawker food is popular at lunch with the office crowd.

water or strong tea boiled in milk with sugar. In the evening, makeshift stalls appear on the Strand and on the Maidan opposite the Victoria Memorial Hall, serving soft drinks, ice cream, *sal moori*, a spicy combination of puffed rice, potato and cucumber, *puchka*, a crisp round paper-thin dough ball filled with spicy potato, cummin, and chilli flavoured tamarind water, *bhel puri* or *batata puri*, and other similar forms of snacks. Street food is not always safe, however, except milk tea which is usually boiled for a long time and is served in *peekey putts*, hand-made little clay cups that are thrown away after use.

Wherever one is travelling out of Calcutta, the place to stop for a meal is the **roadside Sikh** *dhaba*, easily recognised by the numerous trucks parked in front. The standard menu there is *tarka*, *dal* fried with eggs and chilli, *firni* for dessert and *nabe mil ke cha*, a strong tea meant, as its Hindustani name indicates it, to keep the driver going without feeling tired for 90 miles.

No meal, be it Bengali or from any other part of India, is complete without **paan**, pieces of areca nut mixed with lime, tobacco and wrapped in a betel leaf. There are many varieties of *paan*. The Bengali type is sweet, the Southern Indian strong and bitter. Calcutta has a lot of *paan* stalls with some even selling such varieties as *paan* with gold or silver leaf, supposed to be a sexual stimulant, the best known one being *palangtod paan* (break-the-bed *paan*).

Incidentally, Calcutta is also the tea capital of India, the place where one drinks the freshest Darjeeling or Assam teas as those are all exported through the city. Five o'clock tea is served at the Oberoi Grand in the second-floor lounge decorated with early prints of Calcutta.

Calcutta used to be the place in India to eat **Western food**. Many Calcuttans still remember such restaurants as Firpo's or Maxim's at the Great Eastern Hotel. Western meals are served in major international hotels but the quality is not there any more as strict regulations prevent the import of key components. The remark applies to **Chinese food** which is served in many restaurants around town as well as in unlicensed ones operating in the Chinese suburb of Tangra.

121

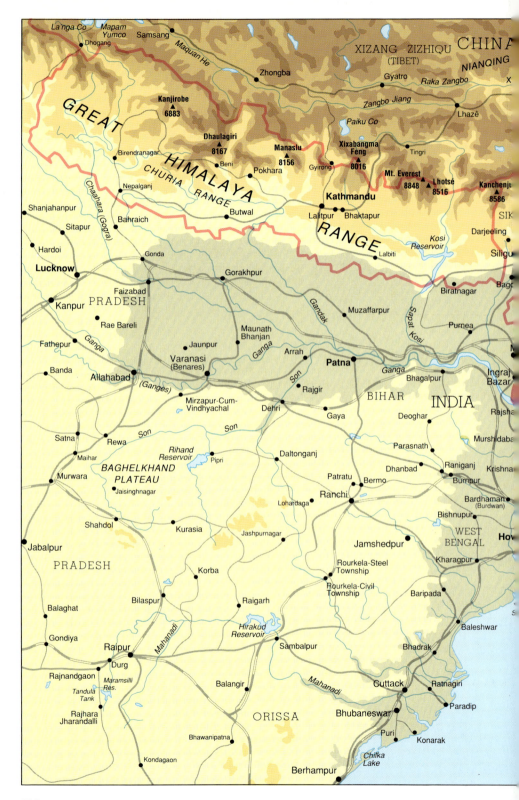

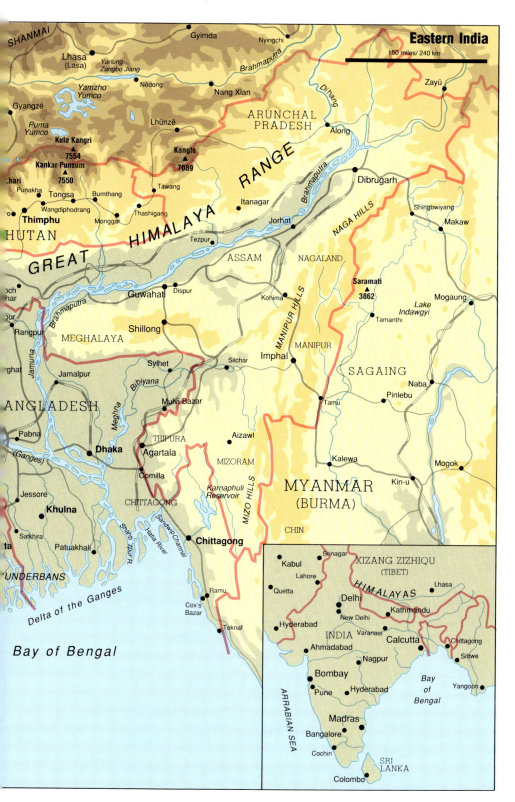

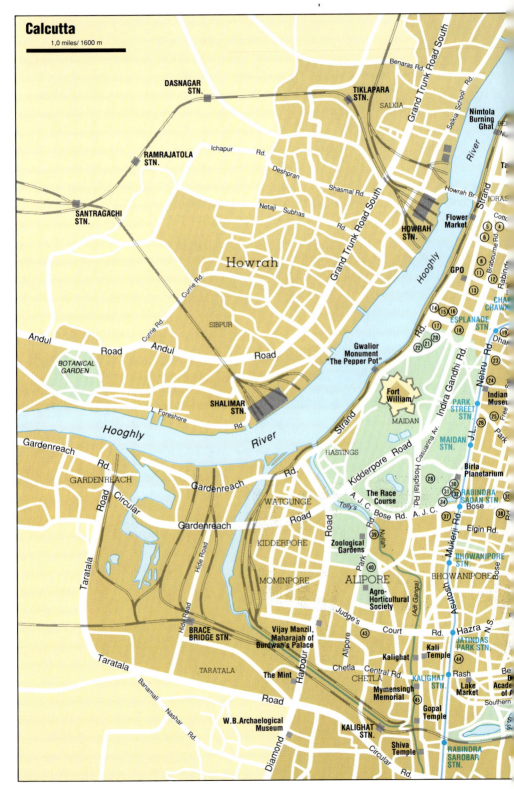

INTRODUCTION TO PLACES

Calcutta is a vast juxtaposition of neighbourhoods, each totally different with its peculiar ethnic profile, trade or style of architecture.

Calcutta was traditionally divided in three areas.

The **White Town** corresponds to the former village of Kalikata. Most of the Europeans would work and live there. The style is Palladian, for the older buildings (Old Mission, Seamen's Chapel, St Andrew's, Raj Bhavan); *capitalisme triomphant* (Standard Chartered Bank, Hongkong Bank); neo-Moghul (Legislative Assembly), Italian Renaissance (Telegraph Building, Eastern Railway); and Gothic (High Court, St Paul's). The **Black Town** covering the site of Sutanuti is what used to be called the 'Native Town' by opposition to the Cantonment. Most of the bazars and trades are established there. The bazar areas are ethnically mixed globally, but each trading community actually lives in a distinct pocket. The architecture is a mixed Palladian-Bengali for the older palaces, all incorporating a large interior yard for religious ceremonies (Marble Palace, Raja Nobo Kissen Deb's palace), or Art Deco-Moghul (most old high-rises of Barabazar), with elements of Gothic (Tagore's Castle, a copy of Neuschwanstein in Bavaria), and Roccocco (Jhogra Kothi). The **Grey Town**, east of the Black Town, is a very mixed neighbourhood with a strong Muslim and Anglo-Indian element. The only buildings of interest are around the University. The rest of the area is rather poor. **South Calcutta**, the whole area south of Lower Circular Road, grew mostly in the 20th century. It partly covers the site of the Govindapur village. There are, however,

Preceding pages: a Bengali meal; painted van; Bengal Mounted Police; scene from the Armenian ghat.

Places 131

some much older buildings such as Hasting's House or the Belvedere built in the 17th century or the club house of the Tollygunge Club, one of the very few remaining *neel kothi* or indigo planter's bungalows. Ballygunge, the Lakes and Alipore are residential areas with mansions and bungalows, the rest being middle-class districts with some poorer pockets of refugees from Bangladesh who have settled in Calcutta.

The proposed itineraries give you time to walk. Between less interesting areas, travel by taxi, metro, tramway and rickshaw. Avoid buses; they are packed and excellent fishing grounds for pickpockets. As the Hooghly flows from North to South and the main arteries are either North-South or East-West, you will therefore never get lost when in Calcutta. The only difficulty when visiting Calcutta comes from the confusion between old and new names of streets, buildings and monuments: Calcuttans, taxi drivers, not the least, continue to use names in vigour before 1947. Maps in the book carry the modern official names. The text mentions the normally used ones.

The best periods of the day to visit Calcutta are from 6.00 to 11.00 am and from 3.00 pm onward. In the Monsoon, the temperatures are lower and throughout the year the light better, a very important point in Calcutta where the high degree of humidity of the air makes it difficult to take sharp pictures.

You need at least four days to explore Calcutta. Spend Day 1 in the **White Town**: you can cover the Maidan, Raj Bhavan, B.B.D. Bag, the business district, the High Court, Saint-Andrew's, Saint-John's, Chowringhee, the Indian Museum, Saint-Paul, Park Street and the Park Street Cemetery.

Devote Day 2 to the **Black and Grey Towns**, in North Calcutta. Most of the temples and palaces, Calcutta University, the hub of the intellectual life, are there. At a fast pace you can see in one day New Market, Tiretta Bazar, Hati Bagan, Chinatown, Barabazar, Machuabazar, Sonapatti, Tulapatti, Chhor Bagan all chiefly trading areas, Jorasanko a more residential in the past where most of the places linked with the memory of Tagore, the famous Marble Palace, Shobha Bazar, Rajabazar, Shyam Bazar, bazar areas scattered with ruined palaces, the University, Nakhoda Masjid and Bow Bazar, the jewellers' district.

Spend Day 3 on **the Waterfront**, at a slower speed, seeing the ghats, Howrah Bridge, the synagogue, the Armenian Church, Howrah Station, the Botanical Gardens, the docks area of Garden Reach, the ruined palaces along the river and the Muslim suburb of Metiaburuz, to end up at sunset with a dinghy ride on the river.

On Day 4, visit **South Calcutta**, an area with many places of interest: the Kali Temple, Kalighat, the Mysore Gardens, the Greek orthodox church, the Birla Art Academy, the Ramakrishna Mission, the Zoo, the National Library and the Belvedere, the Birla Temple excepted and at the Tollygunge Club, and a *neel kothi*, one of the few remaining indigo planter's bungalows.

If you have only one day, start early, cross the Maidan by taxi to Armenian Ghat. Spend a good half hour on the ghat and at the flower market. Cross Howrah Bridge on foot. Take a cup of tea at Howrah Station and cross over back by ferry. Continue by taxi to B.B.D. Bag (Dalhousie Square), Netaji Subhas Road and St John's Church. Walk to the High Court. Have lunch around the Maidan.

After lunch, catch a taxi and stop at the Marble Palace, Sobhabazar, the Jain temples, then to the Maidan for a quick visit to the Indian Museum, to the Kali Temple, and finally to Princep Ghat for a sunset dinghy ride.

You can spend the evening dining in one of the many restaurants, attending a concert or visiting an exhibitons. During the Puja festivals take a trip around town asking the taxi driver to show you the best street altars.

Right: Calcutta's top hotels offer service in style.

134 CALCUTTA FROM OCHTERLONEY MONUMENT.

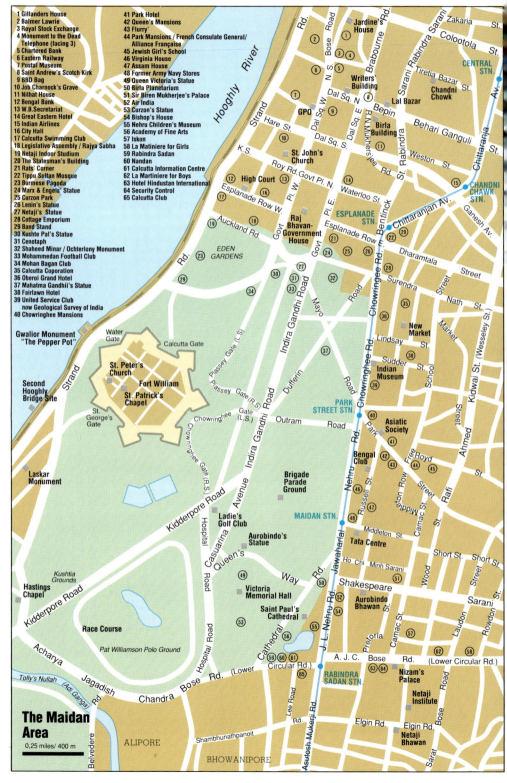

THE WHITE TOWN

The White Town covers those areas in Calcutta where the Europeans lived and worked — the City, the Maidan, Chowringhee and south of Park Street. Take a taxi to the centre of the Maidan early in the morning to see Calcutta wake up. Many British colonial towns had their bund, esplanade, *maidan*, mall or *padang*, a large green area with clubs, English lawns and gardens where expatriate Britishers could be among themselves and relax, away from the unfamiliar native environment.

The **Calcutta Maidan** was set up in 1758 by Lord Clive who cleared tracts of jungle around the new Fort William so that guns could fire freely in all directions from the Fort. Since its creation, the Maidan has been at the centre of Calcutta's life. During the British days, the Maidan was the place to be seen at, riding a horse in the morning or taking a stroll in the evening. Access was limited to upper classes through dress code restrictions barring lower castes. In the middle stood statues of kings, emperors and viceroys. To the west was the Fort; to the north Government House, the Esplanade, a row of administrative and residential buildings and the Ochterlony Monument; to the east Chowringhee, the most elegant street in Calcutta; and to the south the Anglican Cathedral, the Victoria Memorial Hall, the Royal Calcutta Turf Club and Lower Circular Road with the Sadar Diwan-i-Adalat, the former High Court of Civil Justice of the East India Company, now the headquarters of the Calcutta garrison and the Presidency General Hospital where, in 1898, Sir Ronald Ross identified the female anopheles mosquito as the carrier of malaria. Changes to this British cosmogony came in the 19th century. On several occasions, Bengali Revolutionaries deployed the French Tricolour flag at dawn on top of the Ochterlony Monument and Nationalists received the right to organise a traditional fair on the Maidan, the *Hindu Mela*, with concerts of Indian music, dances and plays as well as speeches. Tagore read poems here at the age of 15, making it his first public appearance.

Since Independence with no bars to its access, the Maidan has become a 24-hour scene. Before dawn, Bihari Muslims herd across the Maidan to the abattoirs cattle just arrived by train from Uttar-Pradesh. At sunrise, there are already people jogging, doing yoga exercises or training for the weekend's cricket or football game. The West Bengal Mounted Police do a bit of polo practice and golfers a quick nine-hole before breakfast. At night, the square opposite the main entrance to Victoria Memorial Hall, with a statue of Aurobindo in the middle, becomes a meeting place where people come for a drink, a stroll, or a hackney ride on the Maidan. Later in the night, when the pace slows down, *coolies* cross silently the Maidan carrying goods to the bazar area in North Calcutta, while prostitutes ply their trade in Curzon Park.

On weekends and holidays the Maidan becomes an all-day fair, the *Maidan Mela*. There are matches of football, cricket, hockey and golf, snake-charmers, monkey shows, acrobats, magicians, wrestlers, political speakers, fortune-tellers, preachers, musicians and singers. Stalls sell food, drinks, books and toys. Hundreds picknick on the Maidan and stay there the whole day. The Maidan is also a place for shopping. Trade fairs are organised in the southeastern corner throughout winter and Chowringhee, bordering the Maidan on the eastern side, is one of the busiest shopping arteries of Calcutta. Neither the cultural tradition of the Maidan initiated with the *Hindu Mela* has died. Every year the Calcutta Book Fair on the Maidan attracts over one million visitors. There are regular exhibitions at the Academy of Fine Arts, and shows at the Rabindra

Preceding pages: View of Calcutta from the Ochterlony Monument.

Sadan concert hall, on Cathedral Road. Finally, the Maidan is a popular venue for commemorations and events of all sorts. The Republic Day Parade of January 26th takes place on Indira Gandhi Road (Red Road). Every year, on the night of *Dussehra*, the Sikhs burn here a huge effigy of Ravan. The most impressive happening on the Maidan are the mass meetings of the CPI(M), the Communist Party, a splendid example of crowd management where over a million assemble and disband without incident. The western part of the Maidan is occupied by the second **Fort William** named after Prince William of Orange, like the first fort further north which destroyed by Siraj-ud-Daula.

The construction of the new fort was started by Clive on the site of the Govindapur Kali Temple in 1757 after the East India Company had recaptured Calcutta, and completed in 1773. A well-preserved example of the French military architecture of the 18th century developed by Vauban, it is star-shaped, with no dead angle and no structure above ground. The architect was Georges Coleman who became known as 'Coleman of Singapore' for his work in the Straits.

The Fort is off-limits to visitors. It houses several elegant buildings with distinctive 19th century architecture such as St Mary's Catholic chapel, the St Peter's Anglican church and Lord Kitchener's House. Only the Eastern Command Stadium is open to the public on such occasions as the start of the annual Statesman's Vintage Car Rally or equestrian events. South of the fort is the race course of the Royal Calcutta Racing Club. Races are mentioned as early as 1780 in Calcutta. The present course opened in 1819. In the middle are the Pat Williamson and Bahadur Singh Polo Grounds where the game have been played since 1861. After a stroll on the Maidan, catch a taxi on Red Road (now called Indira Gandhi Road). It was used as a runway during World War II. The Republic Day military parade takes

Taking five on the Maidan.

place there every year on January 26th. Get off at the Cenotaph. Erected in 1920 to commemorate the Dead of World War I, it is a replica of the London Cenotaph. In the middle of the square stands a statue of Netaji Chandra Bose where ceremonies are held every year on January 23rd to commemorate his birthday. At the corner of Government Place East and Esplanade East, is Esplanade Mansions, once one of the poshest block of flats in Calcutta.

To the east stands the massive dark neo-classical structure of the former **Military Secretariat**. Opposite, behind the tramway terminal is **Curzon Park**, with a statue of Lenin, a monument to Marx and Engels. The park is famous for its **Colony of Rats** living at the corner facing Esplanade Mansions on a small piece of land devoid of any vegetation, full of holes, the tip of a huge network of underground galleries said to reach across the street. The rats have become the pets of Calcuttans and let themselves be fed by the public. Attempts by the Municipality to remove them have been opposed by peddlers who sell grain and nuts to feed the rats.

Behind Curzon Park stands **Shaheed Minar** (**Ochterlony Monument**), a tower built in 1828 in the shape of a minaret, to commemorate the memory of Sir David Ochterlony, a general born in Boston who joined the East India Company and won the Nepalese Wars. Steep, narrow steps lead in the dark to the top of the tower. The taking of photographs is forbidden but the view is worth the climb. The tower is used as a minaret for a huge prayer meeting on *Idulfitr* and *Backraid*. The annual May Day Rally too takes place at Shaheed Minar. On Independence Day, August 15th, the national Tricolour flag is hoisted in the morning to the top of the monument. **Raj Bhawan** or **Government House** was built in four years from 1799 to 1803 after Lord Wellesley, dissatisfied with his former residence, decided that India should be "governed from a palace, not from a

Keeping goats on the Maidan.

counting-house, with the ideas of a prince and not with those of a retail dealer in muslin and indigo". Drawing its design from Kedleston Hall in Derbyshire, the property of Lord Scarsdale, it has more than 60 rooms, public halls, council chambers, a throne room used by King George V during his visit in 1911, with Tippu Sultan's silver throne brought back by Warren Hastings, after the fall of Seringaptnam, and a ballroom with 68 cut glass chandeliers. Government House became the residence of the Lieutenant-Governor of Bengal, when the capital was moved to Delhi. Raj Bhawan saw some premieres in Calcutta. Lord Curzon introduced the lift, Lord Elgin gas, Lord Northbrook hot water. "Lord Curzon's lift" is still in working condition and visitors to Raj Bhawan are allowed to take a ride in it.

Access to Government House is guarded from the north by a Chinese bronze cannon from the Opium Wars. Lord Curzon found Government House to be "the finest Government House occupied by the representative of any Sovereign or Government of the world".

Follow Government Place East and stop at the **Great Eastern Hotel** for a cup of tea. The Great Eastern is an old glory of Calcutta. Mark Twain stayed here. It was known for its belly-dancers, Maxim's French restaurant, and gypsy band. Explore the hotel, and you will discover marble floors, doors with heavy brass door-knobs, wood panelled corridors and other architectural details of the 1930s.

Continue along Government Place East. You then reach B.B.D. Bag. This unusual name stands for Binoy, Badal and Dinesh, three Young Revolutionaries hanged for having conspired to kill Lord Dalhousie, the Lieutenant-Governor of Bengal. The square is equally known as **Dalhousie Square**, its pre-Independence name. The first Fort William was located between the square and the river. The pond in the middle of B.B.D. Bag, Lal Dighi, 'the Red Tank', was the main water-point.

The snake charmer — still part of the street scene in Calcutta.

The square is surrounded by elegant 19th century and pre-World War II buildings but the architectural harmony has been ruined by the ugly concrete Telephone Bhawan and when the square, once the terminal of the first animal-drawn tram service in 1860, became a bustling tramway and bus terminal. There are plans to beautify the square and the tank. At the northern end of B.B.D. Bag is **Writers' Building**, the seat of the West Bengal Government. The present building has replaced the former building in 1776 where once lived 'writers', the clerks of the East India Company. Writers' Building is a maze dark corridors, archive rooms stacked with files bundled together by Red Tape, and offices filled with clerks sleeping, chatting or reading newspapers. There are no organised tours to Writers' Building. Simply ask the policemen on guard for any department. Trying to find out where the department really is, will give you enough time for a unique trip to Kafkaland.

Writers' Building — seat of the State Government.

The **GPO**, to the west of the Tank, reminds of St Paul's in London with its massive dome and Corinthian columns. It was built in 1868 on the site of a wing of the first Fort William. The infamous Black Hole of Calcutta is located inside the building. A tablet to the victims of the tragedy has been fixed on the wall of the facing B.B.D. Bag.

The Hong Kong & Shanghai Banking Corporation, the Royal Insurance Building, McLeod House, on B.B.D. Bag, the Chartered Bank, Balmer Lawrie, Coal Bhawan, Gillander's House, Jardine Henderson, Duncan Brothers on **Netaji Subbhas Road** (**Clive Road**), behind Writers' Building, all erected between the mid-19th century and World War II, in the same style as the Bund in Shanghai, give an idea of how impressive the business district looked when Calcutta was the second city of the British Empire.

The solemnity of the buildings is offset by the bustling activity on the street: traffic jams, food and tea stalls,

hawkers and peddlers selling office supplies, religious images, pornographic books, cigarettes and honey, fortune-tellers, peons carrying despatches, and tiffin carriers bringing lunch boxes to offices.

The most remarkable buildings are the **Eastern Railways**, built on the site of a bastion of the first Fort William, in the 19th century, in Italian *sgraffito* style with panels representing the allegoric figures of Architecture, Sculpture, Music and Commerce; and, across the street, the **Royal Stock Exchange**, the **Allahabad Bank** and the **Chartered Bank**. At the corner of Lyon's Range, named after the former owner of the area with the Royal Exchange. Erected in 1917, it houses the Stock Exchange, the Bengal Chamber and Industry, the Indian Tea Association, and other professional bodies.

The Chamber was founded in 1853, five years before the East India Company withdrew from India, by several Managing Agency Houses, as private businesses were called during the years of the Company's monopoly. Most of the founders were Scots who had settled in India, such as Gillanders Arbuthnot, Begg Dunlop, Mackinnon Mackenzie, James Finlay, Shaw Wallace, Duncan Brothers, and Jardine Skinner. At the entrance of the building is one of Calcutta's most original monuments, the **Memorial to the Dead Telephone**, built in 1984 by the Telephone Consumers Guidance Society of India. Every year, a mourning ceremony is organised here to mark the collapse of Calcutta's telephone network.

Behind the Standard Chartered Bank building, on Exchange Lane, is the open-air secondary market. Buyers sit in small booths in a wall, equipped with a telephone, and shout back at sellers standing in the middle of the street.

Back on B.B.D. Bag, St Andrew's Church was built on the site of the Old Court House in 1818 in a climate of controversy. Bishop Middleton, then the Anglican bishop of Calcutta, tried to

The High Court is a distinctive landmark in the city.

142

prevent the erection of the spire as he believed that only the Church of England had the right to do so. St Andrew's has the best organ in India and is probably the only entirely air-conditioned church in India. Inside are brass and marble slabs honouring eminent Scots and regiments (Royal Scott Fusiliers, Queen's Own Camerons) who had served in India. Instead of continuing into B.B.D. Bag, take R.N. Mukherjee Road (**Mission Row**). The Old Mission, built in 1770 by a Swedish missionary, is the oldest surviving Protestant place of worship in Calcutta. The tall building there is **Birla House**, the headquarters of the House of Birlas, the largest private group in India. The next building is **Nilhat House** where the tea auctions take place. Visitors are admitted and also shown the tasting rooms. An appointment can be arranged by phone by calling a day ahead.

Entering **Stephen's House** on Mission Row, you will come out on B.B.D. Bag. On your left is the West Bengal Tourist Development Corporation. Stop there to collect information on festivals and shows going on, as well as on excursions in and out of town, organised by the bureau.

Take a short taxi ride to Government Place West, behind Raj Bhawan. **St John's Church** stands next to the **Bengal Secretariat**, an impressive office building of the 19th century housing services of the Government of West Bengal. St John's was built in 1787. Its churchyard was the first burial ground in the city and was used for the Governors of Fort William, the Chief Justices of Bengal, and employees of the East India Company. Job Charnock, William Hamilton, the surgeon who obtained the East India Company's firman, and Viceroy Sir Michael Brabourne are buried here. The **Halwell Monument** to the victims of the Black Hole, that stood previously at the corner of Writers' Building, has been moved here. Inside the church hangs a *Last Supper* by Zoffany.

18th century palaces can still be recognised on Chowringhee.

At the corner of Esplanade West and Government Place West, the **City Hall**, completed in 1814 under Lord Minto, houses now the Municipal Courts. There are plans to restore the building and convert it into a museum of the heritage of Calcutta.

On the same street, the **High Court of India** was established in 1862, taking over from the abolished Supreme Court of the East India Company. It shifted to its present site from Dalhousie Square in 1872. The High Court is probably one of the most unexpected pieces of architecture in Calcutta. It was built in Gothic style by Walter Granville on the model of the belfry at Yepers in Belgium. The High Court is also the seat of the Sheriff of Calcutta. Sheriffdom was established in 1774. It is an honorary function bestowed for one year to a wealthy and prominent citizen of Calcutta. The Sheriff meets visiting dignitaries on behalf of the Citizens of Calcutta, supervises the Presidency Jail and heads the procession of the High Court, bringing with him its symbols — the Silver Oar of the Admiralty, the Silver Mass of Law and Order, and the Silver Sword of Honest Justice.

Across the street, **Assembly House**, now the **Rajya Sabha**, was built in 1931 after the West Bengal Legislative Council opted to have premises of their own. The H-shaped building, reminiscent of the mixed Euro-Moghul architecture of New Dehli, is conveniently located near the Executive (Writers' Building) and the Judiciary (High Court). Visitors are not allowed inside but the gardens open in winter for flower shows. Following the British tradition. The Council of Ministers and members of the ruling party sit to the right of the Speaker, the Opposition to his left. The Assembly Secretary and the Official Reporters of the House are opposite the Speaker. The 15-kilogramme (33-pound) silver mace was donated by the Maharaja of Santosh, Raja Manmatha Nath Roy Chowdhury.

Take a taxi across the Maidan to

An old print of the first Grand Hotel which was burnt in 1911.

Tippu Sultan Masjid at the end of Esplanade East. The small Shiite mosque, erected in 1842 by Muhammad, Tippu Sultan's son, in honour of his father, is a copy of the Ghulam Muhammad Masjid at Tollygunge in South Calcutta. This is where **Jawaharlal Nehru Road** starts. Nobody calls it that name. Everybody says **Chowringhee**. Chowringhee used to be a path leading to the Kali Temple. After Clive cleared the jungle to establish the Maidan, mansions appeared and the country path soon became the most elegant street in Calcutta. In the 19th century, residential blocks of flats, hotels, clubs, shops, department stores, restaurants and corporate headquarters had replaced or hidden behind them the 18th century neo-classical mansions.

Chowringhee has managed to retain much of its charm and grandeur until the late 1970s when the trees along Chowringhee were removed to allow for the digging of a metro line. Ugly concrete structures, such as the Chatterjee International Building that has sprung up after the imposing facade of the Bengal Club was sold to developers and the totally unesthetic 'temporary' **New Market Extension** opposite the Indian Museum, are very much a part of the comtemporary Chowringhee. In the recent years, however, efforts have been made to give Chowringhee back some of its past charm. Buildings have been restored, ballustrades added along the Maidan, and trees replanted.

The first half of Chowringhee, starting from Tippu Sultan Masjid, is the busiest. The unrestored Bristol Hotel, Firpo's Restaurant, Whiteway and Laidlaw Department Store have been divided, sub-divided and sub-let into shops, flats and offices. The pavement is invaded by hawkers offering second-hand clothes, bags, old copies of *National Geographic* and sex manuals, by shoes-shine boys, professional beggars and touts. There is along this part of Chowringhee a permanent flow of people, mostly shoppers, from dawn to

In the courtyard of the Indian Museum.

past dinner time.

You can break Day I at this stage. Have lunch at the **Oberoi Grand Hotel** for instance. The present hotel replaces an older, much smaller one destroyed by a fire in 1911. The first owner was Aratoon Stephen, an Armenian. M.S. Oberoi, the founder of the Oberoi hotel chain, bought it in 1943. During World War II, the hotel was used to accommodate 2,000 Allied soldiers. The 'Grand' has been restored, retaining its hydraulic lift, its staircase decorated with Dutch tiles and its Palm Court designed after the one at 'the Raffles' in Singapore. You can also have lunch at the Fairlawn Hotel, on Sudder Street, a charming little hotel set in a small garden and run by a British couple.

The **Indian Museum**, also called Garughar, 'the house of marvels', two blocks after the 'Grand', was founded in 1814 by Nathaniel Wallich, a Danish botanist. It is said to be the largest museum in India. Not to be missed in the Archaeological section are the Ashoka capital with four lion heads, at the entrance; a 2,000-year-old red sandstone gateway and ballustrades from the Bharhut Stupa in Madhya Pradesh; plaster casts of the Jain caves of Udayagiri and Khandagiri; Buddhist sculptures from Bihar and Orissa of the Gupta and Magadha periods; Bengali black stones; and a rare sculpture of a boar incarnation of Vishnu. Exhibits of interest in the other sections include paintings from the Company School, Kalighat *pats*, rare textiles, Tibetan *tankas*, Murshidabad ivory, dioramas on aboriginal and hill tribes, and windows on opium, indigo and tea.

One block down Chowringhee is a big neo-classical building, the former **United Services Club** now the **Geological Survey of India**. **Chowringhee Mansions**, next block, now **El Hadj Mansions** is another example of the exuberant architecture of Calcutta in the early 20th century.

Take a taxi to the **Victoria Memorial Hall** or 'V.M.' as it is usually called.

The interior of St Paul's Cathedral.

St Paul's has retained its orginal stain-glass windows.

The decision to build a memorial to Queen Victoria, Empress of India, was taken by Viceroy Lord Curzon who wanted to follow the Moghul tradition. The project was commissioned in 1906. The architect Sir William Emerson blended European and Moghal styles. The dome is 55 metres (182 feet) high and is surmounted by a revolving statue of Victoria, 5 metres (16 feet) high, weighting 3 tonnes and revolving on a sphere 0.6 metres (2 feet) in diametre. The white marble was entirely imported from Markana in the Jodhpur State.

The project was suspended by Lord Minto, the successor to Lord Curzon, officially on financial grounds, but in fact it is believed the reasons were personal as there was rilvary between the two viceroys. Attempts were made to have the project restarted in Delhi, the new capital. Lord Curzon fought in London to resume the project in Calcutta, finding an ally in Lord Morley, the then Secretary of State for India. Finally, in 1921, the Victoria Memorial was inaugurated by the Prince of Wales. The monument was hailed as the '20th Century Taj' and all the more welcome as it replaced an eyesore on the Maidan, the Presidency Jail. During World War II, the Victoria Memorial was a potential target for the Japanese planes which bombed Calcutta twice, and it had been envisaged for a while to paint the building black.

The Victoria Memorial houses a collection of Victorian memorabilia, objects and documents related to the history of Bengal — weapons, portraits, battle scenes, early prints of impressions of India and Kalighat *pats*. There are also paintings by Zoffany, Company School, the largest collection in the world of Danniell's, and a huge painting of the 'Prince of Wales' visit to Jaipur in 1876 by the famous Russian orientalist, Vereschtshagin.

The Victoria Memorial is surrounded, as a Mughal mausoleum must be, by gardens. On the Maidan side, a statue of 'Maharani Victoria' — the

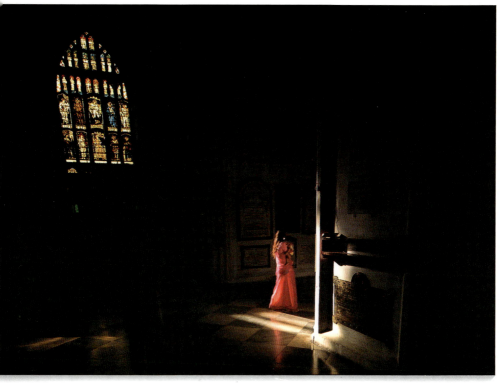

The White Town 147

Empress of India — sitting on her throne, greets the visitor. Statues of King Edward VII and Lord Curzon stand at the southern side.

Across Cathedral Road, next to the **Rabindra Sadhan** concert hall built in memory of Rabindranath Tagore, is the **Academy of Fine Arts**. A private art foundation, started by Lady Ranu Mukherjee, the wife of the late industrialist, Sir Biren Mukherjee, the academy holds exhibitions of young Bengali artists and has a permanent collection of textiles, weapons, Patna School miniatures on mica, Company School, Kalighat *pats*, works by Tagore and modern Bengali painters, and sketches on Calcutta by Desmond Doig.

The Gothic **St Paul's Cathedral** was completed in 1847. The spire was damaged in the 1934 earthquake and was replaced in 1938 by a bell tower on the model of the one in Canterbury. The building is impressive, especially inside — a high wooden ceiling from where hang a battery of fans; wood-panelled stalls; seats made of heavy wood; a window-glass by Burne-Jones, *The Destruction of Sodom*; and rows of commemorative slabs to viceroys and various, religious, civilian and military figures. They read as if taken from pages of a by Rudyard Kipling novel: 'John Paton Davidson, Captain of the Bengal Staff Corps, 1st Punjab Infantry, who fell in command of the Craig picquet at Umbeylah Pass in 1863'. The Cathedral is the Seat of the Bishop of the United Church of Northern India.

The **Birla Planetarium** right next to the cathedral, has daily shows in English, Bengali and Hindi.

Take a taxi to Park Street. On the way, you will pass by the immaculate **Virginia House** on Chowringhee, headquarters of Indian Tobacco Corporation and Tata Centre where the Tata group's management for Eastern India is based. **Park Street**, named after Sir Elijah Impey's deer park on nearby Russell Street, used to be a path leading to a Christian cemetery; hence, its first name European Burial Road.

Houses and mansions soon appeared as Calcutta developed — the Asiatic Society, the 'Star of the East' Masonic Lodge, the oldest in Asia. The Asiatic Society was founded in 1784 by Sir William Jones. The original building, erected in 1808, still stands behind the new aisle built in 1965. The Society has a small museum exhibiting old books, prints and manuscriprts, as well as an extensive library on Oriental languages and culture.

By the turn of the 20th century, Park Street had become, with Chowringhee, one of the most fashionable arteries of Calcutta, with luxury shops, jewellers, restaurants, exclusive night-clubs and such residential blocks of flats as Stephen Court, Galstaun (now Queen's) Mansions and Park Mansions Chowringhee.

Ask the taxi to take you straight to the **South Park Street Cemetery**, the oldest remaining cemetery in Calcutta, dating back to 1767. Many famous historic figures are buried there. They include Major General Charles "Hindu" Stuart; Robert Kyd, the founder of the Botanical Gardens; a Rose Aylmer who died of eating too many pineapples; the poet Henry Derozio, founder of the Young Bengal Movement; and William Jones, the founder of the Asiatic Society. Slabs from the nearby French Burial Ground, destroyed by a real estate project, have been moved here too. Further down on 32, Park Street is **Archbishop's House**, a neo-classical mansion built in the 1830s, the residence of the Catholic Archbishop of Calcutta.

You can now slow down. Take a taxi to the beginning of Park Street and walk around the area, or ask a taxi to drive you around the south of Park Street area along Harrington Street (Ho Chi Minh Sarani), Russel Street, Theatre Road (Shakespeare Sarani), Middleton Row, Loudon Street, and Rawdon Street that have retained a good number of 19th and early 20th century mansions.

Right: a cynical look at Calcutta's defectuous telephone system.

148

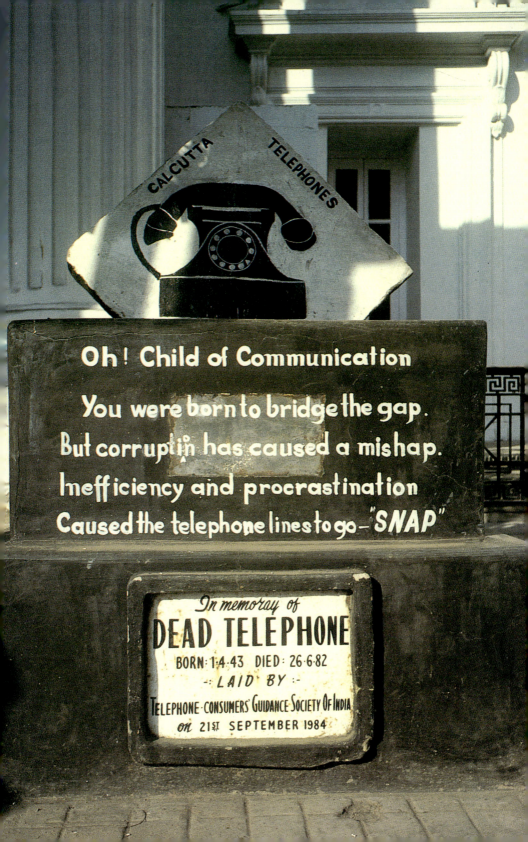

Colonial Cemeteries And Haunted Houses

On either side of the river Hooghly are cemeteries crowded with massive pyramids, obelisks and cupolas in the mixed western and oriental styles typical to colonial funerary architecture. They tell the story of hazardous lives, untimely deaths and of the undaunted spirit of the early European settlers in the East. The Company's servants, free booters and Boston ice merchants fell to the excesses of high living and insalubrious climate as did, so tragically, their young women and infants. Their hopes and aspirations rest in the decaying masonry within the rusty railings of God's Little Acres.

St John's Church (1787), was erected on the **old English burial ground,** over the graves of the early architects of Calcutta, Job Charnock

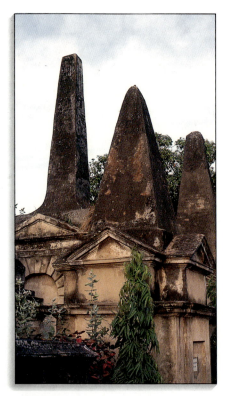

(1693), the founder of the city, his two daughters, and surgeon William Hamilton whose cure of the Emperor Farrukh Sivar earned him the reward of trading privileges for the English in Bengal, share a mausoleum. Charlotte Becher, an ancestress of William Makepeace Thackery; Admiral Watson, Clive's naval commander; and the Grande Dame of Calcutta, Begum Johnson, four times married and mother of the first Earl of Liverpool, were interred here.

The **Holwell Memorial** to the victims of the controversial Black Hole of Calcutta stands by the west wall. Under the west porch is an ornate tombstone inscribed to Lady Canning. She was buried in **Barrackpore Park** where her equestrian husband in bronze watches over her plain tablet.

A high rate of mortality and the fast decomposition of corpses leading to unhygienic conditions made the Calcutta Municipal Commissioners rule that burial grounds be situated outside the city's municipal limits. **South Park Street cemetery** stands alone among the four that were thus opened in the 18th century.

A private association recently took up the cause of this historical though derelict graveyard, and transformed it into a haven of tranquility. Gnarled mango trees, vibrant bougainvillae and grassy paths give peace to Sir William Jones, founder of the Asiatic Society, and to Rose Aylmer, sweetheart of Walter Savage Landor: the sentimental epitaph on her grave was composed while her poet lover cleaned his teeth before going to bed — so much for romance! The model of a Hindu temple is the monument over Indophile General Sir Charles Stuart. Cholera, the scourge of the day, took 23-year-old Henry Vivian Louis de Rosio, the Eurasian poet, inspiration of the Young Bengal Movement. Tablets of historical importance including that of Walter Landor Dickens, second son of the novelist, have been re-sited at South Park Street.

An 18th century mausoleum at the Park Street Cemetery.

Evidence of missionary activity and western learning speaks on the tombstones of many Indian converts, including poet Michael Madhusudan Dutta in Lower Circular Road cemetery. The **Scottish Cemetery** was opened to accommodate members of this thrifty community who, although they controlled the majority of business in mercantile Calcutta, found it too expensive to bury their dead in the English burial grounds!

"Padre's Godown" was the soldiers' name for the **Military Burial Ground** in Bhowanipore. The War Graves Commission cares for the uniform row of crosses over victims of World War II buried at the far end of this cemetery. Across the river, where he took refuge in Danish **Serampore**, William Carey, Baptist missionary, naturalist and visionary, lies with his missionary brothers Joshua Marshman and William Ward. Crumbling monuments in French **Chandernagore**, Dutch **Chinsurah** and Portuguese **Bandel** complete the chapter on colonial cemeteries in Bengal.

While graveyards spell eternal rest, some of the old buildings in Calcutta harbour ghosts who are loath to leave the 'City of Dreadful Night'. When the moon is full, the restless spirit of Warren Hastings, first Governor General of Bengal, rides up in a coach and four to the porch of **Hastings House**, his country seat in Alipore. He searches frantically for important papers lost during his tumultuous time in Calcutta. As if in complement, Maharaja Nundcoomar, Hastings' arch enemy, hanged for forgery, walks sighing for justice in the old building of **Loreto College** where his death sentence was signed. Or so the girls said.

Members of Tipu Sultan's family were deported to Calcutta from Mysore after his death in Srirangapatnam. There are tales of ghosts of dancing girls revelling at **Thana House**, **South Lodge** and **Aldeen** in Tollygunge where they were kept State prisoners.

Hasting's house in Alipore is said to be haunted.

Colonial Cemeteries

PALACES AND BAZARS

Bishop Heber of Calcutta described the native town in 1820 as "deep, black and dingy, with narrow crooked streets, huts of earth baked in the sun, or twisted bamboos, interspersed here and there with ruinous bricks, bazars, pools of dirty water, coco trees and little gardens, and very few, very large, very fine and very dirty houses, the residences of the wealthy natives". The good Bishop omitted to mention the indomitable urge to live that vibrated through the town. These bazars proved gold mines with the development of Calcutta. New trading communities arrived, such as the Marwaris and the Gujaratis. New fortunes were made. Palaces and commercial buildings appeared, transforming radically the traditional Bengali village of Sutanuti where Job Charnock established a factory in 1690. North Calcutta is indeed the core of today's Calcutta. The inhabitants of North Calcutta, the Gothis, are considered the original Calcuttans. Many families were already well-established here even before 1690.

As Calcutta grew, the centre of activities moved south. The Europeans established themselves at the villages of Gobindapur and Kolikata, erecting a 'White Town' there. North Calcutta with its native population became known as the 'Black Town'. Today, the difference is still striking between the formal European Palladian architecture of the city proper and the Oriental atmosphere of North Calcutta.

Start early as the previous days and catch a taxi to **New Market**, a red-brick Gothic complex with a tower clock erected in 1874 "for the greater glory of God and the British Empire". One could buy here the best quality of many Indian products as well as imported foodstuffs and fashion goods. A corner of the building was destroyed by a fire in 1985. To house the sinistered shops, an ugly 'temporary' structure was built on the Maidan opposite the Indian Museum while plans have been drawn to erect some day a new complex behind the existing market building. The range of goods available at New Market is now more limited but still the best florists and cake shops (Nahoum, Flurry) can be found there.

To the west of New Market stands the Lighthouse Cinema. Built in 1938, it incorporates elements of Bauhaus architecture. Behind stand the **Central Municipal Offices**, the seat of the Calcutta Corporation since 1905.

Take again a taxi and head north. **Bentinck Street** is where most of the Chinese leather and shoe shops are located. Start walking from **Lal Bazar**. *Lal* means red in Hindi. The area used to be the brothel area of a regimental bazar. The red brick buildings of the Police Headquarters stand sentinel-like, as if to reprimand the riotous past.

Proceed along **Rabindra Sarani**, the old Chitpur Road, the shortest of the parallel north-south thoroughfares and once the pilgrims' route to the Kalighat Temple. Almost opposite the police building is **Tiretta Bazar**, once the property of Edward Tiretta, a companion of Casanova exiled from Venice. He came out East to seek his fortune and ended up as Superintendent of Roads and Buildings and enough money to buy a bazar. Jewish, Armenian, Greek, Portuguese and Eurasian bird and beast fanciers came there to choose pets for their private menageries while fastidious smokers sniffed their worth of Havana cigars. Tiretta went bankrupt and the market was auctioned to the Maharaja of Burdwan. The birds and beasts moved to reappear with potted plants and tropical fish on Sunday mornings at **Hati Bagan** further north. Tiretta's Bazar now sells electrical fittings and music instruments. Behind the bazar and down **Chhatawala Gully** (Umbrella Lane) are the remnants of Chinatown. At daybreak, a small Chinese market is held there on Tiretta

Preceding pages: the flower market at Armenian Ghat. Left: ruined palace in North Calcutta.

Bazar Street. Cantonese women sell pork, Chinese vegetables, soya bean curd, rice noodles and jasmine tea. Hawkers serve *wonton* soups and *dim sum*. Most of the Chinese buildings are gone now, except the run-down Nanking Restaurant, the Taoist Sea Ip Temple on Chatawala Gully, a few clubs, a Chinese newspaper press on Metcalfe Street and Chinese shops on Sun Yat-sen Street. The Tibetan Hotel opposite Nanking Restaurant used to be Ta Fa Shung, the best opium den in Calcutta in the 1930s. An unlicensed restaurant would operate on the ground floor, serving whisky from tea-pots, while opium-smoking would take place upstairs.

The area used to be much more residential in the 19th century. The family of the defeated Nawab of Mushidabad styled themselves a mish-mash of ornamental stucco and coloured glass panes at 6, Rabindra Sarani, at the corner of **Bepin Behari Ganguly Street**. Within its gilded walls, they entertained with pomp and circumstance the foreign dignitaries who disembarked upriver and would arrive by *palki* (palanquin) to Chitpore for a day of regal entertainment. Many small establishments now do business in the 'royal' apartments. J. Mondal's music shop sells sitars, tablas and violins. The owner's claim to fame lies in a certificate from Yehudi Menuhin, for repairing the maestro's violin string. An entourage followed the Nawab's court in exile. Courtiers and flatterers, dancing girls, performers and musicians, pimps and whores, beggars and mendicants set themselves in Chitpur. The parvenu 'Babu' of Calcutta learnt the art of indulgence from the decadent nawabs. In and around Chitpore sprouted the seeds of dalliance. Elaborate mansions, lawns full of marble statuary, tanks for fishing away hours of idleness became the fashion of the day in the area. Follow Bepin Behari Gangully Street towards Brabourne Road. Behind the Catholic cathedral of Our Lady of the Rosary starts **Bara-**

Machhuabaza is now a fruit market.

bazar, crossed by Mahatma Gandhi Road ('M.G. Road') running east-west, joining the two railway stations of Howrah and Sealdah. It is the oldest and richest bazar in Calcutta. Before the British came to Bengal, Portuguese trading vessels anchored at nearby Sutanuti for revictualising and Job Charnock made his legendary mid-day halt nearby, at the eastern end of the thriving fishing village that stood there.

The bazar that already prospered then, grew into a permanent place of business. Traders, Bengalis, Marwaris, Parsees, Gujaratis and foreigners assembled there and it became the nerve centre of the city's business. The three- and four-storeyed town houses with cast iron railings which rise above the shopping arcades are largely the residences of Marwari businessmen. On Armenian Street, where Gujarati traders sell *bidi* leaves, stands **Jhogra Kothi**, a building so extremely baroque that there were demonstrations of protest on its commissioning. **Macchuabazar** on Ram Lochan Mallik Street, a predominantly Punjabi Muslim area, is a fruit market selling apples from Kashmir, pomegranates and dates from Afghanistan, and dried apricot and raisins from Kashmir and Pakistan. Alleys and byways run into each other on either side of Mahatma Gandhi Road making up a huge pattern of *pattis* or individual wholesale entrepots named for particular commodities reaching right up to the river on the west.

Continue your walk through the terrifying traffic of rickshaws, *coolies*, *hath gari* (man-pulled carts), each emanating its own shout or brand of noise to get right of way. Although big time crime is not a problem, one must be constantly vigilant of snatchers and pick-pockets. In the dark cubby holes of **Sonapatti**, the goldsmiths sit cross-legged on *taktaposh* (low padded divans) before huge iron chests speaking millions. Here gold ornaments are bought, sold, exchanged, melted down and fashioned as they have been for generations. Priceless gems lie in the vaults and pearls are sold by the weight. The cotton bale market of **Tulapatti** is now held where ships loaded and unloaded opium in the days of the China trade. The area is also famous for magnum-sized, yellow *laddu* sweetmeats, a speciality of Barabazar. Refresh yourself at a roadside shop before continuing to **Joransako**, a Bengali area with veranda houses on Sir Hariram Goenka Street, and palaces around Kali Krisna Tagore and Jadullal Mullick streets. The craziest is **Tagore's Castle** on Darpanarain Tagore Lane built in 1867 and reminiscent of Neushwanstein in Bavaria. Overbuilt structures have unfortunately altered its silhouette. In the *alu posta* (potato market) area, on Kali Krishna Tagore Street, stands the **Bain Kunth Temple** built in white marble in the style of the South by the Bangurs, a rich Marwari family of Calcuta. At the end of Dwarka Nath Tagore Lane is the **Tagore Thakurbari**, the 18th century family mansion of the Tagore family built by the poet's grandfather, Raja

Tagore's castle has Bavarian features.

Palaces and Bazars

Dwarkanath Tagore. In the centre, the main building, **Rabindra Mancha**, where Rabindranath was born in 1861 and died in 1941, now houses the **Rabindra Bharati Museum** devoted to the poet's life and to the Young Bengali Movement as well as a collection of almost 2,000 paintings by Tagore. On the left of the compound is the building of the **Rabindra Bharati University**, the only State University in West Bengal offering art courses and running a research cell on Tagore's life and works. The **Bichitra Bhawan** pavilion to the right of Rabindra Mancha derived its name from the Bichitra Club where Tagore held recitations, discussions and staged plays. Every year in September, the Government of West Bengal organises there the *Karashilpa Mela*, a festival of traditional performing arts in the Tagore tradition. There are also dances, plays, songs. Every year on Tagore's birthday on May 15th, as well as on Saturdays and Sundays in the evening, a *son-et-lumière* is held there.

Chhor Bagan, the 'thieves' market' across Rabindra Sarani in the east of Josaranko, got its name back in the days when the bamboo groves that covered the area were a hideout for anti-socials. On Muktaram Babu Street, Raja Rajendro Mullick built his **Marble Palace** in 1835. The orphaned child of a rich merchant, Rajendro was a ward of the courts. His English tutor encouraged the boy's love of all things beautiful, both live and static. Rajendro combined his education and business genius to amass enough money to set up a marvellous repository of Oriental and Western artefacts. Indian and European builders worked according to Mullick's own master plan. The result was a colonaded mansion built around a rectangular yard with a *thakur dalan*, a raised platform for religious functions, at one end, as it is customary for Bengali Hindu families to have a temple to their tutelary deity within their homes. A magnificent *porte cochère* leads into an interior of moulded and carved ceilings and walls,

Tagore's Palace is an 18th century family mansion.

and floors of patterned Italian marble. It is said that the palace draws its name from almost an order by enthusiastic Lord Minto, then the viceroy to Raja Mullick: "Call it the Marble Palace!". In the rooms, gigantic gilt-framed Belgian mirrors, Venetian and Bohemian glass chandeliers, Dutch tiles, pieces of Company School, and Satsuma vases can be picked out from among more mediocre exhibits. There are said to be a Napoleon by Houdon, one Arnold, one Gainsborough, three Rubens and a statue by Michelangelo. In the hall and on the first floor are cages with the family's collection of parrots, doves and mynas. The small zoo in the garden is believed to be the oldest in Calcutta. Maestro Ravi Shankar chose the grand Durbar Hall for a performance, famous photographer Raghubir Singh. The Marble Palace became the model for many 'palaces', in varying degrees of extravagance, that came up in North Calcutta.

Nearby, at 166, Chittaranjan Avenue stands **Tagore Mahajati Sadan**, a concert hall with an audience capacity of 2,500, staging chiefly Bengali cultural performances. The hall was first planned by Netaji Subhas Chandra Bose to be an assembly house for the Congress Party that he was then heading. The foundation stone was laid by Rabindranath Tagore in 1939.

Continuing further north on foot or by tram, you reach **Shobha Bazar**. Jarasanko has a mixed Bengali-Marwari population, Barabazar is a mosaic of communities while Shobha Bazar is a purely Bengali neighbourhood. The area belonged to the Debs. **Raja Nobo Kissen Deb Bahadur**, was an advisor to Lord Clive. For his invaluable services during and after the Battle of Plassey in 1757, he was amply rewarded with government positions and property in North Calcutta. It was in the courtyard of Nobo Kissen's palace on Naba Krishna Dev Street that the first public *Durga Puja* in Calcutta was held.

With the family's growing fortunes,

The ornate Marble Palace on Muktaram Babu Street.

Radha Kanto, Nobo Kissen's son acquired a fabulous library and the house elaborated into a labyrinth of rooms and corridors. Aged lions and a cannon from the Battle of Plassey now guard the arched gateway to the decaying palace. The *Durga Puja* carries on and is part of the tour organised by the Tourism Department of the Government of West Bengal to traditional *Durga Pujas* in old North Calcutta homes during the festival. Heavy taxation and family feuds saw much of the splendour of the North Calcutta palaces go but still but some of the past glory is recaptured during religious festivals. The courtyards are then filled with men in finely pleated white *dhotis* and shirts elegantly creased at the sleeves, and women in beige and red Bengal silk sarees and jewellery.

Many palaces in Calcutta are in streets and lanes shooting off from the main arteries. The best architecture can be seen on Noba Krishna Deb Street, Grey Street (Aurobindo Sarani), Amherst Street, Cornwallis Street (Bidhan Sarani), Beadon Road, Sobha Bazar Street and Chitpore Road (Rabindra Sarani). On D.K. Deb Street are several Deb palaces. The main one is guarded by stone lions. On Cornwallis Street stand the Sadharan Arya Samaj and the Star Theatre, the oldest in Calcutta. There are some well-preserved houses at 39/9 and 47 Beadon Street. It was at 6, Beadon Street, in the Great National Theatre, that Tagore's first drama, *Raja Basanta Roy*, was played.

Feel free to enter and explore the courtyards of the palaces. No visitor is turned away from a Bengali home. He is welcomed with a cup of tea or a glass of sherbert and entertained with leisurely conversation. Shobha Bazar actively celebrates *Durga* and *Kali Pujas* and is one of the few venues in Bengal for the *Charak Puja* festival, on the eve of the Bengali New Year. At the Chatu Babu Bazar near the corner of Beadon Street and Chittaranjan Avenue, men attach themselves now by ropes, not by hooks as before, to giant swings that symbolise the cycles of life. Nearby, a small fair sells toys and clay figurines. Avoid the red light district of **Sonagachi**, once fashionable, where Kanch Kamani, 'the Glass Lady', entertained the male elite of Calcutta in her glazed veranda, and continue to **Shyambazar**. There are some more palaces in this Bengali area that was also a stronghold of the Debs.

On Balaram Ghose Street, is probably the maddest house of Calcutta, a vertical box more than 2 metres (7 feet) high, made of iron strips, standing on the sidewalk and only entered from the top. The owner, known as 'Hamilton Sahib', says it is a ship and it will flow down the Hooghly at the next freak flood. The **Five-Point Crossing**, with a statue of Netaji Chandra Bose riding a horse in the centre, is one of the most congested places in Calcutta.

Take now a taxi to the **Jain temples** on Badridas Temple Street. There are four Jain temples belonging to the Digamber sect, dedicated to Sital Nath, Chanda Prabhu, Dada Guru and Kusul Maharaj, prophets of the Jain religion.

The Jain temples set in an elaborate garden.

They were all built at the end of the 19th century and form a complex called Parasnath Mandir. The main temple, the best known, is dedicated to Sital Nath, the 10th of the 24 Jain prophets. Built in 1867, it is set in a garden with a large fish pond and is open to the public in the afternoon. The style is a mixture of Moghul, Baroque and neo-Classical. The floor is made of Italian marble. The walls are covered with mirrors and small pieces of reflecting glass. A huge chandelier, with more than 100 branches, hangs over the image of the Tirthankara.

It is now time to head straight south along Bidhan Sarani to **Boitak Khana**. Stretching along **College Street**, the area may be called the arts and intellectual centre of Calcutta. Job Charnock's mid-day halt under a pipal tree, slightly inland of Suttanuti, is thought to have taken place here. The population of the area is mixed, with a strong percentage of Muslims. The oldest educational institution to be set up in Calcutta was the **Madrasa**, founded by Warren Hasting in 1748 to teach Arabic and Persian, and moved to Wellesley Square in 1874. The **Sanskrit College** was founded in 1824 and the building erected in 1826. The **Calcutta University** — the second foreign one in India, after the Serampore University founded by the Danes in 1825 — was established much later in 1857. The first building, Senate House, completed in 1872, was shamefully destroyed in the 1970s. Later buildings, Presidency College (1874) and the Eden Hindu Hostel (1886) are still standing and in use. The hardly known Ashuntosh Museum of Indian History, founded in 1937, is located in the Century Building. It houses a collection of Bengali art, Buddhist statues of the 10th century, rare Buddhist manuscripts, *kanthas*, Baluchari sarees, scrolls from Bankura and Birbhum, black stone sculptures, bronzes, folk art and temple terracottas.

College Street and Albert Road carry almost no other trades than in books and

The famous Albert Street coffee shop, popular meeting place of the Bengali intelligentsia.

Palaces and Bazars 161

college supplies, selling syllabuses, text books, old English books and magazines. The **Albert Hall Coffee Shop** on Albert Street (Bankim Chatterjee Street), the meeting place of intellectuals, reminds one of a Left Bank café in Paris, with its hanging cloud of cigarette smoke and animated conversations lasting hours around cups of coffee.

Cross Chittaranjan Avenue behind Calcutta University. The area around **Zakaria Street** like Macchhua Bazar further north is predominantly Muslim but Islam is the only common point to the Barabazar Muslims who belong to a wide range of communities — Bihari, Bengali, Rajasthani, Lucknawi, Punjabi, Pathani and Gujarati. **Nakhoda Masjid** at the corner of Zakaria Street and Rabindra Sarani, offered in 1927 to the Muslims of Calcutta by the small community of Sunni Memons from Kutch in Gujarat, is Calcutta's largest mosque. It was built for 10,000 worshippers on the model of Akbar's tomb at Sikandra. It has four floors. *Sufis* and *fakirs* stay usually on the ground floor. You can buy in the shops nearby perfume essence, *khol*, velvet waistcoats and caps worked in gold thread, embroidered *kurta* shirts, glass bangles, carved *Koran* stands, sarees, *unani* (traditional medicine), *sewai* (sugar vermicelli), dates, pomegranates, dried fruit and even sweet tobacco paste for *hookah* pipes. There are also some good Muslim restaurants around such as the one at the Royal Hotel known for its *biryani* and *firni* rice dessert.

On the eve of Muslim festivals, a commercial fair takes over Zacharia Street and closes it to traffic, while a market selling goats from as far as Agra is held on Colootolla Street (Maulana Shokat Ali Street) and Canning Street.

Take a taxi to **Bowbazar**, your last stop, an area also known as Dharamtola, the 'mat' market, or Jan Bazar. It is famous because of its owner in the days of the East India Company, Rani Rashmoni. A rich widow who also built the Dakshineshwar Temple north of Calcutta, she was known for her strong and daring character. Once, during a *puja* festival, foreigners complained of the noise made by the continuous beating of drums in the area. She fenced off the whole area and forbid foreigners to enter it. The fences were removed only after she received apologies.

Dharamtola is famous for its jewellery shops. Bengalis are considered the best diamond-setters and gold-workers in India. They work in Surat, Bombay. In Calcutta the gold shops are concentrated on Bipin Behari Ganguli Street in Bowbazar. Shops like B. Sarkar & Sons or P.C. Chandra will execute orders within 24 hours. The Portuguese already lived in Bowbazar in 1690. The Ferringhi Kali Temple near the crossing of B.B. Ganguly Street and Chittaranjan Avenue, was named after a Portuguese who worshipped Kali here in the 16th century, and the Church of Our Lady of Dolours at 147 Bowbazar Street was built by the Portuguese in 1809.

Left: 'Hamilton Sahib' built his floating house in North Calcutta. He now waits for the Big Flood. **Right**: The onion-shaped domes of Nakhoda Masjid dominate the skyline.

THE LOOSHAI EXPEDITION: SHIPPING ELEPHANTS ON BOARD THE SIMLA AT CALCUTTA.

THE WATERFRONT

One cannot get a real feeling of the city without having explored the Waterfront and been on the Hooghly.

Being a part of the Holy Ganga, the Hooghly has always been at the centre of the religious life of Calcutta. Some rituals are no longer practised such as *antarajali* when one, feeling that death was close, would be brought to a ghat and be lowered waist-deep into the water to wait there for the end. Rich ladies in *purdah* are no more taken to the river in closed palanquins that were immersed to let them have their daily bath without being seen. Gone, too, are the days when a *Boishnab Charan Seth* would sell *Ganga Jhol*, water from the Ganges and despatch it from Calcutta in sealed jars all over India.

Still, everyday, early in the morning and at sunset, people continue to gather for prayers and ritual ablutions at neo-classical and neo-moghul ghats and waterfront temples built by rich religious Hindu families. Several burning ghats have remained active. Many Hindu festivals end up on the ghats. On *Shivaratri*, women bathe in the river to gain fertility. On *Chhat Puja*, lower caste Biharis accompanied by Hijras, eunuch dancers, take a sunset dip. On the Bengali festivals of *Kali*, *Durga*, *Lakshmi*, *Vishvakarma*, *Sarasvati* or *Manasha*, hundreds of processions converge to the river to immerse clay statues of deities.

The Hooghly and the Waterfont were, for a long time, the hubs of the commercial activity and of the social life of Calcutta.

As the city's wealth remained for a long time based on its convenient location at the end of inland trading routes and international sealanes, most trading companies had their headquarters, godowns and docks on the waterfront where opium and tea clippers stood at anchor. At the same time, space being limited with Salt Lakes in the east, marshes in the south, and the crowded Native Town in the north, Europeans also lived near the Waterfront not far from Fort William where they could take refuge in case of trouble. The only 'safe' open spaces were then the Maidan, the Strand, a promenade built along the Hooghly by Hastings for European ladies to take an evening stroll, and the river proper where parties were organised up to the late 19th century aboard *budgerows* with their usual lot of dancing girls, ganja, wine, opium and whisky.

As Calcutta developed, rich Bengali families also built palaces, most of them neo-classical, on the Waterfront, in North Calcutta, while a commercial port was built in the south at Garden Reach and Kidderpore. Upstream from the city, and on the other side of the river jute mills appeared in the 19th century. During that period, one figure stood out — Rani Rashmoni. The widow of a rich Bengali landlord, she opposed the East India Company on a number of occasions, several incidents taking place on the Hooghly. When the Company forbid fishermen along the Calcutta waterfront, she leased a part of it and let the fishermen along it, and in retaliation, she put up a red signal, forbidding the Company ships from sailing along the stretch of the river under her control.

The Hooghly in Calcutta is not as active as before. The river is now shallower. Most cargo ships unload downstream at Kidderpore or Haldia. The social life has spread since the 19th century to other parts of the city but the Waterfront remains a testimony to the city's past grandeur with its commercial buildings of the 1930s, deserted wharves and godowns, ruined palaces of the 19th century and neo-classical ghats.

Start the day early, around 7.00 am, and take a taxi to **Eden Gardens**, a public park established by the sisters of Lord Auckland on the site of Respondentia Walk, a fashionable promenade along the Waterfront. **A Burmese Pagoda** stands there. It was disassembled

Preceding pages: Early morning at Armenian Ghat. Left: Calcutta served as a basis for British expansion in the East.

and brought from Prome in 1856 after the Second Burmese Wars. Nearby is the 19th century **Band Stand**. Behind the park is **Eden Gardens Cricket Stadium**, the Mecca of Indian cricket. The world record attendance to a cricket match was broken here in 1982 when 394,000 fans watched England play an Indian Selection. England also played Australia there in 1987 for the finals of the Reliance Cup.

Continue again by taxi, past the former Bank of Bengal building at the corner of Esplanade Row, past the Palladian Metcalfe Hall, now in ruins, the former Imperial Library, Babu Ghat and Koliaghat, Calcutta's oldest ghat, Inchcape House at the end of Fairlie Place, Customs House, the Port Commissioner's Building and abandoned godowns, all testimonies to the past shipping activity on the Hooghly.

Turning into Canning Street, you reach **Old China Bazar**, an area where various minority groups were settled in the days of the Company as it was located almost on the Waterfront, near one of the most active ghats at that time. Parsees have an agiary (23 Ezra Street), Borah Ismailites a mosque (28A Brabourne Road) and Digamber Jains a temple (46 Canning Street). There are three synagogues. The oldest one, Maghen David, on Canning Street was built in 1884 by Elias David Joseph Ezra, a wealthy merchant, and looks like any 19th century Christian church from the outside, except that it has no cross atop its spire. Off Old China Bazar Lane, the **Armenian Church of Our Lady of Nazareth** was built in 1707 by public subscription among the Armenian community, on the site of a much older Armenian cemetery where the oldest grave dates back to 1630. The church has the oldest working clock in Calcutta. The shops in the streets around the church are the main shopping area for firecrackers and flares during the *Diwali* festival. The **Catholic Cathedral of Our Lady of the Rosary** on Brabourne Road stands at

The Pontoon Bridge, ancestor of the Hooghly Bridge.

The Pontoon Bridge on the Hooghly, Calcutta.

Murghihatta, 'the chicken market', a piece of land given to the Portuguese in the late 17th century by the Nawab of Bengal. They first built a thatched mud chapel here. The present building was erected in 1798.

Turning back to the river, **Armenian Ghat** is one of the most colourful in Calcutta with its temples, flower market, religious shops, tea stalls, traditional gymkhana in the early morning, and Saddhus. The ghat is right under the **Howrah Bridge**, one of the main landmarks of Calcutta. A first pontoon bridge was set up in 1874. Supported by a chain of barges moored one to the other, it was designed to have a life of 25 years and was finally replaced by the present cantilever steel structure in 1943 under pressure from the US forces headquartered in Calcutta who insisted on decent infrastructure to carry men and weapons to Assam for the Burma offensive. The bridge is 97 metres (295 feet) high and 705 metres (2,150 feet) long. The suspended span between the cantilevered arms is 172 metres (564 feet) long. It is the largest cantilever bridge in the world. Walking across the bridge one can feel the whole structure vibrate because of the heavy traffic of buses, trams, double-deckers, taxis, hand-pulled carts and pedestrians.

From the middle of the bridge, the view of the Calcutta skyline, of the crowded ghats and of the river with ferries, steam launches, budgerows, dinghies and straw barges sailing under the bridge, is unique. With a bit of luck, you will see dolphins that swim in with the tide as far upstream as Calcutta to get rid of salt water parasites.

Your next stop is **Howrah Station**, the terminal point of the Eastern Railway. The original East India Railway was formed in 1845 and the first service between Howrah and Hooghly, some 50 kilometres (31 miles) north, was opened on August 15th, 1854. The present station was built in 1906. Have tea in the hall and watch as waves of commuters arrive, clerks going to office, peas-

The Hooghly Bridge — a study in steel structures.

ants and fishermen coming to the city markets. The station has a terrible reputation of masses of starving people sleeping on the tracks and on the platforms, a cliche dating back to the Bangladesh War of 1971, not true any more.

Take a taxi from the station along the busy Grand Trunk and Angul roads to the **Shibpur Botanical Gardens**, founded in 1786 by Col. Robert Kyd of the Bengal Engineers on the site of Mouckwah Thanna, a moghul fort built to protect local villages against the Arakanese pirates operating from the Sunderban jungles in the Delta. Spreading over 109 hectares (269 acres), the gardens are famous for the Great Banyan Tree, about 150 years old, said to be the largest in the world. The central trunk had to be removed in 1925 after it was damaged by lightning. Over 1,500 offshoots remain, forming a dome almost 30 metres (98 feet) high.

From Botanical Garden Ghat, take a ferry to Metiaburruz Ghat, then catch a taxi to town.

Metiaburuz is a Shiite neighbourhood that developed into a mini-Lucknow when the British exiled here Hezrat Wajed Ali Shah, the last Nawab of Oudh, in 1856. Nowadays, the same variety of Urdu as in Lucknow is spoken there and the same Shiite festivals are celebrated. Wajed Ali Shah is buried at the **Sibtainabad Imambara**, a mosque built in 1864. It is the starting point for Shiite processions during *Muharram*. A camel market is held nearby for the *Bakraid* festival. The most impressive building is **Wajed Ali Shah's palace**, now the headquarters of **South-Eastern Railways**, a huge red building surrounded by five smaller buildings, the Serail Houses, where the Nawab's wives lived.

Next to Metiaburuz is the Port area, with Garden Reach, a ship-building centre, and the Kidderpore docks built in 1884. They were bombed by the Japanese in 1942. Although a large chunk of the shipping activity has moved downstream to Haldia, the

An old Johnston & Hoffman print of the largest banyan tree in the world.

docks remain active. With their operations still largely under-mechanised, they give a genuine image, especially on a foggy winter morning, of what the London Docks could have looked like some 50 years ago.

Kidderpore is also known for its **Five Star Market**, Calcutta's largest shopping area for smuggled goods on Circular Garden Reach Road, the Orphangunj cattle market, very active before Muslim and eastern Hindu festivals, and finally the ill-famed red-light district of Munshigunj where foreigners are not welcomed.

You return to Calcutta through the suburb of Hastings, an old cantonment area where the Indian Navy is nowadays quartered. The oldest monument there is the 18th century Seafarers' Chapel. The **Lascar War Memorial** on the Waterfront was erected in memory of the 896 sailors from Bengal, Assam and Upper India lost at sea during World War I. Takhta Ghat nearby is an embarkation point for steam trips on the river. At one end of Hastings, construction of the **Second Hooghly Bridge**, started on the late 1970s, still drags on. The bridge might be finished one day. In the meantime, Khanna Buddo gypsies have set up camp on the site, while the 61st Cavalry and several other regiments stable their horses under the access flyovers during the Horse Season in winter.

After lunch, catch a taxi to **Nimtola Ghat**. Rabindranath Tagore was cremated there in 1941 next to the small Tara Baba Temple. The small Buro Mahadev Temple of Beniatola at 16 Mohammed Ranjan Lane, off Nimtala Ghat Street, with its Shiva Lingam, is a pilgrimage centre.

You can now walk along the ghats all the way up to **Baghbazar**. Rich Bengali families built palaces along the Waterfront in the 19th century as well as private ghats such as Banamali Ghat at Kumartuli. Most palaces are in disrepair, shedding off their coat of plaster. They are usually squattered, such as the

The central trunk of the banyan was hit by lightning but the old shoots remain.

Bhagyakul Roy Palace on Chapatala Ghat, known as Bhooter Bari, 'the haunted house', as a ghost is believed to live there, or Putulwala Buri at Sobhabazar Pier with its nude Greek statues on top.

At **Kumartuli**, behind Kumartuli Ghat, lives a community of potters and clay statue makers. They use mud from the river. The straw to structure the statues is bought by barges from the paddies south of Calcutta. The best time to visit Kumartuli is before a *puja* when workshops are producing hundreds of statues of deities for the altars erected throughout the city. Further north is Baghbazar Ghat, the mooring point where the barges unload straw for Kumartuli. Straw barges sail in with the tide, attached in pairs loaded with a huge stack of straw in which the crew digs out a cabin.

Located on the site of Sutanuti, **Baghbazar**, once Captain Perrin's Garden where the East India Company's servants took the evening air, may be called the home of the *Rosogolla*, Calcutta's most famous delicacy, invented in 1868 by Nabin Chandra Das who lived here. His descendants carry on the trade. The house opposite theirs on Baghbazar Street is perhaps one of the oldest in Calcutta. The Mahratta Ditch, a moat dug around Calcutta to ward off marauding Mahrattas, start at Baghbazar. It was used as a hideaway by young revolutionary fugitives during India's struggle for freedom.

The most prominent figure of Baghbazar was Babu Pradhyumma Mullick. He drove in an open carriage drawn by a pair of zebras and had fourteen Rolls Royces in the 1920s, the largest collection in the world at that time. His palatial home on Baghbazar Street is now the property of a charitable hospital. Baghbazar Street has kept several palaces of the Bengali landed gentry, some in rather good condition such as politician Pashupati Bose's mansion with its art nouveau glass door panes imported from Germany painted with figures of Hindu Gods. Nationalist meetings were held in the vast courtyard supported by mammoth Corinthian pillars. Beyond the ditch, further north is Cossipore Ghat where Ramakrishna was cremated in 1896.

To finish the day, get back downtown to Princep Ghat by Circular Rail and hire a dinghy there. The one or two-hour sunset boat ride on the Hooghly will take you upstream along the Strand, all the way to Outram Ghat and back. Between Outram and Princep Ghats stands the Gwalior Monument, nicknamed 'the pepperpot' because of its shape. It was erected in 1847 by the Earl of Ellenborough to commemorate the Gwalior Campaign in 1843 against the Sindhia.

On Sundays, instead of hiring a dinghy, you can alternatively take a sunset cruise at 7.30 pm on a steam launch operated by the Government of West Bengal from Outram Ghat. During *pujas*, special night cruises are organised by the West Bengal government along the ghat where clay images of deities are immersed into the Hooghly.

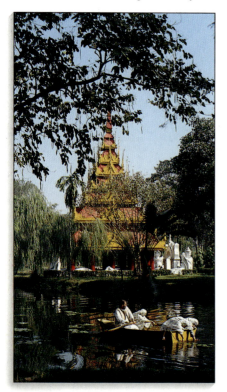

Left: the Burmese pagoda in Eden Gardens. **Right**: traditional gymnastics.

SOUTH CALCUTTA

South Calcutta is a mixture of residential areas with parks, lakes and clubs, of middle-class Bengali neighbourhoods and of overcrowded poorer pockets inhabited by refugees from East Bengal.

South Calcutta starts after the steel Zeerut Bridge crossing **Tolly's Nullah**, a canal starting in the suburb of Hastings at the Hooghly and continuing south of Calcutta. Also known as Adi Ganga, 'the real Ganges', it flows along the old bed of an arm of the Ganges. The *nullah* was dredged by a Colonel Tolly in 1775 to set up a link between Calcutta and the Malta River in the east of the Delta. He had planned to use it to collect a toll. The scheme never took off but the *nullah* is still used by boatsmen to carry goods on oar-propelled barges, plying with the tide, between the Hooghly and south of Calcutta.

First, take a taxi to the residential suburb of Alipore that starts after the Zeerut Bridge. Opposite the luxurious **Taj Bengal** hotel, opened in 1989 and decorated using Bengali designs and handicraft, are the **Zoological Gardens** inaugurated in 1876 by the Prince of Wales. It draws over 100,000 visitors a day on weekends and holidays. The main attractions are the White Tiger, a mutant species, not an albino; the Tigon, a cross between a Bengal tiger and an African lioness; and the Litigon, born of a lioness and a tigon. The zoo has a good sampling of Indian wildlife. Main attractions include the Royal Bengal tiger, ghavial, one-horned rhino, chittal, barking deer, sambar, Indian lion, black buck, langur, gibbon, cobra, rock python, adjutant crane and Indian elephant. Thousands of migrating birds from Siberia fly in every year to spend winter on the zoo lake.

The **Belvedere**, next to the zoo, is the former Vice-Regal Lodge where the viceroy would reside until 1911 when the capital was transferred to Delhi. He would stay at the lodge every winter and hold his annual Christmas Ball here, even after the capital was moved to Delhi. The building dates back to the last years of the 17th century but has received many additions. It became Government property in 1854 when it was acquired to serve as a residence to the then Lieutenant-Governor of Bengal. After Independence, the Belvedere became the National Library. The last viceroy's two long mahogany dining tables have been retained and are now used in the reading rooms, the former ball-room and banquet hall. Over two million books are stored here. The park is open to the public and is normally not crowded, except on weekends.

East of the Belvedere is the Presidency Jail where most of the political hangings carried out by the British during the fight for Independence took place. Nearby is the Bhowanipore Cemetery, nicknamed Padre's Godown, where a section has been allotted to Commonwealth War Graves from World War II. Immediately south of the Belvedere the **Agri-Horticultural Society's Gardens** were founded in 1820 by William Carrey, the Baptist missionary of Serampore fame.

Some of Calcutta's richest families live in Alipore. Their 'bungalows' can be seen along Alipore Road, Penn Road, Judge's Court Road, Burdwan Road and Raja Santosh Road. The Maharajahs of Cooch Behar and Burdwan, and the Rajah of Santosh had their palaces in Alipore. The Burdwan palace, **Vijay Manzil**, built in 1903, had once more than 50 servants and stables for about 60 horses. Viceroys would dine here. One of the best examples of Calcutta's heritage, the palace is now threatened by a real-estate project. Vijay Manzil can be seen across a small lake from Burdwan Road, not far from where it connects with Diamond Harbour Road.

Hasting's House on Judge's Court Road, the former country seat of Warren Hastings, was purchased as a State

Preceding pages: sunset on the Lakes during the Monsoon. Left: The Belvedere, previously residence of the viceroy, is now the National Library.

guest house by Lord Curzon in 1901. It has now become an educational institution. The house is said to be haunted. At midnight, people say they can hear Hastings' horse-drawn cart pull up under the porch.

Hasting Road crosses Tolly's Nullah into **Kalighat**. Kalighat Road starts on the left immediately after the bridge and leads to the **Kali Temple**. According to a legend, Daksha, a son of Brahma and Shiva's father-in-law, spoke ill of Shiva in the presence of his daughter Sati, Shiva's wife. Overcome by emotion, she died of shock. On hearing of this, Shiva rushed to take Sati's dead body in his arms, went into trance and started to dance with such a frenzy that the Earth began to tremble. The Gods, afraid that he might destroy the world, decided to cool him down by making the body disappear. Vishnu, using his solar disc, chopped Sati's body into 51 parts that scattered all over the Earth. Each of the places where a part of Sati's body fell became a *pitha*, a pilgrimage centre for Shakti Hindus. The temple is said to stand on the spot where the little toe of Sati's foot fell.

The Kali Temple was built in 1809 along Tolly's Nullah on the spot of a former 16th century Kali temple by the Sobarna Chowdhury family, landowners from the nearby village of Barisa. The temple is an important centre of Sakti worship. The main deities of the temple are Kali and Shiva. The temple to Kali, an avatar of Sati, is in the centre. The black marble statue of the Goddess with four arms, garlanded with a chain of human heads, rests on a block of red granite. Her hand, tongue and eyebrows are made of gold. Eyes and tongue are painted scarlet red.

There is a *Shivalingam* to the northeast of the compound where women pray for fertility. In front of the temple is a little enclosure where *boli*, the sacrifice of animals, is performed. The usual *boli* consists of one goat, although it can be a buffalo, on *Durga Puja*.

The temple is an active pilgrimage

An old print of the Kali Temple. It has not changed much.

centre. Prayers are performed around the clock. It is still owned by the founders' descendants, the *paladas*, who have the monopoly over conducting rituals. There are now more than 600 *paladas*. They take turns to perform at the temple. Pilgrims come mainly from Eastern India. They first offer Kali a mixture of milk, mixed with holy Ganga Water and *bhang*, a paste made of cannabis indica leaves. Many bring a goat as an offering to Kali. The goat is first washed and garlanded with red hibiscus flowers, the flower of Kali. The pilgrim then whispers to the goat a wish, a message to take to the Goddess, and brings it into the sacrificial enclosure where the goat's head is fastened, facing east, sprinkled with water, and chopped off by a special attendant.

On a Sunday morning a few dozens *boli* are performed, more during festivals. Filming or taking pictures of sacrifices is forbidden. As the place is a *pitha*, at least a sacrifice a day has to be made. If no pilgrim makes a sacrifice, the priests have to offer one from their own earnings of the day. Sensitive souls are advised not to watch if the sight of blood upsets them.

The area along the *nullah*, consisting mainly of shops and small shrines as well as a wooden boat bridge, has been neatly restored in the late 1970s.

Nearby in a temple dependency is Mother Theresa's Nirmal Hridoy Manzil, 'the abode of the tender heart', where the Poor and the Destitute are given a roof to peacefully spend their last moments. It is not a tourist attraction. Visitors with cameras are not welcome, but volunteers to take part in the daily chores and join in the prayers are definitely welcome.

Kalighat is famous for its style of painting, the Kalighat *pat*, that developed from the mass demand for holy souvenir images by pilgrims to the Kali Temple. Examples can be seen in South Calcutta at the Gurusaday Museum and at the Birla Academy of Art and Culture. The shops on Kali Ghat Temple

A sradh ceremony at the Kali Temple.

Street, selling all sorts of religious souvenirs, are the ones that in the past used to sell the famous Kalighat *pats*. At the end of the street, on Shyana Prasad Mukherjee Road, stands the Greek orthodox church of the Transfiguration of Christ on Mount Thabor, built in 1926 to replace a much earlier church built in the north of the city in 1781, 10 years after the first Greek settled in Calcutta. There is one Greek left in the city. The last pope left in the 1960s and no services are held in the church now.

Continue through the Kalighat market to the Chetla Bridge. Chetla Avenue is a busy commercial artery. On the other side of the bridge is the Calcutta burning ghat. The statesman Chittaranjan Das was cremated here and a *Samadhi* has been erected in his memory.

Next to the burning ghat is a memorial to the Maharajahs of Mymensingh, built in the 19th century in the traditional Bengal *panch-ratna* style and the **Mysore Gardens** built along Tolly's Nullah by the Maharajah of Mysore in the memory of two Mysore princes who were murdered in Calcutta. The Maharajah himself was cremated here in 1897. Take a taxi at this stage on Tollygunge Road and follow the *nullah*. You will pass by several traditional Bengali temples, including the **Gopal Mandir** and the **Shiva Mandir**, built in the late 19th century by the rich local Mondal family.

Turn into Deshapran Sasmal Road. Run by Bob and Anne Wright, a couple of *ko-hais*, as old India hands are called, the **Tollygunge Club** was first a *neel kothi*, the residence of an indigo planter, Richard Johnson, then housed Prince Gholam Muhammad, the son of deposed Tippu Sultan. The club house was built in 1791 and the Tollygunge Club was formed in 1895. It is Calcutta's only country club and offers tennis, golf, horse-riding, clay-shooting and squash. There are several restaurants and an exellent bar serving the best pink gin in town. The club house is surrounded by an immense park with a rich wildlife

Below, left: a Kalighat pat; **right**: the Chetla Temple.

and various species of trees. The club accepts visitors on a temporary basis, provided they are introduced by another member or introduce themselves to the Managing Member or the Secretary. Stop here for lunch.

Further south, at the junction of Netaji Subhas Road, are the Indrapuri Film Studios where the best Bengali movies were shot. Take a rickshaw for a quick look at the **Royal Calcutta Golf Club** ('The Royal'). Established in 1827, it is the oldest golf club outside the British Isles. Next, catch a taxi to Rabindra Sarovar ('the Dhakuria Lakes'), a residential area with parks and several rowing and social clubs.

At the corner of Prince Anwar Shah, off Deshapran Sasmal Avenue, stands the Shiite **Ghulam Muhammad Mosque**. Built in 1835, it is the first of a series of mosques constructed in Calcutta by descendants of Tippu Sultan. Nearby, a Hindu temple and a Muslim Holy Man's grave stand side by side.

On Southern Avenue is the **Birla Academy of Art and Culture**, one of Calcutta's most pleasant museums, founded by the wealthy Birla family of industrialists. It has pieces of every period of Indian Art and holds exhibitions of Classical, Modern Arts and folklore festivals.

Near the museum entrance is a small but active temple, the **Lake Kali Bari**, at 108 Southern Avenue, a Tantric worship centre. There are several mansions and palaces around the lake, the most remarkable ones being the steamboat-shaped building at Southern Avenue, Dr Meghnad Saha's mansion on 125 Southern Avenue and the ruined palace on the right of Southern Avenue just before Gul Park. On Lake Road, the Buddhist temple is also worth a detour. Around the lake, the Nehru's Children Museum operates a toy train. North of the lake at 29B Hazra Road is a Sri Saraswata Gondiya Asan and Mission, an elaborately decorated Vaishnab Temple, one of the few in Calcutta.

The **Ramakrishna Mission Insti-**

The Tollygunge Club was once the residence of an indigo planter.

tute of Culture on Gul Park was founded in 1936 by the Ramakrishna Movement. It has a school of languages teaching Persian, Sanskrit, Bengali and Hindi; a library; a museum of Indian Art; and a Universal Prayer Room.

From Gul Park, take another taxi along Gurusaday Road in the district of **Ballygunge**. Stop and keep the taxi waiting at the **Birla Industrial & Technological Museum**. The building has been given to the State by Raja Baldeo Das Birla, founder of the House of Birlas, to be turned into an educational museum. There is an incredible variety of exhibits making it worthwhile to visit: the first disc-recording machine, the first one-sided disc-cut of a Tagore song, a steam-beam and a narrow-gauge engine, old wall telephones, vintage Rolls-Royce and Fiat cars, Douglas and NSU motorbikes, and models of early ships, a rajah's pleasureboat, and *Indian Boom*, the warship of the East India Company. There are also dioramas of Calcutta in the 18th century, of a village in the Indus Valley at the time of Mohenjo Daro, of the Assam oil fields in the 19th century, and of a pigeon-post in India in the old days, a life-size mock-up coal gallery and several snake-pits.

Further down Gurusaday Road is the **Laksmi Narayan Temple** that the Birla family is building on the model of the Lingaraj Temple at Bhubaneshwar in Orissa. The temple will be air-conditioned. The Birla Samaghar Hall in the basement has already opened. Conferences and shows of traditional performing arts take place there regularly. According to tradition, the temple may not be completed until a propitious site for another temple is found by the oldest woman in the family.

The **Calcutta Cricket and Football Club**, the oldest cricket club outside the United Kingdom, was founded in 1792. Nearby on Ballygunge Circular Road, usually called B.C. Road, opposite the Jesuit St. Lawrence School, is the Maharajah of Tripura's palace, and at 55

The Roychowdhury Temple with its 12 Shiva shrines.

B.C. Road, Chitrakoot, one of Calcutta leading modern art galleries.

Jhowtola, around Park Circus, used to be a residential area. The Muslim aristocracy of undivided Bengal built there superb mansions. Many of the city's prominent citizens lived there. Fazul Haq, once the Mayor of Calcutta, lived at 88/2 Jhowtola Road. He was also Chief Minister of Bengal from 1937 to 1943, an active member of the Indian National Congress, then a leader of the Muslim League which he represented at the First and Second Round Table Conferences, and after 1947, the Governor of East Pakistan. The Bangladesh Deputy High Commission, at 3 Park Circus, is the former palace of Husain Shahid Suhrawardy, Chief Minister of Bengal in 1946 and founder of the Awami League in Pakistan. Khwaja Nazimuddin, another Chief Minister of undivided Bengal and Governor of East Pakistan, Prime Minister of Pakistan in 1951 and Governor-General at Jinnah's death in 1948, lived at 50 Syed mir Ali Avenue.

The area is now a mixed neighbourhood of Muslims, Anglo-Indians, Armenians, Bengalis and Tamils. Nearby is Karaya Road which used to operate the poshest brothels in town with expensive prostitutes coming from France, Britain and Romania.

Continue by taxi to Lower Circular (L.C.) Road, heading west. On the right hand side is the **La Martinière College**, which is separated in two by Laudon Street. The college was founded in 1836 by Major-General Claude Martin, a former French Army officer in Pondicherry who later entered the service of the East India Company and rose to the rank of Major-General. He died in Lucknow and left money to set up three schools, one in Lucknow, one in Calcutta, and one in the French city of Lyons where he was born. All three are still in operation today. La Martinière Calcutta opened in 1836. It is run, like the Lucknow school, by the United Church of Nothern India. The boys' building has a rotunda that

Ah Chi's grave facing the Ganges — good *feng shui* for the first Chinese settlers.

once supported a dome with a chapel. The girls' building has the only 'elephant balcony' left in Calcutta. It is a two-storey porch, high enough for elephants to come under it and allow people to disembark from the back of the elephant at a balcony on the second floor. Behind La Martinière, on Short Street, is Calcutta's other prestigious school and competitor of the La Martinière, the **Saint-Xavier's College**, which was built and has been run by Jesuits since 1860.

Near the **Hindustan International Hotel** is the **Nizam's Palace**, the former house of a rich Armenian family, the Galstauns, later purchased by the Nizam of Hyderabad, then taken over by Government of India. The former **Chinese Consulate**, a yellow Art Deco building, is now occupied by the office issuing visa extensions and Darjeeling Permits. Across Chowringhee, the **Calcutta Club** was founded in 1907 by a group of British and Indian personalities such as Maharaja Nripendranarayan of Cooch Behar, Maharajadhiraj of Burdwan, Sir R.N. Mukherjee and Lord S.P. Sinha, who were opposed to the concept of a 'whites only' club. The position of club president was rotated between a British and an Indian every alternate year. The club boasts lawn-tennis courts, the best smoked *hilsa* in town and the only men-only bar in Calcutta, known as the 'Dirty Bar'.

Behind L.C. Road, **Netaji's House** on Elgin Road, from where Netaji Chandra Bose escaped in January 1941, is now a museum. The car in which Netaji fled is in the yard. Under the porch stands a replica of the Singapore Memorial to the Martyrs of the Indian National Army blown up by the British when they reoccupied the island in 1945. Celebrations are held in front of the house on Netaji's Birthday, on January 23rd, every year.

South and west of Alipore are areas too far to be all squeezed into a one-day tour of South Calcutta. The suburb of Behala starts after Alipore at Diamond Harbour (D.H.) Road. **Shahbani Begum Mosque** at 49/1 D.H. Road, built by Shahbani Begum, Tippu Sultan's granddaughter, is almost a replica of Ghulam Muhammad Masjid at Tollygunge. It is double-aisled, multidomed and rectangular, in the style of Bengali mosques that have absorbed elements of the local Bengali *chandni* and *dalan* Hindu temple architecture. At 1 Satyendra Nath Roy Road, off D.H. Road, housed in a 19th century palace is the well-maintained but relatively unknown to the public, **West Bengal Archaeological Museum** with exhibits from the Paleolithic, Bronze Age, Pala-Sena, Maurya and Moghul periods as well as Kalighat *pats* and black stone Hindu sculptures.

At Barisa, further south, along D.H. Road, the main feature is the Annapurna Temple with an Annapurna shrine and 12 smaller Shiva temples. It is located on K.K. Roychowdhury Road, near the Barisa Girls' School. Barisa is also known for the puppet shows that take place here at the Shoker Bazar Chandimela during *Kali Puja*. Some 15 kilometres (9 miles) south, along D.H. Road, is Thakurpukur, where a former civil servant, Gurusaday Dutt, who had been collecting Bengali folk art during his life, set up a museum. The **Gurusaday Museum of Folk Art** houses an exhibition of Kalighat *pats*, black stones, wooden sculptures from Comilla, aboriginal *pats*, terracotta panels saved from ruined brick temples, some dating back to the 10th century, wooden village toys, *sandesh* pastry moulds, and *kanthas* or quilts embroidered for years to be presented on such formal occasions as a wedding.

Branching off from D.H. Road, Taratala Road leads to Achipur, near Budge-Budge, where the first Chinese settler Ah-Chi is buried. His grave, on a high bank facing the Hooghly for good *feng-shui*, and the nearby Taoist temple are now pilgrimage places for the Chinese of Calcutta on the 15th day of the first Lunar month.

Right: the Burdwan Palace, Vijay Manzil, is threatened by a real estate project.

THE BIRLA ACADEMY OF ART AND CULTURE

There are many art collectors in India, but few have given thought to the establishment of a museum or an art academy. One of India's leading industrialists, B.K. Birla, and his wife Sarala, began collecting art treasures in the 1940s. Over the years, as their collection grew, they conceived the idea of setting up a permanent home for it in Calcutta. **The Birla Academy of Art and Culture**, a Public Charitable Trust, was thus founded in 1962 to collect, preserve and exhibit art treasures for public benefit. With the establishment of this academy, Calcutta has the privilege of possessing one of the best private art galleries in India.

The Birla Academy is located on Southern Avenue beside the Dhakuria Lakes. Its museum is quite distinctive in character, as it permits a visitor to catch a glimpse of Indian art through the ages, from the distant past to the living present. Although there are more than 4,000 art objects in the collection, only a balanced selection of works, covering each art form, is displayed at any one time.

The collection comprises Indian stone sculptures, bronzes and terracottas from 300 BC to the 16th century; Indian miniatures of various schools such as those that can be classified as 'Rajasthani', 'Pahari' or 'Mughal'; and old Jain and Persian palm-leaf manuscripts. Certain folk styles of painting and textiles from Kalighat, Paithan and Tanjore are also included.

Works of contemporary Indian art are gradually being acquired though artists of eminence like Rabindranath Tagore, Abanindranath Tagore, Gaganendranath Tagore, Nandalal Bose, Hussain, Bendre, Hebbar, Ganesh Pyne, Bikash Bhattacharjee, Jogen Chowdhury and others, are already represented. Among contemporary international artists, works of Jean Arp, Nivola, Dorothy Dehnar and Olav Beartling, deserve mention.

The Birla Academy also serves as a link between artists and their public. It organises and sponsors exhibitions for public benefit. Throughout the year, it presents various exhibitions which help to whet the immense cultural appetite of the city. This is the only gallery in Calcutta where one can enjoy international exhibitions. In addition, the academy arranges lectures, seminars and workshops for art teachers and students in the city as well as runs a short course on aesthetics. It also circulates educational material outside the academy and provides guided tours on request. At the same time, the Birla Academy offers courses on Indian classical dance, including the rare Manipuri School.

Visitors are welcome to participate in all the activities of the academy. The museum itself is open in the afternoons from 3.30 to 6.00 pm every day except on Mondays.

On display at the academy are all styles of Indian statuary (left) as well as a collection of miniatures from Rajasthan (right).

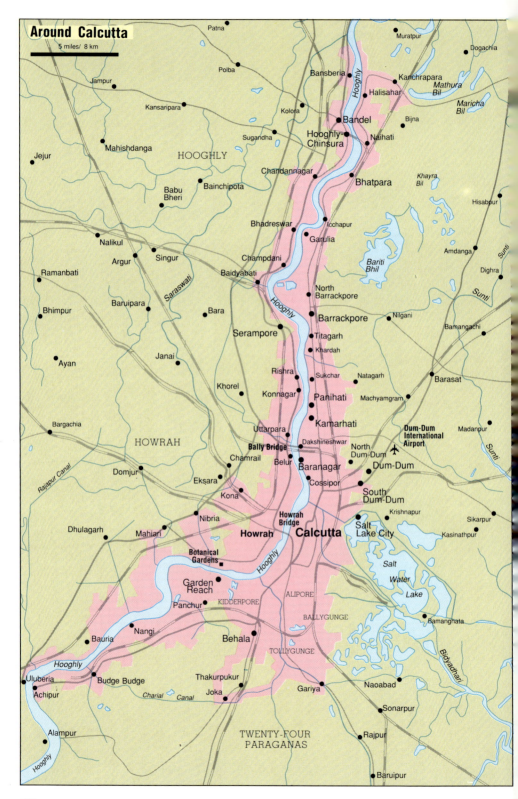

SIDE-TRIPS

Calcutta can be the starting point to a whole range of destinations. The State of **West Bengal**, stretching from the Delta of the Ganges to the Himalayas, offers a number of possibilities. Immediately north of Calcutta, at Habra, are the ruins of the city with stupas and a wall that have just been discovered. Excavations are going on and a small museum has been set up in the village. The origins of the city are unknown as its existence was unsuspected. Further north, along the Hooghly River, are the remains of several foreign settlements forming what is now called the Hooghly Heritage. **Serampore** was Danish, **Chandernagore** French, **Chinsurah** Dutch and Armenian, and **Bandel** Portuguese. Further north, **Tribeni**, at the confluence of the Ganges, the Jamuna and the Saraswati Rivers, is a pilgrimage centre where a festival in honour of Varuna, the God of Water is held every year at *Dusserah*.

Past Tribeni, **Nawadwip**, built on nine formerly distinct islands on the Ganges and the capital of Bengal in the 11th and 12th centuries, is also a centre of Vaishnab worship. Lord Chaitanya, the founder of the movement was born and preached there and the ISKON movement is headquartered at **Mayapur**, on one of the islands. Every year over 500,000 pilgrims perform *padakrama*, a pilgrimage on foot that takes them along a 50-kilometre (30-mile) loop over the nine islands. Some 45 kilometres (28 miles) west of Tribeni, the town of **Burdwan**, the capital of a former princely state, has retained an impressive wing of the Maharaja Dhiraja's palace.

Some 145 kilometres (90 miles) north of Calcutta, on the right bank of the Hooghly, is **Plassey**, where a monument marks the site of the battle where Clive defeated the forces of Siraj-ud-Daula, on June 23rd, 1757. About 50 kilometres (30 miles) further north, **Murshidabad** became the capital of Bengal in 1705, when the Nawab of Bengal decided to move from Dacca, until 1773 when it was shifted to Calcutta after the East India Company had secured the *dewani* rights of Bengal, Bihar and Orissa. Hazarduari, the Nawab's palace, built in 1837, is now a museum. There are plans to restore it. Other points of interest are the Katra mosque, the Deorhi palace where Siraj-ud-Daula was assassinated, his grave at Khusbagh, and the Baranagar terracotta temples. Some 120 kilometres (75 miles) north, is **Malda**, also known as **English Bazar**, a former trading centre where the British, the French, the Dutch and the Armenians had factories. Nearby, are the ruins of **Gaur**, the former Pala and Sena capital of Bengal and of **Malda**, the former Nawab's capital where several Muslim monuments were built, using elements from the Hindu temples of Gaur. Only the western point of Gaur can be visited as the

Preceding pages: snow caps Mount Kanchenjunga in Sikkim; a temple bas-relief of Portuguese soldiers. *Right*: a waterway on the Delta.

border with Bangladesh cuts the site in two. The most interesting monuments, however, are on the Indian side.

West and north-west of Calcutta are some of the finest terracotta temples of Bengal. **Tarkeshwar**, 67 kilometres (42 miles) west of Calcutta, is a pilgrimage centre. Ever year during the *Kasta Mela* festival, devotees walk all the way there from Calcutta, bringing water from the Hooghly. They converge at the temple, built around a black stone considered to be the *lingam* of Taraknath Babu, an avatar of Shiva, and pour the water over the statue. **Vishnupur**, 201 kilometres (125 miles) west of Calcutta, was the capital of Bengal during the Malla kings in the 17th and 18th centuries. The finest temples are Rasmancha, Radhagovind, Radhamadhab, Shamroy, Madan Gopal and Madan Mohan Mandir, all well preserved examples of the terracotta temple architecture.

The main festival is *Jhapan* in August. It is both a tribal and a Hindu festival. On that day, in the past, neighbouring Santhal tribes used to converge at Vishnupur for the annual ceremony of allegiance to the local Raja. Although there is no raja any more, the Santhals continue to mark that day, holding celebrations in the city. For Hindus it is *Manasha Puja*, the festival of the Goddess of Snakes. In this rice-growing area, she is an important deity as she can protect peasants harvesting rice in the paddies towards the end of the Monsoon from being bitten by snakes. The festival is an impressive one, as snakes are brought to temples, let to wander freely and fed with milk and eggs.

North of Vishnupur, 136 kilometres (85 miles) from Calcutta, is **Santiniketan,** the open air university founded by Rabindranath Tagore. A former *ashram* founded by his father, it was converted by Rabindranath into a university in 1921 with the financial backing of the Maharaja of Tripura. The objective was to revive the traditional Indian way of teaching, in the open, under a tree, in close contact with Na-

A 2,000-year-old stupa at the Bhadra.

ture. Santiniketan has become one of the hubs of the intellectual life of India.

The Chancellor of the University is traditionally the Prime Minister of India. Faculties offer studies in Bengali, Hindi, Pali, Sanskrit, Tibetan, Chinese, Indian History, philosophy, Arts, music, dance and handicraft such as *batik*. Every change of season and Foundation Day are marked by festivals with traditional songs and dances in praise of Nature and the Supreme God of Man. **Kendulbilwa**, near Santiniketan and the birthplace of Joydeb, a great Bengali poet and Vaishnab preacher, is famous for its *Baul Mela*, where Bauls, the bards of Bengal, gather for three days of songs non-stop. South of Calcutta is the **Delta of the Ganges** and of the Brahmaputra famous for its mangrove jungle, the largest in the world, the *Ganga Sagar* annual festival, and the Sunderban Wildlife Reserve.

West of Bengal is the State of **Bihar**. **Patna**, the capital, a city of 500,000, built along the Ganges is the former Pataliputra, the former capital of the Magadha Empire that once stretched under Emperor Ashoka in the 3rd century BC from Afghanistan to the Bay of Bengal. Before, it had been invaded by the Greeks of Bactriane in the 2nd century BC and the Hayataleh Huns, in the 5th century. The Bihar State Museum has a rare collection of Buddhist bronze and stone sculptures of the Maurya period. Not to be missed are the statues of Vishnu and George V standing side by side under a tree in the garden. The main monuments are, in Patna, the Maharaja's palace, now the Bihar Tourist Development Corporation office, the Bihar Secretariat, both built in the neo-Moghul style of the early 20th century, the Golghar, a granary built by the British in 1786; and in Patna Sahib, the old Patna, Harmandirji, the second holiest Sikh shrine in India after the Golden Temple at Amritsar, the former opium godowns of Gulzaribagh, and, at Maner, 30 kilometres (19 miles) west, a complex of Moghul sufi graves. A huge

A riverside temple at Atbara, north of Calcutta.

cattle fair, the **Sonepur Mela** takes place every year at Konhara Ghat, on the north bank of the Ganges, at the confluence of the Sone River. The fair, the largest in the world, larger even than the *Pushkar Mela* in Rajasthan, starts on the full moon of the month of *Kartik* and runs for a month.

Bihar draws its name from *vihar*, which means a temple in Sanskrit. The religious past of the state is, indeed, rich. Two religions take their roots here. The Lord Buddha reached Illumination in what is now Bodhgaya, and taught at Rajgir. Mahavira, the 24th *tirthankara* Jain prophet lived and died in Bihar. The main Buddhist sites in Bihar are **Bodhgaya**, **Rajghir** and **Nalanda**, the former Buddhist University and gaya where Buddha stayed before going to Bodhgaya. All are south of Patna, the capital. Among the Jain places, the most important are the **Parasnath Hills,** near the border with Bengal, where 20 out of 24 Jain *tirthankaras* reached Nirvana. The hills are accessible by taxi from the Dhanbad railway station and Pawapuri, 86 kilometres (53 miles) south of Patna; a white marble temple in the middle of a lotus pond marks the spot where Mahavira was cremated in 477 BC.

South of Patna on the **Chhotanagpur Plateau**, a mostly tribal area of Mon-Khmer stock are **Ranchi** and **Jamshedpur**, two steel cities. Jamshedpur, the oldest, was built as early as 1912 by Jamshed Tata, the founder of the House of Tata's, which has become the first or second largest business group in India. It is an extremely well managed and maintained city, and probably the neatest in the whole country.

South of Bengal is the State of **Orissa**, the former kingdom of Kalinga. Orissa is an intensely religious state. The main deity is Lord Jagannath, an incarnation of Vishnu. Orissa temples have a distinct style: at the entrance of a temple compound stands a hall of offerings, the *Bhoga Mandap*; next come a dancing hall, the *Nata Mandir*; frontal porches, the *Jagamohana*; and, finally,

Bari Dargah at Maner.

the sanctum, called *Deul*. **Bhubaneshwar**, the state capital, is a city of temples. The largest concentration is around the Bind Bindusagar Lake. The Lingaraj Temple, built in 1114 to the glory of Shiva, is the largest with its 45-metre (148-foot) high *deul*. Like the other temples, it is decorated with a profusion of sculptures of deities, nymphs and amorous couples. Access is prohibited to non-Hindus, but there is a good view from the terrace of the neighbouring **Chitrakatini Mandir**, a small temple with a *bas-relief* scene of a camel procession, a rather unusual feature in Eastern India.

The other temples in the lake area, Parasuramesvara, Rajarani, Markandeyesvara, Sisiresvara, Uttaresvara, Ananta-Vasudeva Mandir, and Vaital Deul, open to non-Hindus, are worth a visit as they too are all elaborately decorated with *bas-reliefs* and sculptures. **Markandeyesvara Mandir** has representations of the Nine Planets, of amorous couples and of a drunken man, Vaital Deul of Durga Mahishasuramardini, of Chamunda, sitting on a corpse with an owl and a jackal at her sides, of Shiva and Parvati, and of Durga Mandala sitting on an elephant. Vaital Deul is also famous for its shape, that of an upturned boat, said to be a rare example of the original architecture of Hindu temples of Eastern India. **Ananta Vasudeva Mandir** has friezes with military processions and hundreds of elephants, each in a different position. The oldest temple is Parasuramesvara Mandir, built in the 7th century BC. **Mukhteshvara Mandir**, not far from the lake, is the gem of the temple architecture of Orissa with its latticed windows, erotic scenes as well as representations of dancing girls, *nagis*, which are half-human and half-snake, elephants, and monkeys in comical situations. Each side of the *deul* has a *Bho*, a sort of coat-of-arms typical of Orissa, with a grinning lion flanked by two dwarfs. The nearby smaller temples of Kedaresvara, Siddesvara and Gauri

Mukhteshvara Mandir — the gem of temple architecture in Orissa.

Side-trips 197

Mandir are of minor interest. Other monuments not to be missed are the Rajarani and Brahmesvara temples. The Orissa State Museum, the Tribal Research Institute, the Jain cave monasteries at **Khandagiri** and **Udayagiri**, and **Dhauli Hill** with a stone elephant bearing Emperor Ashoka's Edict and a stupa at the top built by Japanese Buddhists.

Bhubaneshwar is the starting point for the Golden Triangle of Orissa. Pipli, 10 kilometres (6 miles) south, is a small village famous for its applique work in vivid colours. **Puri**, 55 kilometres (34 miles) south, is one of the biggest pilgrimage centres of India. First known as Dantpur, a major Buddhist centre, and the port from where the Lord Buddha's tooth was sent to Sri Lanka in 543 BC, Puri became a centre for the cult of Jagannath, a Hindu god of tribal origin. Jagannath, was first a log-god from the tribal Daru tree cults. It was assimilated progressively to Rama and Krishna. The **Jagannath Temple** was built by King Anantavarman Chudaganga Day in the 12th century. It is known as the White Pagoda because of its 65-metre (210-foot) high, white plastered *deul* surmounted by the Dharmachakra, the wheel of religion and time, and Vishnu's banner. It has been recently discovered that the white coating dates back to the days of expansion of the Moghul Empire. Under the layers of plaster are stone sculptures that were thus hidden from the eye of the invaders. Some 5,000 monks and priests live in the compound. The temple is off-limits to non-Hindus. The main event here is the *Rath Yatra* Festival, celebrated late in June or early in July. Statues of Jagannath, his brother Balabhadra and his sister Subhadra, are taken from the Lingaraj Temple aboard three 13-metre (42-foot) high wooden chariots to Gundicha Mandir, a temple to Lakshmi, a mile away. They stay there one week, then return to the Jagannath Temple. This fertility festival is attended by an ecstatic crowd of nearly one million. Puri is also a seaside resort

Erotic bas-reliefs at the Sun Temple, Konarak.

that developed in the Raj Days. The place to stay is the colonial-style 'BNR', or 'Bengal Nagpur Railway Hotel'. There are cheaper hotels along the beach on Tirthankara Road or in the old city towards the Jagannath Temple.

Marine Drive, a 30-kilometre (19-mile) road, runs through a landscape of casuarina plantations and sand dunes to **Konarak**. The Sun Temple, erected in the 13th century on the seashore by King Langula Narasimha Deva to replace an older one built in the 9th century, had a 70-metre (230-foot) high *deul* and a 40-metre (130-foot) *jagamohana*, representing the chariot of the Sun. The chariot, drawn by seven impetuous horses, representing the days of the week, had 12 pairs of wheels, the fortnights, each wheel having eight spokes, the three-hour periods of the traditional Hindu clock. Today the temple no longer stands on the seaside, the sea having receded over the centuries. The *deul* collapsed in the 19th century and one horse is missing, but most of the erotic statuary and *bas-reliefs*, more within reach of the visitor, and in larger numbers than at Khajurao, have remained intact. The Government of Orissa operates a tourist guesthouse at Konarak, allowing these visitors to stay overnight for the *son-et-lumiere* show and to see the sunset at the temple. Near Bhubaneshwar, the two hills of **Lalita Giri** and **Ratna Giri**, some 20 kilometres (12 miles) from **Cuttack**, the former capital of Orissa, off the road to Paradip, is the site of the former Buddhist University of Pushpagiri. Excavations have unearthed a number of sculptures of the Buddha, including two huge stone heads, over one metre-high, of stupas and the ruins of the main building of the university.

Inhabited by a variety of Aryan, Mon-Khmer and Tibeto-Burmese communities, difficult of access because of travel restrictions and of the need, in most of the cases, to have an Inner-Line Permit, the northeastern states of Arunachal-Pradesh, Assam, Manipur,

Buddhist ruins unearthed at Lalita Giri.

Meghalaya, Mizaram, Nagaland and Tripura, the "Seven Sisters" as they are known, remain untouched by tourism. **Assam**, the former kingdom of Kamrup, is the most accessible as the Inner-Line Permit is not required from visitors. It spreads along the valley of the Brahmaputra. The main sites are **Kamakhya Mandir**, a tantric temple on a hill dominating the river, in the suburbs of Guwahati, the capital; the **Kaziranga game reserve**, the only place where there are at the same time elephants, rhinos and tigers; **Sibsagar**, the former capital, where temples and palaces built by the Tai Ahom kings in the 16th century; and the tea gardens of Upper-Assam. **Meghalaya** is a hilly state that the British used as a resort and the summer capital of Assam to escape from the overheated valley of the Brahmaputra during the summer and the Monsoon. **Shillong**, the capital, with its English cottages, Christian boarding schools, Botanical Garden, Anglican Church, and Governor's Lodge, is a typical Raj hill resort. Other places of interest are **Cherrapunji** the wettest place in the world (1,150 centimetres/ 453 inches of rain per year) and **Mawphluang**, a barren plateau covered with monoliths and dolmens.

Spreading along the Chinese border, **Arunachal-Pradesh** was the scene of heavy fighting during the Indo-Chinese war of 1962. When the Dalai Lama escaped from Tibet in 1957, he entered India there through the **Bomdila Pass** and his first stop was the 17th century **Tawang Monastery** where the sixth Dalai Lama was born. **Nagaland** is the home of the Nagas, a generic name for Tibeto-Burmes tribes, some of which were head-hunters. **Kohima**, the capital, the furthest point reached by the Japanese during World War II. In the Commonwealth War Cemetery, a memorial is engraved with the famous inscription: "When you go home tell them of us and say, for your tomorrow we give our today". At **Dimapur** are the ruins of the Cachar kingdom wiped out by the Ahoms in the 16th century. The neighbouring state of **Manipur**, a former kingdom that once dominated Burma, was also the target of the Japanese that reached but could not take **Imphal**, the capital. Manipur is famous for its indigenous form of polo from which modern polo is derived, for its religious Hindu festivals and dances, tribal as well as classical and the **Loktak Lake**, home of the black-antlered deer. **Mizoram**, the former Lushai Hills, is inhabited chiefly by tribes related to the Shans of Burma. There are no large cities. In **Tripura**, the former princely state of Tiperah, the capital Agartala boasts a maharajah's palace built in the 1920s.

Four itineraries are recommended in the guide. Two that can be covered in one or two days from Calcutta, the Hooghly Heritage and the Delta of the Ganges, while the two others, the Buddhist sites of Bihar and the **Eastern Himalayas** are usually omitted from most tourist guides.

Left: Avalokitesvara Buddha at Lalitagiri. Right: sunrise on the Brahmaputra.

THE HOOGHLY HERITAGE

North of Calcutta, on a 60-kilometre (37-mile) stretch along the Hooghly River, are the remains of the former foreign settlements. The British, indeed, were not the only foreigners to carry trade in Bengal. Other nations also took part. The Armenians were the first to come. They settled in Chinsurah. Then came the Danes to Serampore, the French to Chandernagore, the Greeks to Rishra, the Prussians to Bhadreshwar, the Portuguese to Bandel and Satgaon. Some of these settlements have retained a fair concentration of 18th and 19th-century colonial architecture, but also of traditional Bengali brick-temples with terracotta *bas-reliefs*, constituting what is called the **Hooghly Heritage**, an entity that the Indian Government is now trying to preserve. Most of the sites can be seen in one day. Rent a car or a taxi and start early in the morning to beat the traffic. Drive along the Barackpore Trunk Road to the Bally Bridge at **Dakshineshwar**. The Kali Bhavatarini Temple complex north of the bridge, on the left bank of the river, was built in 1855 by Rani Rashmoni, a rich widow of Calcutta, in reaction to the wave of conversions to Christianity that was sweeping Calcutta at that time. In the beginning, she had trouble finding priests for the temple as she was not herself a Brahmin. Two Brahmin brothers finally accepted. The younger one, Gadadhara Chattopadyay, who assumed the name of Ramakrishna, became one of the greatest religious philosophers of Bengal. The complex includes a tall Nava-ratna temple to Kali, probably the highest in Bengal, another dedicated to Radha and Krishna, and 12 smaller Shiva temples. Ramakrishna's room is now a museum. The small park next to the complex literally swarms with Hanuman Rhesus monkeys that expect to be fed bananas, peanuts and biscuits by pilgrims and weekend crowds. Dakshineshwar is indeed a popular place as it combines the Kali, Radha-krishna and Ramakrishna cults. On *Shivarati* in February, women take a dip in the river and pray for fertility. On *Novoborsho*, the Bengali New Year that falls on April 13th, businessmen bring their *halkata*, new account books, for blessings. On the same side of the river but south of the bridge, the **Tagore Villa**, a *neel khoti*, one of the few remaining indigo planters' bungalows in India, was built in the 18th century and purchased later by the Tagore family who added a Chinese tea pavilion, a moongate, Italian marble statues, an orchid house and a rose garden. The villa is off-limits to visitors but can be seen from the bridge.

Across the river, slightly to the south, is **Belur Math**, the headquarters of the Ramakrishna Mission, founded in 1938 by Ramakrishna's disciple Vivekananda. The main Ramakrishna temple, a 75-metre (246-foot) long, and 35-metre (115-foot) high structure, was de-

Preceding pages: Sunrise at a ghat in Serampore. **Left**: the Dakshineshwar Temple. **Right**: arms of the Dutch East India Company.

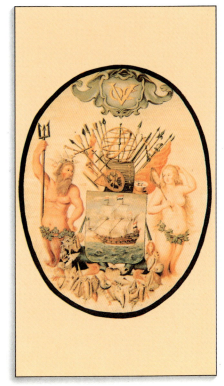

signed in such a way as to appeal to all major religions. The gate is Buddhist, the facade Hindu, windows and balconies Muslim, and the ground plan is in the shape of a Christian cross. The temple stands in a complex containing other minor temples, gardens, study rooms, and residences for the members of the orders. The main festival here is Ramakrishna's birthday on February 21st and *Kumari Puja*, on *Mahastami*, the day after *Durga Puja*.

Further north along the Grand Trunk Road to **Serampore**, a former settlement of the Danish East India Company from 1699 to 1777 and Danish colony thereafter until 1845. The colony of Fredericknagore, as Serampore was named, to honour King Frederick V, never really took off. British competition was too strong. The East Indian Company occupied the colony twice, each time Britain was at war with Denmark, and reduced its activity to nil by restricting access to opium and salpetre, the two main commodities the Danes were trading in. While a commercial failure, Serampore was an important cultural centre. As the British were not allowing missionaries to preach to the natives, Serampore, being in Danish hands, became a centre of missionary activity. In 1799, William Carey, an Englishman, and two fellow Baptist missionaries, established a press there and started printing Bibles in several Oriental languages, including Sanskrit, Bengali, Burmese and Persian. In 1819, Carey founded the Serampore College. It was incorporated later in 1827 by Royal Charter, placing it at par with the Danish universities of Copenhagen and Kiel, 30 years before Calcutta University was founded, becoming the first modern university in Asia. The college is now a Baptist theological institute. Its massive neo-classical structure, built in 1821 on the high bank of the Hooghly, houses a library with books of the 18th and 19th centuries and a museum displaying Carey's personal effects, as well as copies of his works such as the

Left: the gates of **Chandernagore**, a former French settlement. **Right**: the Hooghly Imambara.

Universal Dictionary of Thirteen Indian Languages, *The Sanskrit Dictionary* and the *New Testament* in Bengali.

Other points of interest are the 18th and 19th-century mansions along the waterfront, the St Olaf Church, the former Danish Army barracks, and the cemetery where several former governors and Wallich, the famous botanist, are buried. Serampore is a centre of Vishnu worship. The Jagannath Temple in the suburb of Mahesh is the second most important in India after Puri's in Orissa. A *Rath Yatra* procession is held every year in June-July.

Opposite Serampore, reachable by the local ferry, **Barrackpore** used to be the country residence of the viceroy in office. Built in the 18th century, once Lord Wellesley's country villa, the Viceroy's Palace, 'Lat Bagan' is now a police academy and therefore off-limits. A garden annexe stores several of the statues of former British Kings, Viceroys and Governors removed from the Maidan and streets of Calcutta. Nearby are the very quiet 19th century Annapurna Temple and Gandhi Ghat where part of the Mahatma's ashes were scattered in 1948 after he was cremated. All Faith's prayers are held here at 8.00 am on Independence Day, on August 15th. Barrackpore is the only town along the Hooghly where accommodation can be arranged. The West Bengal Tourist Development Corporation runs a tourist bungalow and bookings can be made in Calcutta.

North of Serampore, **Bhadreswar** has no remains left by the Prussian traders who used to operate here but the Kothari Foundation, a small temple complex in a park, built on the high bank of the river by a Marwari jute millionaire, is worth a stop. It is well kept and has immaculate white marble temples to Lakshmi Narayan, Shiva and Ganesh.

A gate bearing the motto of the French Republic, *Liberté, Egalité, Fraternité*, marks the entrance to **Chandernagore**, the earliest French

Left: Hamsheshwari Mandir at Bansberia. Right: the Lourdes grotto at Bandel.

settlement in India. The city became French in 1673. In 1757, the East India Company's fleet, commanded by Admiral Watson, attacked Chandernagore and destroyed Fort d'Orléans, the French fortress. Chandernagore was returned to the French in 1763, retaken in 1794 and restored in 1815. In the opium days, Chandernagore would be a sourcing point in opium for the French, who would export it to China, and, in increasing quantities in the late 19th century, to Indochina. At the turn of the century, over 55 percent of the budget of the French Indochina was derived from Chandernagore-supplied opium. Chandernagore also played a role in the fight for India's Independence. Revolutionaries and activists, fleeing the British police, would seek refuge in the French territory. The philosopher Aurobindo, who later founded the *ashram* at Pondicherry, lived here for a while during the time he was still Aurobindo Ghosh, the revolutionary.

Between the World Wars, Chandernagore become a favourite spot for rich Calcuttans who would drive there for a good meal and to buy vintage wines, duty-free. Chandernagore was also well-known for its French-managed brothel. At Independence in 1947, all the five *Etablissements Français en Inde* were granted local autonomy within the *Union Française*, a French attempt to set up an equivalent of the British Commonwealth. On June 19th, 1949, a referendum was held by the French Government on the future of Chandernagore. The majority voted for an instant merger with India and seized power, expelling the French Administrateur. In 1952, both Governments signed a Cession Treaty confirming Chandernagore's transfer to India. Hardly anybody speaks French nowadays but a French atmosphere still pervades along the shaded quai Dupleix, now Strand Road, with its public benches, replicas of the ones in Paris' parks. The 18th century former Administrateur's residence houses now

Monkeys at sunset, Dakshineshwar

a library, a French language school and a museum displaying archeological finds, early views of Chandernagore and Dupleix's bed. There are plans to restore the building with French Government assistance.

Other interesting buildings on the waterfront are the former Hotel de Paris, the Couvent Saint-Joseph, and Tagore's house with a low terrace almost at water level. Behind the institute is the *Eglise du Sacré Coeur* reminding of French village churches with its statue of Joan of Arc and a Lourdes grotto. On Rue de Paris, now Grand Trunk Road, towards the north of the city, is a French cemetery where the parents of Madame Grand, Talleyrand's wife, are buried. Finally, there is an interesting 18th century Nandadulala temple at Lal Bagan dedicated to Krishna, a good example of flat-roofed Bengali architecture. The main festival in Chandernagore is *Jagadhatri Puji*, a local variation of *Kali Puja*, held 10 days later.

Chinsurah, further north, was one of the Armenian settlements in Bengal. The Armenians came in the late 16th century. The St John's Armenian church was built in 1695 but graves in its yard date back to the early 17th century. Amongst those buried is Melik Beglaroff, the last independent prince of Karabagh. There are no Armenians left in Chinsurah but the Armenians of Calcutta all gather here every year on St John's Day, one of their most important festivals. The Dutch Vereenigte Oostindische Companie, better known as Jan Compagnie, settled in Chinsurah in 1625 to trade in opium, salpetre, muslin and spices, and ceded it to Britain against Bencoleen on Sumatra in 1825. The 18th-century Dutch church and Fort Gustavius have since been destroyed but there are still remains of the Dutch period, including barracks; a cemetery; the Governor's residence — the house of the famous General Perron, a Frenchman who had served with Daulat Rao Scindia during the Marhatta

The Lord Inchape's Garden House on the Hooghly.

Wars —now the Chinsurah College; and the Factory Building, now the residence of the Divisional Commissioner.

Hooghly, which comes immediately after Chinsurah, is famous for its Shiite Imambara, an impressive mosque of the 19th century, with a tower clock donated by Queen Victoria. Inside the prayer hall are huge crystal chandeliers from Belgium and Bohemia.

The Portuguese founded nearby **Bandel de Hooghly** in 1580. From here they carried on slave trade, buying prisoners from Portuguese pirates of the Sunderbans, and controlled most of the Moghul Empire's foreign trade passing through Bengal, until the arrival of other European nations. In 1632, after a siege of three months, Bandel was destroyed by the Moghul Emperor Shah Jahan who had a grudge against the Portuguese. They had not supported him earlier in his rebellion against his father Jahangir and were supplying arms to the enemy Arakan Kingdom. Survivors were taken to Agra. Women were sent to *harems*, men enslaved. A death sentence was carried on officers and priests. They were to be thrown to infuriated wild elephants, but a miracle took place. The beasts became suddenly quiet and one of them delicately lifted a priest on its back. Moved, the Emperor ordered the Portuguese to be released and to rebuild Hooghly, giving them privileges and money. No revival took place, however, as the Portuguese were now too weakened to face competition from other European nations. Already in 1640 the East India Company had opened a factory here.

The **Church of Our Lady of Bandel** is the only remains of the Portuguese past. Consecrated in 1599, it was rebuilt after the return from Agra but lacks the usual architectural exuberance of Portuguese churches. When Bandel was captured, the church was already a pilgrimage centre. Christians, Muslims and Hindus would come and pray to the statue of Our Lady of Happy Voyage, before a long trip. During the siege, the statue was lost when the soldier carrying it across the river drowned but it miraculously reappeared on the bank when the Portuguese came back. A cross stands on that spot and the statue has found its place back in the church, attracting pilgrims all year round. On Christmas Eve, a mass is celebrated, drawing extra trainloads of Catholics from Calcutta. Within the church compound is a yard with a small cemetery and a boat mast, used as a flagstaff, presented in the 16th century to the church as an ex-voto.

Some 15 kilometres (9 miles) north of Hooghly, at **Bansberia**, are two temples standing side by side. The small Vasudeva brick temple was built in 1679. Its terracotta tile *bas-reliefs* represent scenes from the life of Krishna — pastoral scenes, images of Parvati and Shiva — and also feature Indian fighting ships, Portuguese galleys and soldiers. The nearby Hangsheshwari temple with its 13 towers, was founded in the early 19th century. Rajah Deb started building it after a dream but died before its completion. His widow who was saved from *sati* at the last moment by religious reformer Ram Moham Roy, founder of the Brahma Samaj movement, finished the temple.

Returning to Calcutta will take you three hours. There are unfortunately no organised cruises on the Hooghly. Groups can, however, charter a steam launch from Calcutta (about 4,000 rupees for the day) and sail up the Hooghly. The boat starts from Takhta Ghat at Hastings and, after half an hour, you pass under the Hooghly Bridge. You will not, if you travel by river, have the time to stop everywhere. As a compensation you will see from the boat the garden houses built by the rich Calcuttans along the river for their weekends, the jute mills, most of them now idle, built at the turn of the century in red bricks in a typically Liverpoldian style as well as several temple complexes, such as Ichhapur, north of Barrackpore, which are invisible from the road.

Right: Sakyajit Ray movie atmosphere at the Annapurna Temple, Barrackpore.

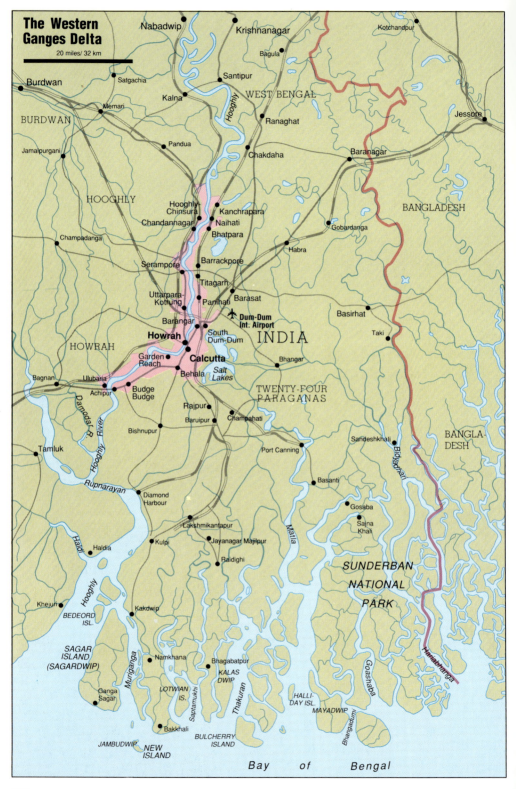

THE SUNDERBANS AND THE DELTA OF THE GANGES

There are several legends attached to the Delta. According to one, Sagar, King of Oudh and 13th ancestor of Rama, had performed 99 *asvamedha jajna* horse sacrifices and was to make his 100th when Indra, the King of Heaven, who had himself managed to reach that number, stole the horse and hid it far away in the cell of a holy man, Kapila, an incarnation of Vishnu, without him noticing it. Sagar's 64,000 sons found the horse and attacked Kapila who, with his supernatural powers, reduced them to ashes and sent their souls to Hell. Sagar's grandson Ansuman pleaded with Kapila to release them. The holy man agreed on condition that the waters of Ganga come up to his cell. Ganga was then residing in the Himalayas in the custody of Brahma. Ansuman prayed for Brahma to release her but died before Brahma had agreed. His son Bhagirat continued to pray and managed to move Brahma. Bhagirat led Ganga down but could not find his way on the last part of the trip. Ganga then divided herself into 1,000 channels. One of them, as planned by the Goddess, reached Kapila's cell and the souls where released. This is how the Delta was formed.

The Delta used to be entirely covered with mangrove. The Sunderban jungle (*Sunder* means mangrove in Bangla and *bon* forest), bordered by marshes, extended all the way to the present site of Calcutta. In the 16th century, hiding in the Sunderbans, Arakanese and Portuguese pirates raided villages and attacked boats, in the Bay of Bengal and in the Delta. The prisoners were sold at the slave market in Bandel, then a Portuguese settlement in Bengal, a part of the Goa-based Estado da India. Pirate attacks were so common that the demon that Durga defeated is often represented in statues of the goddess as a bearded Portuguese pirate wearing an eye-patch. At the end of the 16th century, cultivation started, pushing the jungle limit to the southeast. The 1947 Partition took two-thirds of the Delta from India. Still, the remaining area offers a variety of attractions: the largest estuarine tidal jungle in the world, tigers of man-eating repute, traditional shipyards, a religious festival on attended by 500,000, and black sand beaches.

To those arriving by sea in the old days, land would start at the **Sandheads**, 30 kilometres (18 miles) south of the coast. At **Sagardwip Island**, situated where the Ganges joins the ocean, ships would embark a pilot, sail up through shifting sand bars — to this day marked by indications of shipwrecks on navigational maps — and stop at Khejuri to unload mail and send it by *dakrunners* on horse to Calcutta, before sailing on upriver to the city of Calcutta.

Khejuri, before becoming the first Post and Telegraph Office in India, was

Preceding pages: waterway in the Sunderbans; an aerial view of the Sunderbans, the world's largest mangrove. Right: the Hooghly pilot.

The Delta of the Ganges 215

a Portuguese port in the 16th century. A platform built for a time-gong and parts of a gate still remain as well as the ruins of the British telegraph office destroyed by a cyclone in 1864 and a European cemetery, probably one of the oldest in India, now in a total state of neglect. Access to Khejuri is not easy. One has to travel by bus to Diamond Harbour, then take the ferry to Haldia, Calcutta's new port, a dinghy across the Haldi River and a half-hour rickshaw ride.

The real Delta starts 40 kilometres (25 miles) south of Calcutta. With extensive irrigation, canals and waterways have become a permanent feature of the landscape. All trips, therefore, include a bit of sailing. At **Diamond Harbour** (78 kilometres/48 miles), the Hooghly widens and forms a wide pool where East Indiamen used to anchor to avoid sailing further north for fear of getting stranded. Ruins of a Portuguese fort can be seen on the waterfront. On a late sunny afternoon when enough sailboats are on the river, or on an early misty winter morning, Diamond Harbour and the lower reaches of the Hooghly, carry a definite Conradian flavour.

Diamond Harbour is easily reached by bus from Calcutta. The ride lasts two to three hours. The **Omar Resort**, a group of bungalows set in a lush garden, provides a good base from which to visit the traditional shipyards along the coast still building wooden dinghies and Diamond Harbour boats with their huge orange sails, as well as motorised and bastardised modern versions of the pinnace. Similar hulls carried Hindu trade and civilisation to Southeast Asia and can be found on *bas-reliefs* at the Borobudur temple in Indonesia.

The road ends at **Namkhana** (105 kilometres/65 miles), a starting point for passenger and cargo traffic for the Delta. Small motorised dinghies cross the Hatama-Dounia River to the opposite embankment from where a short bus ride leads to **Bakkhali** (123 kilometres/76 miles), a black-sand beach bordered by dunes planted with casuarina trees. The beach faces full south the Bay of Bengal. The next piece of land is Antarctica. There is a West Bengal Governement tourist bungalow there with a kitchen that one can take over to cook his own meal, using locally-bought fish. On a one-day trip, one can visit the nearby **Frasergunge** fishing village. With two days, it is possible to hire a country boat at Namkhana to the **Lothian Island Bird Sanctuary**, famous for its white-bellied sea-eagle, black-capped kingfisher, whimbrell, tern and curlew as well as the Bhagabatpur Crocodile Reserve. The Reserve was set up in 1976 to incubate the eggs of the saltwater estuarine crocodile, collected on mud flats in the jungle. The crocodiles are released after three years. Over 10 years, the Reserve has let over 70 of them out. The projet also breeds the rare Ridley sea-turtle. A permit to visit the Reserve has to be taken from the Chief Wildlife Officer at Writers' Building in Calcutta.

A Kali beggar at the Ganga Saga Mela.

Some pilgrims even make it by paddle-boats.

The nearby island of Sagardwip has, from time immemorial, been a place for fertility worship probably because of the sexual symbolism of the Ganges penetrating the ocean. Even after the advent of Hinduism, mothers would throw their first babies to sharks and crocodiles there, to be blessed with many more male childen in the future. Every year during the second week of January, half-a-million pilgrims cross Calcutta on their way to the annual *Gangasagar Mela* festival celebrated on Sagardwip. They come from as far as Gujarat or Rajasthan to celebrate the descent to Earth of Ganga and her union with the Ocean. The festival lasts three days and centres around the Kapila Muni Temple built on the site where Kapila's cell was believed to have been located. Kapila's image is a shapeless block of stone daubed with red paint in front of which pilgrims take *darshan*. The climax is at dawn on *Makar Sankranti* Day, January 14th, when hundreds of thousands take a holy dip in the Ganga that washes them from all sins. It is said that at this precise moment a warm current crosses the waters on that chilly winter morning. The easiest and best way to attend the festival, and avoid hours of travel in jammed conditions, is to join the two-day river tour with one night on board, organised by the West Bengal Tourist Bureau.

The mangrove jungle can be reached after a three-hour drive from Calcutta through Lakshmikantapur, Jayanagar and Raidighi (76 kilometres/47 miles). On the way, stop at **Maijhilpur**, near Jayanagar. It is the home of one of the last Bengali puppet companies. Check to see if there is any performance planned or going on in the neighbourhood on the occasion of a festival or a family celebration. **Raidighi**, a small fish market town, is the terminal for country pinnaces plying the Delta. From this point on, this is the only available form of public transport as there are no roads, only *khols* (waterways). The jungle is a two-hour ride on channels

The Delta of the Ganges 217

and *khols* through a landscape of paddy, high embankments and villages of thatched-roofed mud houses built low to offer less surface to cyclone winds.

One hour south of Raidighi on **Jatadwip Island** stands **Jaital Deul**, an 11th century spire-shaped Shiva temple standing amongst paddy. The jungle is reached an hour later after crossing the 3-kilometre (1.8-mile) wide Thakuran River. In the jungle, the boat sails along mud flats afternating with mangrove and shrubs, steering clear of the embankment for fear of an attack by a tiger leaping from a tree or swimming up. The boat usually stops at the **Forest Lodge**, surrounded by chicken-wire to prevent attacks by tigers. It has a small shrine to Ma Bonobibi and Dakshinaroy, two deities related to the tiger-cult of the Sunderbans.

A day's excursion is not long enough to take you deep into the jungle. To get into the core of the Sunderbans, two days are needed and the point of entry is **Port Canning**, 54 kilometres (34 miles) southeast of Calcutta. "Canning" was build in 1858 as an alternate port to Calcutta. It has a small fishing fleet and private boats can be hired there. Canning is also the starting point for organised tours to the **Sunderbans Wildlife Reserve**.

The Sunderbans properly cover an area of 9,630 square kilometres (3,718 square miles) in West Bengal. Mangrove and shrubs, with small patches of dry land represent 60 percent of the total area. Half is submerged at high tide. The remaining 40 percent is permanently under water. Still, men make a living out of this hostile environment. *Mahual*, honey-catchers, roam the jungle in April and May to bring out wild honey. Prawn-catchers spend days waist-deep in water, dragging fine nets to catch minuscule prawns indispensable for prawn-breeding farms. *Darijhals*, fishermen, use tame otters to scare fish into their nets. *Barvalis*, wood cutters, set up camps on stilts deep inside the jungle to bring out goran, a

Raidighi — a typical river port on the Delta.

variety of wood impervious to salt water or termites. Those occupations sustain a heavy toll every year. Men get carried away by crocodiles, eaten by sharks and killed by tigers that view them clearly as intruders and an easy, slow-moving prey.

The Sunderbans is now a wildlife reserve. Apart from the Royal Bengal tiger, rarely spotted, there is plenty of other wildlife to be seen: spotted deer, wild boar, monitor lizard, Rhesus monkey, estuarine crocodile, python, king cobra, jungle cat, fishing cat, otter, fiddler crab, white-bellied sea-eagle, kingfisher, white egret and darters as well as varieties of terns, sandpipers and other shore birds. The nesting period is in June-July. The best time to visit the Sunderbans would be between October and March. The Sunderbans are also famous for the migratory and resident birdlife. The **Sajnakhali Bird Sanctuary** next to the Reserve, welcomes every year open bill storks, white ibises, night herons, little cormorants and large egrets. Below the nests, giant water lizards can occasionally be seen collecting fallen eggs. The right period for a visit is during nesting time between June and September.

Access to the Reserve is restricted. Obtaining an individual permit to hire a boat and enter the area may take time. It is advisable to join the group tours organised by the West Bengal Tourist Bureau. Tours last two days, and include land and river transport, food, trips into the jungle, viewing from a *machan* (observation tower), and a night at the **Sajnakhali Tourist Lodge**.

Near Sajnakhali, and not to be missed during an excursion to the Reserve area, **Gosaba** holds a Sunderban Folk Culture Festival in late December with dances by Adivasi tribals, brought here in the last century as cheap labour to clear the forest. The local museum has a section on the tiger, showing an electrified clay dummy bearing claw marks from the tiger that had attacked it and fled after receiving a rude 'shock'.

The flooded jungle of the Sunderbans.

The Royal Bengal Tiger of the Sunderbans

In 1973, an area of 2,595 square kilometres (1,002 square miles) of the Sunderbans was declared one of the nine Tiger Reserves set up under India's Project Tiger. There is a buffer zone of 1,365 square kilometres (527 square miles) and a core area of 1,230 square kilometres (475 square miles). In the core area, all exploitation of forest resources has been stopped. The buffer zone is earmarked for wood gathering, but in such a way as to be conducive to wildlife management. For instance, only villagers with special passes issued by the Forest Department are allowed to enter the reserve to gather wood, but actually many enter without clearance and every year a number of them disappear, many being killed by tigers.

The Sunderbans, with about 300 Bengal tigers, now contains the largest tiger population in the world.

The Royal Bengal tiger of the Sunderbans (*Panthera Tigris Tigris Bengalensis*) is said to be a man-eater. The first description of the Sunderbans and of the strange habits of its legendary tiger to reach the West were recorded by Bernier in his *Travels to the Moghul Empire* in the 17th century. He writes: "Among those islands, it is in many places dangerous to land for it constantly happens that some person or another falls prey to tigers. These ferocious animals are very apt, it is said, to enter into the boat itself and to carry away some victim, who, if we are to believe the boatmen of the country, generally happen to be the stoutest and fattest of the party."

One scientist recently developed the view that tigers have turned man-eaters because of a mental disorder provoked by the amount of salt that they absorb daily, mainly through drinking murky salt water. Most tigers generally eat wild bear and chittal deer, and while it

The Royal Bengal tiger on a mud flat in the Sunderbans.

is true that there are man-eaters amongst them, their proportion is believed to be not more than 10 percent although the environment is definitely conducive to preying on Man. The tiger has been pushed back by advancing cultivation to an area which, as the land is often flooded and fresh water virtually non-existent, offers little food. Competition among the tigers is fierce as the tide prevents a tiger from spraying trees and delineating its territory. The most easily available food on legs are slow-moving defenceless humans who intrude into the forest in search of wood, honey or to catch fish.

There are no statistics on the number of people jumped by tigers as Government figures take into account only those fishmen, wood or honey-gatherers carrying Government-issued licences. In some villages in the buffer zone surrounding the core area, half of the population has lost at least one relative to tigers. **Arampur**, near Gosaba, is even called the "tiger widow village" as 150 men have disappeared in the last several years.

Not surprisingly, the tiger is on everybody's mind and a tiger cult, followed by Hindus and Muslims alike, has developed. Before a person enters the forest, the *ganin*, a tiger cult priest, will organise a *puja* to pray to Ma Bono Bibi, the Goddess of the Forest, Shiber Kumir, Shiva's crocodile and Dakshinaroy, an ogre, the ancestor of all tigers, having assumed himself the shape of a tiger, to apologise in advance for disturbing them.

Another means of protection is dissuasion. Electrified clay dummies of wood-gatherers or fishermen are left on dinghies in the forest in the hope that tigers will receive a shock and become from then on reluctant to attack humans. But it is too early to conclude whether this method is effective as once a tiger has tasted human flesh, it will always be a man-eater. Attacked dummies are on show at the tiger section of the Gosaba museum near the Sunderban Reserve.

Villagers in the Sunderbans use electrified dummies to ward off attacking tigers.

THE BUDDHIST SITES OF BIHAR

Buddhism was born in India. In the past, Buddhist pilgrims, monks and students entered India through Bengal. Even nowadays, Calcutta remains the main gateway for Buddhist visitors. Religious tours usually include Lumpini in Nepal where the Buddha was born, Bodhgaya where he reached Enlightenment, Sarnath, near Benares, Rajghir and Shravasti where he preached, Kushinagar where he died, the University of Nalanda and the Sanchi stupa. To cover all these places would take more than a week. However, some of the most interesting sites can be covered in two to three days.

Take a night train to **Patna**, or fly in with a morning flight. Check in at the Maurya Hotel, and ask the local ITDC office, located in the hotel, to arrange for a car leaving at dawn on the next day for Nalanda, Rajgir, Bodhgaya and back. You can spend the rest of the day visiting Patna. Attractions in Patna include the Patna Museum, famous for the *Didarganj Vakshi*, a Mauryan sandstone statue of a woman; the ruins of Pataliputra, the former capital of the Magadha Empire; and *Sonepur Mela*, the largest cattle fair in the world, held every year in November, starting on the day of the festival of *Kartik Purnima*.

Alternatively, you can arrange from Calcutta for a car to wait for you at the Maurya Hotel and take you to Nalanda and Rajghir on the first day, leaving the entire second day for Bodhgaya. Make sure in that case that you hold a confirmed room booking at the ITDC Hokke Club Hotel in Rajgir before you leave Calcutta as accommodation is scarce at Rajgir during the pilgrimage season in winter.

Some 90 kilometres (60 miles) south of Patna is the site of the former **Buddhist University of Nalanda**. The university flourished from the 5th century till 1199 when it was ransacked by Afghan invaders. At its apex, it had 2,000 teachers and more than 10,000 students from as far as China, Japan and Java. Teachings first followed Mahayana Buddhism, then from the 8th century Tantric Buddhism, which has survived in Tibet after the destruction of Nalanda. At the end of a road branching off from the road to Gaya, excavations have yielded nine levels of occupation. There are ruins of temples, prayer halls, stupas, one of them containing hair and nail clippings from the Buddha, and monasteries with cells, kitchens and meeting rooms. On the walls of several stupas and inside some *viharas* remain stucco figures of the Buddha and Boddhisatvas. The local museum has an interesting display of Buddhist and Hindu images of Gupta and Pala periods found during excavations.

Further south, spreading over five hills across a valley, is **Rajgir**, 103 kilometres (64 miles) from Patna. The Buddha stopped at Rajgir in search of Enlightenment and impressed King

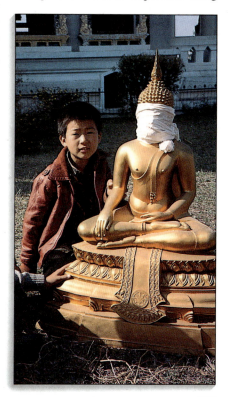

Preceding pages: a festive Mahabodhi temple at Bodhgaya. **Left**: a votive stupa at Bodhgaya. **Right**: this newly bought statue of Buddha will be carried home before the blindfold is removed.

Bimbisara, Emperor Ashoka's father, by his sermons. When he returned after Enlightenment — followed by 1,000 monks — Bimbisara, who had converted to Buddhism, offered the new order a bamboo grove, Venuvana, and built a monastery there. The grove remains one of the few green spots in this dry landscape turned into a desert by cattle grazing and deforestation.

On **Gridhrakuta**, the Vulture Peak, one of the hills where the Buddha preached, Japanese Buddhists built a stupa in the 1970s. A ropeway reaches the stupa in winter. The rest of the year the pilgrims have to undergo a two-hour strenuous walk uphill, with temperatures over 40°C (104°F). On the other hills are other Buddhist sites, such as the cave on Saptapani Hill where the first Buddhist conclave was held.

Other religions are present in Rajgir, at one stage the thriving capital of the Magadha Empire. There are several spots where Mahavira, the 23rd Jain prophet, preached and there is a Shiva temple at the foot of Saptapani Hill, built over hot springs. Rajgir has a Japanese temple, Nipponzan Myohoji, a Burmese one, and a small Thai shrine. There is also a modern Japanese-style hotel, open in winter, operated by the Centaur chain. Accommodation there can be booked in Calcutta.

Gaya is an important Hindu pilgrimage place. Vishnu has conferred upon the city an *asura*, the power to heal from sins. There are 45 temples in Gaya. The main one is the Vishnupada Temple, built by the Maharanee of Indore in 1787 over the footprint Vishnu left on a stone. In the temple compound is a banyan tree, under which the Buddha spent six years. He then decided that mortifications would not bring Enlightenment, proceeded to a cave, then finally took a walk along the Phalgu River and found a pipal tree about 15 kilometres (9 miles) east of Gaya. He sat there to meditate, vowing not to move anymore. Enlightenment came after the first night. The Buddha remained under the

Entrance to the Chinese temple in Bodhgaya.

banyan tree for a week, then took a walk, wondering whether to start preaching, lotus flowers springing from his footsteps.

Bodhgaya grew as a pilgrimage centre around the descendant of the original pipal tree. A stone slab marks the spot where the Buddha meditated. Ashoka erected a shrine behind the tree. It was replaced later in the 2nd century by a larger shrine. The present 54-metre (177-foot) high, spire-shaped temple, is the result of alteration in the 11th, damages in the 12th, and restorations in the 19th centuries. Inside the temple, is a gilded statue of the Sakyamuni Buddha, sitting crossed-legged in *maravi jayasana*, his hands in *bhumisparamudra* with his right hand touching the ground in acceptance of Enlightenment.

Along the north side of the temple is the Chanka Ramana, a platform built in the 1st century BC where 18 slabs with lotuses mark the place where Buddha walked in meditation after reaching Enlightenment. The local archeological museum displays various sculptures, some of them headless, having been mutilated during the Muslim invasion, as well as the original railing that surrounded the temple, a delicate piece of stonework, with scenes from the life of the Buddha. Bodhgaya is a holy city. In winter, thousands of monks and pilgrims, including Westerners, throng the main street, staying in tent villages or in monasteries, built by Governments or Buddhist organisations from Japan, Taiwan, Thailand, Burma, Tibet, Bhutan and Korea. The Dalai Lama himself comes every year for several days to teach in Bodhgaya.

Accommodation in Bodhgaya include a tourist bungalow run by the Government-owned ITDC and guest houses in the monasteries. In both cases you must book well in advance as, here too, accommodation is limited. You can also either take an overnight train from Gaya to Calcutta if you manage to get a berth or drive back to Patna and catch the night plane to Calcutta.

The holy city of Bodhgaya is also home to a Thai temple.

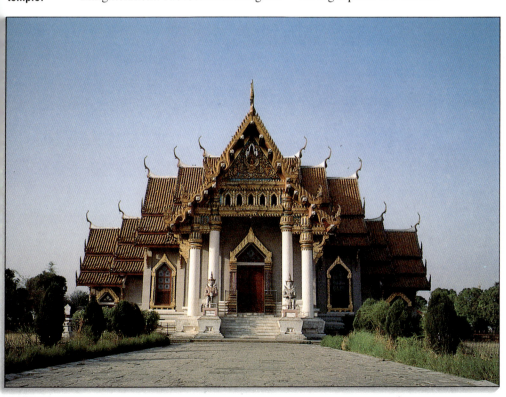

DARJEELING. GROUP OF TWO LEPCHAS.

THE EASTERN HIMALAYAS

Over an hour's flight from Calcutta are the east Himalayas where **Kanchenjunga** reigns supreme over **Darjeeling**, **Kalimpong** and **Sikkim**. The change of scene from the plains is dramatic. Fresh-faced smiling people in colourful costumes appear by the road side. A three-hour drive up from Siliguri in the foothills, on a spiralling hill road, brings you to Darjeeling. The tiny 'toy train' on the narrow gauge chugs up alongside and gets there in six hours.

Having received parts of the Nepali Terai as a reward for his support to the East India Company during the Anglo-Nepalese war, the King of Sikkim gave in return the village of **Darjeeling** to the Company in 1835. The site was set up as a sanatorium for British troops, became the most popular summer resort in the country and acted for a while as the summer capital of India during the Raj days.

You arrive at the motor stand and find the town in three tiers, a mingling of modern India and Raj nostalgia. Weather permitting, leaving on Friday afternoon and coming back on Monday, you can spend a weekend to explore Darjeeling.

Lloyd's **Botanical Gardens** has a marvellous collection of Himalayan flora. You can trudge up the hill to sit on the benches at **Chowrasta**, or join the regulars on their constitutional mile round **Observatory Hill**. If you are feeling energetic, climb the hill and find the curious Hindu-Buddhist **Mahakal Mandir**. Have a milk shake at **Keventer's** milk bar or lunch at **Glenary's**. Half a day must be spent at the **Himalayan Mountaineering Institute** on **Birch Hill**, adjacent to the **Himalayan Zoo** with its high altitude fauna. The museum has memorabilia from **Everest** and other mountaineering expeditions. Close by, at **North Point**, is the first passenger ropeway in India, connecting Darjeeling to **Singla Bazar** in the Little Rangeet Valley. Up and down the ropeway you get a fine view of mountains and of the famous Darjeeling tea gardens. The evening can be spent at the **Mall**, contemplating the residents and the tourists who gather to gossip or ride round Observatory Hill on small, scrawny *tattoo* ponies. The shops around the Mall have been there for years. **Habeeb Mullick's** curios and **Oxford Bookshop's** array of Himalayan literature demand a browse. Standing in a *hawa ghar* (covered shelter), you can get a nostalgic view of red-roofed cottages and rolling tea gardens while the streets reflect modern India's "jeans-and-*kurta*" culture.

A pre-dawn visit to **Tiger Hill** (45 minutes away by Land Rover) to see the sunrise on the snows tells you what the mountains are all about and makes you decide whether they should be a label on your suitcase, or a further experience for trekking or jeeping to closer views at **Sandakphu** and **Phalut**.

Extending your stay to include **Kalimpong** and **Sikkim** across the Teesta River, would involve more days. The drive to **Kalimpong** down the Peshoke Road from Darjeeling and up the Teesta valley from Siliguri is fantastically beautiful as the river changes mood with every turn until it reaches **Teesta Bazar**. After a hot cup of tea at the bazar, a steep uphill climb brings you to Kalimpong, the town of flower nurseries, and the bi-weekly *haat* (market), a Himalayan microcosm, on Wednesdays and Saturdays. From two ridges on either side, the centre of town is dominated by the **Tharpa Choling Monastery** and **Dr Graham's Homes**, a boarding school started by a Scottish missionary. There is also a **Bhutanese Monastery** on the 12th Mile, which is how some roads are named in Kalimpong from the days the city was the entrepot for Tibetan trade. At **Holumba**, 9th Mile, you get an armchair tour of the region and a cup of tea with the charming owners, together with

---

Preceding pages: the Happy Valley Tea Garden spreads on the outskirts of Darjeeling. **Left**: the Lepchas are the indigenous community of Darjeeling.

your bulbs and orchids.

The Teesta road also reaches **Gangtok**, the capital of Sikkim. It is best to place yourself in the hands of the Sikkim Government's Tourism Department whose office in the bazar, manned by a knowledgeable and helpful staff, has everything chalked out for the tourist, from treks up to **Dzongri** to helicopter flights over the mountains. On the way up, you have seen **Saramsa Gardens**, an orchidarium and garden of medicinal plants. At **Deorali**, the manuscripts and exhibits at the **Institute of Tibetology** give a good introduction to Tibetan religion and philosophy present throughout Sikkim.

In Sikkimese homes and in monasteries, prayer flags whisper sacred messages to the winds. For Sikkim was once a Buddhist kingdom. The reigning *Chogyal* accepted the British protectorate. Sikkim became an Indian protectorate in 1947 before being incorporated into India in 1975 as the 22nd state.

It is in mountains and monasteries that the Sikkim survives. Not far from Gangtok is **Rumtek Monastery**, the seat of the *Gyalwa Karmapa,* head of the Kagyupa sect of Buddhism. Visitors are welcome and there is even a small 20-room lodge to accommodate them opposite the monastery.

Eight kilometres (5 miles) from Gangtok, on the North Sikkim Highway to Nathu La Pass, is **Tashi View Point**, an excellent spot to see **Kanchenjunga**, the sacred mountain of Sikkim. She qualifies for any superlative in the dictionary. Dances are performed to honour her in September and October at **Tsuklakhang**, the royal chapel in Gangtok. The famous Mask Dances of the Himalayan monasteries are performed at **Phodang** (and further north at **Kagyet**) in December. But the cradle of monasteries is in the west where Buddhism entered Sikkim. **Pemayangtse**, the house of the "royal" *lamas,* is situated on a ridge commanding a panoramic of the mountains with towering **Pandim** near the tourist lodge

The Anglican Church runs South Point at Darjeeling ...

of the same name. Nearby are **Tashiding**, the most sacred monastery in Sikkim, where the *Bumchu* (sacred water) festival is held; and **Dubdi**, the oldest. At **Yuksam** is the stone where the first *Chogyal* was consecrated, and the wondrous lake nearby (at **Kechiperi**) is said to possess mystical qualities. From **Pemayangtse** starts the trek to **Dzongri** up to 4,030 metres (13,222 feet) through rhododendrons, paddy fields and yak herders' villages. *En route* to **Bakhim** and **Yuksam** are bungalows for night halts.

Reachable from Calcutta by air or from Darjeeling in a day-long drive, **Bhutan** is a kingdom tucked in the Himalayas. About the size of Switzerland (47,000 square kilometres/18,500 square miles) for one million inhabitants, it is one of the rare countries in Asia which is underpopulated. Its capital, **Thimphu**, counts only 15,000 people and most of Bhutan is mountainous and covered with forest. No hectic nightlife, no fantastic shopping opportunities, no five-star restaurants, but an unspoilt country, smiling and gentle people, a beautiful architecture, and the freshness of an unpolluted air — all these make it a perfect place for a few days of quiet relaxation. Bhutan, or *Druk Yul,* as the locals call it, is today still a mysterious and unknown destination. Hidden in the southern folds of the Himalayas and for centuries forbidden to foreigners, Bhutan has succeeded in preserving its independence and its ancestral way of life.

The kingdom is protected by natural obstacles: in the north, the Great Himalayan range forms the border with Tibet (China) and is pierced with few passes, most of them snowbound in winter. In the south, a thick tropical forest infested with wild animals and many kinds of leeches, constitutes a very efficient buffer between the central valleys of Bhutan and the Indian plains of Bengal and Assam. Till the completion of the first road in 1962, it was a strenuous five-day journey from India to the

... while the Jesuits run North Point.

centre of the country. Like Nepal, Bhutan is a gigantic staircase: from the 300-metre (1,000-foot) altitude of the southern fringe, the landscape soars up to 7,600 metres (25,000 feet) along the border peaks, just 150 kilometres (93 miles) away.

Change in ecological patterns over a short distance are commonplace in Bhutan. These sharp contrasts are one of its main attractions. A one-day trek is sometimes sufficient to go from subtropical valleys, where rice and banana trees grow, to yak pastures. But for all its variety, Bhutan remains a uniformly traditional country, so uniform, in fact, that the people, by law, go to work in national dress. The one million Bhutanese are mainly Buddhist and hold traditional values. They believe in hierarchy and deferring to authority.

Bhutan is divided into three main zones: the foothills, which have a tropical climate and luxuriant vegetation; the inner Himalayan valleys, which enjoy cold sunny winters and warm humid summers; and the high Himalayas. Foothills and low altitudes (till 1,600 metres/5,250 feet) are mainly inhabitated by 'Southern Bhutanese' who are Bhutanese of Nepali origin, while the rest of the country is populated by *Drukpas*, a generic term which gather different Mongoloid populations more or less closely affiliated to Tibetans.

All the mountain chains except the border Himalayan range, run from north to south, forming real barriers between the different parts of the central area. This area can be divided longitudinally into three zones — Western, Central and Eastern Bhutan.

Western Bhutan, consisting of the valleys of Ha (2,800 metres/9,240 feet), Paro (2,250 metres/7,425 feet), Thimphu (2,320 metres/7,590 feet), Punakha and Wangdiphodrang (1,300 metres/4,290 feet), is the rice basket of Bhutan. Situated along gentle slopes are orchards producing apples, plums and peaches. Coniferous forests cover the higher part of the mountains. Blessed by relatively fertile lands, the Western Bhutanese, called *Ngalong*, are the most prosperous of all the Bhutanese. Their language, the *Dzongkha*, which is closely affiliated to Tibetan, has become the national language. In the northern regions of Laya and Lingshi, live yak-herders who come in autumn to the valleys to sell their yak products.

Central Bhutan (Tongsa, Bumthang, Shemgang, upper part of Lhuntse) is a mosaic of regions linked by a common language akin to ancient Tibetan. It has regional variations: *Bumthangkha*, *Khyengkha* and *Kurtoekha*. As rice cannot grow in Bumthang which is at a higher altitude, the main crops are wheat, barley and buckwheat. Big herds of sheep and yaks share the highland pastures, while in the lower Shemgang region, semi-tropical jungle, with a few clearings for paddyfields, covers the mountains.

Eastern Bhutan, which includes the districts of Mongar, Tashigang, Samdrupjongkhar, Pemagatshel and

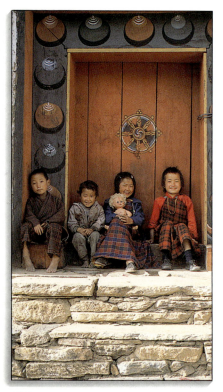

Smiling children in Thimphu.

the lower part of Lhuntse, is the land of the *Sharchops*, "the people from the East". A warmer climate, steep slopes which are bare in many places, villages perched high in the mountains and fields of maize, are the distinctive features of this area.

The whole southern belt, populated by Bhutanese of Nepali origin, is prosperous with paddy-fields, orange orchards and cardamon fields.

The State religion is Mahayana Buddhism in its tantric form which has many religious schools. In Bhutan, the official religious school is the Drukpa Kagyupa. The Head Abbot is the *Je Khenpo*. The Nyingmapa school is also very important, especially in the centre and the east of the country. Hinduism is practised among the Southern Bhutanese, who are akin to the Nepalese.

Bhutan's history begins in the 7th century. According to the Bhutanese tradition, the Tibetan King Songtsen Gampo built two temples, one in the valley of Paro and one in the valley of Bumthang. These were the first Buddhist establishments in the country but Buddhism was not really introduced on a large scale until the 8th century when the Indian tantrist Padmasambhava (or Guru Rinpoche) propagated what would become the Nyingmapa religious school. After two centuries of obscurity following the fall of the monarchy in Tibet, Buddhism revived in Bhutan in the 11th century through the activities of Tibetan missionaries. The Lhapas, a branch of the Kagyupa school, arrived first in Western Bhutan followed by the Drukpas, another branch of the Kagyupas. From the 13th century, other schools came from Tibet to settle in Western Bhutan. Besides the Nyingmapas, the Lhapas and the Drukpas, there were the Sakyapas, the Nenyingpas and another sub-sect of the Drukpas. The Drukpas and the Lhapas, the latter backed by the other schools, fought for religious and economic predominance over Western Bhutan till the 17th century when the Drukpas

The Yellow Hat sect is dominant in Sikkim.

The Eastern Himalayas 235

emerged victorious. As for Eastern Bhutan, it was composed of petty kingdoms without any unity.

Everything changed with the arrival in 1616 of the *Shabdrung* Ngawang Namgyel (1594-1651). Ngawang Namgyel, who belonged to the ruling family of the Drukpas, fled Tibet because of persecutions and took refuge in Bhutan. He took the title of *Shabdrung* ("to whose feet one submits") and started bringing Western Bhutan under the Drukpa hegemony. At the same time, he faced and repelled many Tibetan attacks. The *Shabdrung* devised a judicial and political system for the country.

With much political sense, and help from local allies, the *Shabdrung* gradually had the central and eastern parts of the country unified under the Drukpa rule. The country then took the name of Druk Yul, 'Land of the Drukpas'. When he died in 1651, the *Shabdrung* left an original dual system of government which lasted until Bhutan became a monarchy in 1907. Under the *Shabdrung's* authority, the temporal power was held by a *Desi* while the religious affairs were headed by a *Je Khenpo*.

In the 18th and 19th centuries, this system of government led to political inertia and inter-factional struggles, allowing the governors to increase their powers. In the ensuing struggle, *Tongsa Penlop* (Governor) Ugyen Wangchuck defeated his opponents in 1885. He thus became the strongman of Bhutan and in 1907, he was proclaimed king. The monarchy signalled an end to years of internal feuds, and brought a guarantee of stability. Ugyen Wangchuck died in 1926 and was succeeded by his son Jigme Wangchuck, who reigned peacefully until 1952. His son King Jigme Dorje Wangchuck, considered the 'Father of Modern Bhutan', gradually opened the country to the world, starting economic and social development in 1961 and having Bhutan admitted to the United Nations in 1971. Since his father's death in 1972,

The Brahmaputra Gowahatt.

the present king, His Majesty Jigme Singye Wangchuck, has continued to promote this progressive programme of development, while maintaining the ancestral and cultural values of the country.

Because of strict regulations which started on the January 1st, 1988, it is not possible for foreigners to visit the interiors of most of the temples, monasteries and *dzongs* (fortresses).

Paro Valley is so beautiful that there is something unreal about it. The clusters of white farmhouses with shingle-roofs or the gaily painted houses of the new Paro village, the patchworks of the paddy fields surrounded by slopes covered with blue pines, the small irrigation canals shadowed by willows, the white mass of Paro *dzong* dominated by its elegant watchtower which contains the National Museum, the silence and the lightness of the atmosphere when disembarking at the small airport — all these contribute to an atmosphere of peace, beauty and enchantment.

Among the most famous temples of the Paro Valley is **Kyichu Lhakhang** which appears amidst a forest of prayer flags. It was built to suppress a demon by the Tibetan King Songtsen Gampo in the 7th century.

Taksang, 'the tiger's lair', takes its name from the tiger that Guru Rinpoche supposedly rode when he arrived there. From the valley, Taksang, a small building clinging to the face of a vertical rock, 800 metres (2,625 feet) above the valley, looks almost impossible to reach. To have a breathtakingly close view of the complex, it takes one and a half hours of strenuous walking through a beautiful forest. A fascinating ruin, Drukyel *dzong,* stands at the end of the Paro Valley, barring access to the north. Built to commemorate a Bhutanese victory over Tibetan armies in the 17th century, it was accidentally burnt down in the mid-1950s. In clear skies, the snow-clad peak of the Jomolhari (7,315 metres/24,136 feet) can be seen on the horizon, like a sentinel on the road to

Taksang takes a while to get to, naturally.

Tibet. A visit to the **National Museum** located in the watchtower, or **Tadzong**, is a must. The traditional architecture enhances the beauty of the items on display, ranging from statues and paintings to stamps and artifacts of daily life.

Thimphu, the capital, is also the Big City of Bhutan. It is situated at 2,320 metres (7,920 feet) in the fertile valley of the Wang River, which is still largely devoted to agriculture. Formerly the summer capital and since 1955 the permanent capital of Bhutan, Thimphu has grown rapidly in the last decade. However, there is nothing congested about Thimphu, and except for the main street, most of the houses and buildings have gardens where chillis, maize and potatoes grow. On the banks of the river, among roses, weeping willows and terraces of ricefields, stands the **Tashichhodzong**, the fortress which is Bhutan's central secretariat and the Drukpa monk-body's headquarter. Built in 1641 by the *Shabdrung* Ngawang Namgyel, the "fort of the auspicious religion" was rebuilt by the third king in 1969 to house the nation's secretariat. The architectural features of the old building were faithfully maintained.

A characteristic feature of Thimphu is the tall white *chorten* crowned by golden canopies which was built in 1974 in memory of the third king, Jigme Dorje Wangchuck. Inside, the three storeys filled with paintings and statues are dedicated to the most important teachings of the Nyingmapa religious school and the representations are highly symbolic.

The main street of Thimphu is lined with shops which seem to sell the same things, smelling of butter, betel, tea and dried fish. Anybody can enter, look around and leave without buying anything without offending the shopkeeper. The Indigeneous Hospital, the Painting School and the National Library are also worth a visit as well as the small zoo above the Motithang Hotel where the takin (*bos taxicorla*), an animal unique to Bhutan, can be seen.

On Saturday afternoon but especially on Sunday morning, most of the local population congregates. It is a wonderful occasion to mingle with the people as they buy their foodstuff for the week. Vegetables, heaps of chillis, cheese, fruit, dried fish, rice as well as artifacts, chinaware and traditional books are displayed. In a corner, religious men chant prayers in front of a portable chapel.

The road to **Punakha** crosses a high pass, the **Dochula** (3,000metres/10,000 feet) which has a beautiful view of the Himalayan summits, but only on winter mornings. The two to three-hour drive through a dense forest takes the visitor to the low valley of Punakha (1,300metres/4,290 feet), which enjoys a warmer climate and is dotted with paddy fields, banana and orange trees. The central monk-body spends the winter months in the huge *dzong,* built in 1637 and the one-time capital of Bhutan. Half an hour's drive south of Punakha is **Wandiphodrang** (1,300 meres/4,290 feet), the last western *dzong* before the Pelela, the pass which traditionally separates Western and Eastern Bhutan. Built in 1638 and recently renovated, the *dzong* has a beautiful shingle roof. The small town which has sprouted near the *dzong* is besieged by howling winds for most of the year.

For most of the visitors, the discovery of Bhutan will stop here but for the more adventurous, **Tongsa** and its gigantic *dzong*, Bumthang, the east and the wild north offer other possibilities.

They are a unique chance to watch religious dances, *cham,* which are performed by monks or laymen wearing colourful costumes and impressive masks. A lot of these festivals are called *Tsechu,* and commemorate the great deeds of Guru Rinpoche. During some of these festivals a huge appliqué and embroidered banner is displayed for the benefit of the people. The dates of the festivals follow the lunar calendar and change every year. They are available from the Bhutan Tourism Corporation.

Right: a mandala at the Royal Palace, Thimphu.

TRAVEL TIPS

GETTING THERE
- 242 By Air
- 243 By Rail
- 243 By Road

TRAVEL ESSENTIALS
- 243 Visas & Passports
- 244 Money Matters
- 244 Health
- 245 What to Wear
- 245 What to Bring
- 245 Customs
- 246 Bond Facilities
- 246 Prohibited Articles
- 247 Unaccompanied Baggage
- 247 Export of Articles

GETTING ACQUAINTED
- 247 Time Zones
- 247 Climate
- 248 Culture & Customs
- 248 Weight & Measures
- 248 Electricity
- 248 Business Hours
- 248 Holidays/ Festivals
- 248 Religious Services

COMMUNICATIONS
- 249 Media
- 249 Postal Services/ Telephone & Telex

EMERGENCIES
- 249 Security & Crime
- 250 Medical Services
- 250 24-Hour Medical Shops
- 250 ambulance
- 250 Blood Banks

GETTING AROUND
- 250 Orientation
- 251 Maps
- 251 Public Transport
- 252 Private Transport

WHERE TO STAY
- 252 Hotels
- 253 Youth Hostel

FOOD DIGEST
- 253 Where to Eat

THINGS TO DO
- 256 City
- 256 Country
- 256 Tours Operators
- 257 Tour Guides

CULTURE PLUS
- 257 Museums
- 259 Art Galleries
- 259 Concerts
- 259 Theatres
- 260 Movies

NIGHTLIFE
- 260 Pubs & Bars
- 260 Discos
- 260 Cabarets

SHOPPING
- 260 What to Buy
- 261 Government Emporia

SPORTS
- 262 Clubs

PARKS & RESERVES
- 263 Parks & Gardens

SPECIAL INFORMATION
- 263 Doing Business
- 263 Children
- 264 Pilgrimages
- 264 Photography

LANGUAGE
- 265

FURTHER READING
- 267 General
- 267 People
- 267 Arts
- 268 Culture
- 268 History
- 268 Religions
- 268 Guidebooks
- 269 Outside Calcutta

USEFUL ADDRESSES
- 269 Tourist Information

Getting There

BY AIR

Calcutta is linked to the major Indian cities and is a feeder centre for the Indian East and North-East by the three national carriers Air-India, Indian Airlines and Vayudoot. Calcutta is internationally connected to Dhaka and Chittagong in Bangladesh, to Pavo in Bhutan, and to Amman, Bangkok, Beijing, Dubai, Hong Kong, Kathmandu, Kuala Lumpur, Singapore, Osaka, Tokyo, and Yangon in Asia; to Belgrade, Frankfurt, London, Moscow, New York, Paris and Rome by Alitalia, Bangladesh Biman, Druk Air, Gulf Air, JAT, Malaysian Airlines, Royal Air Nepal and Singapore Airlines.

DOMESTIC CARRIERS

Air-India, 50 J.L. Nehru Road (Chowringhee), Tel: 442356, Airport Tel: 572611 Ext. 346.
Indian Airlines, 39, Chittaranjan Avenue, Tel: 260730, 263390, Airport Tel: 572633.
Vayudoot, 28-B, Nilambar Bldgs., Shakespeare Sarani, Tel: 447062; Dum Dum Airport, Esso Sub-station Bldg., Tel: 572611, Ext. 472, 576582.

INTERNATIONAL CARRIERS

Aeroflot Soviet Airlines, 58 J.L. Nehru Road, Tel: 449831
Air Canada, 35 A, J.L. Nehru Road, Tel: 298353
Air France, 1, J.L. Nehru Road, Tel: 296161
Air Mauritius, GSA Air India, 50, J.L. Nehru Road, Tel: 442356
American Airlines, Hotel Hindustan International, 235/1, A.J.C. Bose Road, Tel: 442329
Alitalia, 2/3 Chitrakoot, 230, Acharya J.C. Bose Road, Tel: 447394
Bangladesh Biman, 1, Park Street, Tel: 292832
British Airways, 4l, J.L. Road, Tel: 293434
Burma Airways Corpn., 8/2, Esplanade East, Tel: 281624
Cathay Pacific, 1, Middleton Street, Tel: 293211
Druk Air, 51 Tivoli Court, 1-A, Ballygunge Circular Road, Tel: 441301
Japan Airlines, 35/A, J.L. Nehru Road, Tel: 297920
KLM Royal Dutch Airlines, 1, Middleton Street, Tel: 292451, 297462
Lufthansa, 30A/B, J.L. Nehru Road, Tel: 299365
Pan Am, 42, J.L. Nehru Road, Tel: 295001, 295020, Airport Tel: 573931
Qantas, Hotel Hindustan International, 235/1, A.J.C. Bose Road, Tel: 442329.
Royal Nepal Airlines, 41, J.L. Nehru Road, Tel: 298534
Scandinavian Airlines System (SAS), 18/G, Park Street, Tel: 249696
Singapore Airlines, 18/D, Park Street, Tel: 299293, 291525
Swissair, 46 C. J.L. Nehru Road, Tel: 444643
Thai Airways International, 18/G, Park Street, Tel: 299846/7/8/9.
Yugoslav Airlines, 21, Camac Street, Tel: 441561

GSA for **Gulf Air, Kuwait Airlines, Philippine Airlines, Royal Jordanian Airlines** and **Trans World Airlines:** Jetair Pte. Ltd., Chitrakoot, 230A, A.J.C. Bose Road, Tel: 447783, 445576.

Dum Dum, Calcutta's Airport, is 22 kilometers (14 miles) from the city. There are shops, an exchange counter, a restaurant, a bar, a duty-free with a limited choice of goods, and a hotel, the Ashok International. Taxi and bus vouchers for the city can be purchased in advance inside the airport.

The Foreign Travel Tax is INR100 for most international flights and only INR50 for Bangladesh, Bhutan and Nepal.

Transit passengers are exempt provided they do not leave the bounded area.

BY RAIL

Regular services link Calcutta to New Delhi, Bombay, Madras, to most major cities, the neighbouring States and the rest of West Bengal. Services to Dhaka in Bangladesh have not resumed since 1971. Information on schedules can be obtained and tickets purchased at the stations or at booking centres in town.

South Eastern Railway Booking & Information Centre, Esplanade Mansions (opposite Raj Bhavan), Tel: 289530
Computerised Booking Office for Eastern and South-Eastern Railways. Rabindra Sadan, 61, J.L. Nehru Road, Alexandra Court
Round-the-clock Railway Information: For incoming trains: Tel: 203445 to 203454. Other information: Tel: 203535 to 203544. For reservations on trains, Tel: 280370 (9 a.m. - 9 p.m. on weekdays, Sundays 9 a.m. - 2 p.m.).
Rabindra Sadan Booking Counter, Alexander Court, 61 J.L. Nehru Road, Calcutta 13
Howrah Station, 1st Floor
New Koilaghat, 14 Strand Road, Calcutta 1, Tel: 234676/72/7254
Sealdah Station, 1st Floor, Open 9 a.m. - 9 p.m. on weekdays; 9 a.m. - 2 p.m. on Sundays & National Holidays.
3 Koilaghat Street, Calcutta 1, Tel: 289494
6 Fairlie Place, Calcutta 1, Tel: 222789/4025

Most trains depart from Howrah Station, located near the Hooghly Bridge. Some, however, like the Darjeeling Mart and a good number of trains to West Bengal leave from Sealdah Station in the East of the city. Do not forget to check from which station your train is leaving. If it is Sealdah, make sure you leave well in advance to avoid being delayed by traffic jams.

BY ROAD

Calcutta is connected to the National Highway network through G.T. (Grand Trunk) Road and the Bombay Trunk Road. Roads in Bengal and neighbouring Bihar are in a poor state with many pot-holes. The average travel speed in the state rarely exceeds 30 kilometres (19 miles) per hour. Roads in Orissa are good and speeds up to 100 kilometres (62 miles) per hour can be reached between Calcutta and Balasore. It takes 12 hours to reach Dhaka in Bangladesh, 180 kilometres (112 miles) away as several rivers have to be crossed by ferry. Detailed itineraries can be obtained from the **Automobile Association of Eastern India** (3, Promotesh Barua Sarani, Tel: 475131).

TRAVEL ESSENTIALS

VISAS & PASSPORTS

Foreigners desirous to visit India must obtain a visa from the Indian mission in their country of residence. Passports due to expire within 6 months must be renewed before applying for a visa. Usually a tourist visa valid for 90 days is granted. Entry into India must take place within 6 months from the date of issue of the visa.

Groups of not less than 5 persons and sponsored by an approved travel agent can apply for a group visa. They may split into smaller groups upon arrival but must reassemble for departure.

Foreigners coming on tourist visas for a maximum stay of 90 days need not register with the Indian authorities. However, they may be required to furnish personal and passport particulars at the hotel where they are staying. Extensions of stay, up to 6 months, can be obtained from the **Foreigners' Registration Office**, 237 Acharya Jagadish, Bose Road, Calcutta-700 001, Tel: 443301. The visitor has to register with the same office upon approval of his extension of stay. A Certificate of Registration is then issued by the Indian authorities. Visitors staying in India up to 90 days do not need a permit to leave India. For a stay above 3 months and up to 6 months, visitors must obtain clearance from the Foreigners' Registration office.

Restricted and protected areas: access to the North-East, the Andaman and Nicobor Islands, Sikkim and 5 districts of West Bengal is limited. Special permits are required for which applications must be lodged at least 6 weeks in advance before leaving for Inda. The Darjeeling permit, however, can be obtained in Calcutta in 2 days. A day permit for a limited area around Port Blair, the capital of the Andamans, is delivered on the spot upon arrival there.

MONEY MATTERS

The Indian Rupee (INR) consists of 100 paisas.

There are no restrictions on the amount of foreign currency or travellers' cheques a tourist may bring into India provided he makes a declaration in the Currency Declaration Form given to him on arrival. This will enable him not only to exchange the currency brought in but also to take the unspent currency out of India on departure. Cash, bank notes and travellers' cheques up to US$1,000 or equivalent need not be declared at the time of entry.

Any money in the form of travellers' cheques, drafts, bills, cheques, etc in convertible currencies which tourists wish to convert into Indian currency should be exchanged only through authorised money changers and banks which will issue an encashment certificate. This certificate is required at the time of reconversion of any unspent money into foreign currency. Changing money through unauthorised persons is not only illegal but also involves the risk of receiving counterfeit currency. Exchanging of foreign money other than through banks or authorised money changers is an offence under Foreign Exchange Regulations Act, 1973.

Tourists have to get an endorsement on the Currency Declaration Form or a certificate from authorised dealers while encashing their travellers' cheques. This would also facilitate reconverting the residual Indian currency at the time of departure. No Indian currency whatsoever can be brought in or taken out of the country. This restriction does not apply to rupee travellers' cheques. Banks abroad do keep rupee balances with their agents in India and a recognised procedure for them to draw upon these balances is to issue rupee travellers' cheques to intending tourists.

Persons holding currencies or travellers' cheques which are not included in the Currency Declaration Form furnished on arrival will not be permitted to take them out of India without written permission from the Reserve Bank of India.

Main banks in Calcutta:

American Express
2 Old Court House St Cal-1
Tel: 286281
Bank of America
8 India Exchange Place Cal-1
Tel: 262352
Bank of Rajasthan Ltd
31 J.L. Nehru Rd Cal-16
Tel: 299336/9573
Bank of Tokyo
2 Brabourne Rd Calcutta 1, Tel: 261125/1763
Banque Nationale De Paris
Stephen House, 4A BBD Bagh (E) Calcutta 1, Tel: 289841
Citibank
Tata Centre, 43 J.L. Nehru Rd, Calcutta 71, Tel: 293425
Grindlays Bank Ltd
19 N.S. Rd, Calcutta 1, Tel: 228346
HongKong Bank
8 N.S. Rd, Calcutta 1 Tel: 221833-36
R.R. Sen & Bros
18A,B,C J.L. Nehru Rd, Calcutta 13, Tel: 297520/6077
R.R. Sen & Bros
11D Kabitirtha Sarani, Calcutta 23, Tel: 452934
Standard Chartered Bank
31 J.L. Nehru Rd, Calcutta 16, Tel: 299731
State Bank of India
33A J.L. Nehru Rd, Calcutta 71, Tel: 297230/7335/16/24723
All 5 Star Hotels have Bureau de Change facilities.

HEALTH

Foreign tourists should be in possession of Yellow Fever Vaccination Certificate conforming to International Health Regulations, if they are originating or transiting through Yellow Fever endemic countries.

Any person (except infants up to 6 months

of age) arriving by air or sea without a yellow fever vaccination certificate, is detained in isolation for a period up to 6 days, if he arrives within 6 days of departure from an infected area or has been in such an area in transit, or has come by an aircraft which has been in an infected area and has not been disinfected. The following countries and territories are regarded as yellow fever endemic.

Africa: Angola, Benin, Botswana, Burundi, Central African Republic, Chad, Congo, Equatorial Guinea, Ethiopia, Cabon, Gambia, Ghana, Guinea, Guinea-Bissau, Ivory-Coast, Kenya, Liberia, Malawi, Mali, Mauritania, Niger, Nigeria, Rwanda, Sao Tome and Principe, Senegal, Sierra-Leone, Somalia, Sudan (south of 15° north), Togo, Uganda, United Republic of Cameroon, United Republic of Tanzania, Upper Volta, Zaire, Zambia.

America: Belize, Bolivia, Brazil, Canal Zone, Colombia, Costa Rica, Ecuador, French Guiana, Guatemala, Guyana, Honduras, Nicaragua, Panama, Peru, Surinam, Trinidad and Tobago, Venezuela.

When a case of yellow fever is reported from any country, that country is regarded by the Government of India as infected with yellow fever and is added to the above list.

The validity period of all international certificates of vaccination or revaccination against yellow fever is 10 years, beginning 10 days after vaccination. Revaccination performed before the end of the validity of the certificate renders the certificate valid for a further period of 10 years starting on the day of revaccination. If the revaccination is recorded on a new certificate, travellers are advised to retain the old certificate for 10 days, until the new certificate is valid by itself.

No other vaccination certificate is required for entry into India.

Although there are no health checks for departing tourists, they are advised in their own interest to obtain valid Cholera and Yellow Fever vaccination certificates if they are visiting a country where these certificates are required. Facility for such a vaccination is readily available at all major ports of departure.

WHAT TO WEAR

The weather in Calcutta is hot and humid from April to October. The monsoon starts after the short and torried Indian summer that lasts from April to June. Light clothes, preferably of cotton and open shoes are recommended. Winter is mild in Calcutta. A woollen jumper is sufficient during the day. Evenings can be a bit chilly (8°C). People, including men, wear shawls made either of wool or of raw, heavy silk (*erri*). The dressing code is casual in Calcutta. Sandals, shorts, T-shirts, however, are banned from the dining-rooms of many clubs or restaurants. Women are advised not to wear shorts and singlets leaving shoulders bare.

WHAT TO BRING

Buy your clothes before leaving for Calcutta as good quality cotton clothes are difficult to find in India where people prefer synthetics. Photographic films, video tapes are available in Calcutta. However, the quality is not regular, especially for slide films and blank video tapes. If possible, buy a stock abroad before arriving.

CUSTOMS

Visitors are generally required to make oral baggage declaration in respect of baggage and foreign currency in their possession. Visitors in possession of more than US$1,000, or equivalent thereof in traveller's cheques, bank notes, or currency notes, are required to obtain a Currency Declaration Form before leaving Customs. They should fill in the Disembarkation Card handed to them.

There are two channels for Customs clearance:

Green Channel – for passengers not having any dutiable articles in their accompanied baggage; they may have imported items through unaccompanied baggage.

Red Channel – for passengers having dutiable articles irrespective of whether they have imported unaccompanied baggage or not. At the airports are separate counters in the Green Channel for issue of TBRE forms to those who do not have any dutiable articles and would be taking back their high value articles.

Articles Allowed Free of Duty

Duty-free import of the following items is allowed: provided that they are for the personal use of the tourist, are carried on the person or in the baggage accompanying the tourist, that there is no reason to fear abuse and that these personal effects, other than what has been consumed during his stay, are re-exported by the tourist on his departure from India.

Personal Effects

Clothing and other articles;
Personal jewellery;
One camera with 12 plates or five rolls of films;
One miniature cinematograph camera with two reels of films;
One pair of binoculars
One portable musical instrument;
One portable wireless receiving set;
One portable sound-recording apparatus;
One portable typewriter;
One perambulator;
One tent and other camping equipment; and sports equipment such as one fishing outfit, one sporting fire-arm with 50 cartridges; one non-powered bicycle, one canoe or kayak less than 5.5 metres (18 feet) long, one pair of skis, two tennis racquets.

Tourists are also allowed to bring free of duty the following articles, provided that a written undertaking is given that these will be re-exported.
(i) Audio-visual aids including slides and films for demonstration and instructional purposes.
(ii) Professional equipment, instruments, apparatus or appliances including cine/television equipment.
Travel souvenirs up to a value of Rs. 500 are allowed provided they are not intended for commercial purposes and re-exported by tourists.

Articles of high value: such as sound-recording apparatus, wireless receiving sets and the like are not allowed to be imported free of duty unless the tourist gives an undertaking in writing to the proper officer to re-export them out of India on his leaving India for a foreign destination, or upon his failure to re-export, to pay the duty leviable thereon.

Every tourist shall be given on arrival and after examination of his baggage, a list of articles of high value brought by him and signed by the proper officer who examines his baggage. Unless the list is produced by the tourist to the proper office at the time of examination of his baggage on his departure from India for a foreign destination along with the articles listed therein, his baggage may not be allowed clearance through the Customs for export.

Gifts: articles up to a value of Rs. 500 for your use or for presentations as gifts. Certain articles like the following will not be allowed free of duty as gifts:
(i) Motorcycle, scooter or moped
(ii) Fire-arms
(iii) Cigarettes exceeding 200, or cigars exceeding 50, or tobacco exceeding 250 gm (9 oz)
(iv) Alcoholic liquor exceeding 0.95 litres (2 pints)

BOND FACILITIES

Any dutiable article imported by a passenger as his baggage may be left in bond with the Customs authorities pending re-export at the time of departure if he does not want to pay duty on it. However, if the baggage is very bulky it may not be possible for the Customs authorities to accommodate it because the storage space at their disposal is limited. Sufficient notice should, however, be given regarding the date of departure if the port of embarkation is other than that of arrival. Passengers should contact their airlines for transferring the items to the port of departure, and inform the Customs authorities.

PROHIBITED ARTICLES

The import of certain articles such as dangerous drugs, live plants, gold coins, gold and silver bullion and silver coins not in current use, is either totally prohibited or restricted. The law provides heavy penalties for infringement of this restriction.

UNACCOMPANIED BAGGAGE

Bona fide unaccompanied baggage arriving in India after the arrival of the passenger, if it was in his possession abroad and was shipped by sea within one month or despatched by air within a fortnight of the passenger's arrival in India, is allowed free of duty subject to the conditions and limitations laid down in the Rules.

EXPORT OF ARTICLES

All articles, brought into India temporarily with the permission of Customs authorities can be exported without any export trade control restrictions.

Any person not ordinarily resident in India may take out from India jewellery made mainly or wholly of gold without limit provided that the jewellery was previously brought into India from abroad, with the permission of the Customs authorities. Such a person may also take at any one time out of India, jewellery made mainly or wholly of gold up to Rs. 2,000 in value purchased by him in India.

Any person other than a person domiciled in India may take out any precious stones or jewellery brought into India without limit; and precious stones or jewellery other than articles wholly or mainly of gold purchased by him in India up to Rs. 10,000 in value.

ANTIQUITIES & ART OBJECTS

There are restrictions on the export of antiquities and art objects more than 100 years old from India. To ascertain whether purchases made by tourists are considered antiquities or not, the following authorities may be consulted:

Superintending Archaeologist
Eastern Circle, Archaeological Survey of India Narayani Building, Brabourne Road Calcutta-700 013

SHIKAR TROPHIES

Skins of all animals, snakes, etc, and the articles made thereof used or unused, as personal baggage, whether accompanied or unaccompanied, are banned. For details, contact the nearest Government of India Tourist Office.

GETTING ACQUAINTED

TIME ZONES

The time difference between Calcutta Time and Greenwich Meridian Time is **??** hours.

CLIMATE

Calcutta has four seasons.

Winter, or the **Cold Weather**, starts in late October – early January. The temperature around New Year's Eve can drop down to 8°C at night but never below 15°C in the daytime. There is often heavy fog in the early hours of the morning. The temperature rises progressively, until *Holi* in March, the festival marking the advent of spring.

Spring is short, never lasting more than a month. The temperature and humidity rise slowly, remaining quite acceptable.

The **Indian Summer** from mid-April to mid-June is the most unpleasant period of the year. The temperature can reach 40°C and humidity nears saturation. Violent thunderstorms, the Nor waters come down from the Himalaya several times a month, from the North, bringing the temperature down in a matter of minutes by 10°C to 15°C. Many catch a bad cold during storms.

The first rains of the **Monsoon** come as a deliverance. Temperatures drop to the range of 25°C – 35°C. The sky is almost permanently grey. It rains virtually every day. Every year the city is flooded knee-high several times. The Monsoon ends in late November with the *Awga Puja* festival.

CULTURE & CUSTOMS

Calcutta being a cosmopolitan city, many cultures and customs coexist. A foreigner is not expected to be aware of all of them. There are, however, several basic rules to observe:

• never shout or lose control of yourself. This will lead you nowhere. The more one loses face, the less cooperative he will be;

• use your left hand as little as possible when giving or receiving something, showing an object or a person, or eating;

• do not point with your index finger: use either your extended hand or your chin;

• when speaking to someone, look into his eyes otherwise it will seem that you are lying or hiding the truth.

• physical contact with women is to be avoided. Avoid shaking hands with a woman or putting your hand on her shoulder;

• do not compliment parents on their children. It is believed you can attract on them the Evil Eye;

• when visiting people, always remove your shoes upon entering their homes;

• in places of worship, be extremely cautious. Here again, remove your shoes. Cover your head in Sikh temples. Avoid wearing leather in Hindu or Sikh places; in mosques, women should cover their heads and shoulders and wear a long skirt;

• dress casually but try not to look neglected or provocative. Women should avoid shorts, singlets leaving the shoulder bare;

• show respect to the old.

WEIGHTS & MEASURES

The metric system is uniformly used all over India. Precious metals, especially gold, are often sold by the traditional tola, which is equivalent to 11.5 grams. Gems are weighed in carats (0.2 grams). Financial outlays and population are usually expressed in lakhs (100 thousand) and crores (100 lakhs or 10 million).

ELECTRICITY

Voltage is 220A C, 50 cycles. The supply is irregular in Summer and during the Monsoon. Daily cuts, of up to 6 hours and more during the worst days in some parts of the city, are tactfully called "Load Sheddings".

BUSINESS HOURS

Offices start at 9 a.m. There is a tea-break in the morning around 11 a.m. Lunch is at about 12.30 p.m. New tea-break at 4.00 p.m. The working day ends at 5.30 p.m. Many companies are open on Saturday mornings. Government offices work two Saturday mornings a month. Banks are open to the public from 10 a.m. to 3 p.m. Mondays to Fridays and from 11 a.m. to 6 p.m. on Saturdays.

HOLIDAYS/FESTIVALS

With so many communities, Calcutta has a core of public holidays and twice as many optional holidays from which one can choose three days. For most religious festivals based on the lunar calendar, the dates change every year. The compulsory holidays are New Year's Day (Jan 1), Netaji's Subhas Chandra Bose's Birth Anniversary (Jan 23), Republic Day (Jan 26) *Saraswati Puja* (late Jan – early Feb), *Holi* (March), Good Friday and Easter (March or April), May Day (May 1), Independence Day (August 1), *Durga Puja* (Oct), *Lakshmi Puja* (Oct - Nov), *Kali Puja* (Nov), Christmas (Dec 25) *Idulfitr* (end of the Ramadan), and *Idul Aza* (return of the pilgrims from the Mecca) which moves 11 days backward every year.

Check in the newspapers and with the West Bengal Tourist Office (3/2 B.B.D. Bag Tel: 285917) for the dates and venues of the coming festivals.

RELIGIOUS SERVICES

Most persuasions are represented. Catholic Mass is said at the Murgihatta Cathedral on Brabourne Road. The Anglican, British

Methodist, Presbyterian, Congregationist and some Baptist Churches have merged into the United Church of North India. Services are held at St Paul's Cathedral on the Maidan, St Andrew's Kirk on B.B. D. Bay and St. John's behind Government House (Raj Bhavan). The main synagogue Moghen David is at the corner of Canning Street and Brabourne Road. Armenians hold their services alternately in three Calcutta churches: Holy Church of Nazareth on Armenian Street, St Gregory's Chapel (Park Circus), Chapel of the Holy Trinity (Tangra) and at Chinsurah, north of Calcutta. A number of visitors attend prayer meetings at Aurobindo Bhawan (on Shakespeare Sarani), at the Ramakrishna Mission (at Gul Park in Calcutta or Belur Morth, in the northen suburb of Belur) and at the ISKON temple (3C Albert Road).

COMMUNICATIONS

MEDIA

The first newspaper, the Bengal Gazette, appeared in 1780.

The press in Bengal has always had a tradition of independence towards the government, and are therefore more interesting to read than those printed in Delhi or Bombay. The main dailies in English are the *Statesman*, the *Telegraph* and *Amrita Bazar Patrika*. They publish every Sunday a colour supplement with articles on culture and history, as well as on contemporary issues. *Calcutta Skyline*, a monthly, runs articles on the history of the city or on a specific area and features up-to-date information on what is going on in Calcutta. *Calcutta Folklore* (at Anglo-Indian Street) specializes in articles on Bengali and Indian folklore or anthropology. It is available only from the publisher. *Chowkidar*, published in the U.K. (76 œ Chartfield Avenue, London SW15 6HQ) runs articles on old European cemeteries and memorials, as well as book reviews on India. Other magazines of interest published in Delhi or Bombay have regular features on Calcutta. *Sanctuary* focuses on wildlife and the environment, The *India Magazine* on anthropology, culture and monuments and Marg, on the arts.

POSTAL SERVICES/ TELEPHONE & TELEX

The General Post Office and Poste Restante service are on B.B.D. Bag. Major hotels have postal facilities. The mailing time for letters and postcards to and from Calcutta take a minimum of a week up to a month. Parcels cannot be closed until their content has been checked. Glue or scotch tape may not be used to seal them as the Indian Postal Service reserves for itself the right to open them for random checks. You will have to use a string to tie up a parcel you want to send abroad.

The Central Telegraph Exchange is on 8 Red Cross Place, the International Telephone Exchange on Wood Street. The main hotels have business centres with telecom facilities. The telecom system is in West Bengal B.M. Shambles. You might have to wait hours before your call gets through.

EMERGENCIES

SECURITY & CRIME

Calcutta is one of the safest cities in India, which does not mean that you should not take precautions against pickpockets, quite active in buses, at markets, and the railway station. You must also avoid the red light districts of Munshigunge, Sonagacchi and Wattgunge where foreigners are definitely not welcome.

Emergency calls:
Police : 100

Fire : 101
Ambulance: 102

In case of theft or aggression contact immediately the Police Headquarters at 18 Lal Bazar Street (Tel. 255900).

MEDICAL SERVICES

The main diseases that can be contracted in Calcutta are malaria, food poisoning, hepatitis, gastro-enteritis, sinusitis caused by changes of temperature between air-conditioned premises and the street, toxoplasmosis and an indigenous form of conjunctivities called Jay Bangla. Most hotels in Calcutta can arrange for a doctor to call on you in your room. There is also an Emergency Doctor Service (Tel: 466770-410604). In case you need to check into a hospital, Calcutta has several decent ones:

Calcutta Hospital, 7/2 D.H. Road, Tel: 453921
Park View Nursing Home, 109 B Park Street, Tel: 248446.
Assembly of God Church Hospital, 123/1 Park Street
Belle-Vue Nursing Home, 9 Dr. UN Brahmachari Road, Tel: 442321
Woodlands Nursing Home, 8/5 Alipore Park Road, Tel: 453951.

24-HOUR MEDICAL SHOPS

Dhanwantary Clinic
6 Diamond Harbour Rd Cal-23 7 a.m. -10 p.m.

Emergency Oxygen Clinic
'Kantashree',
28 Camac St Cal-16

Girlish Pharmacy
167-B Rash Behari Ave Cal-19 9 a.m.-10 p.m.

Singh & Roy
4/1 Shambhunath Pandit Rd Cal-20
Tel: 433770; Open 24 hrs Wed-Sun

AMBULANCE

Ambulance Station
34 Judges Court Rd Cal-27

Dhanwantary Chemists
1 National Library Ave Cal-27 Tel: 456256

Emergency Doctors' Service
A 165 Lake Gardens Cal-45
Tel: 466770/416 24 hrs

Indian Red Cross Society (WB State Branch)
5 & 6 Govt Place East Cal-1
Tel: 233635/36 8a.m. - 8p.m.

Private Ambulance Service
Tel: 392232/223

St. John's Ambulance
1/A Rishi Bankim Rd, Howrah; Howrah Dist. Centre, Tel: 668051

BLOOD BANKS

Assembly of God Church Hospital
125/1 Park St Cal-17

Belle-Vue Nursing Home
9 Dr U N Brahmachari Rd Cal-17
Tel: 442321/692

Calcutta Blood Bank
186A Rash Behari Ave Cal-29 Tel: 468552
Marwari Relief Society
227 Rabindra Sarani Cal-7 Ph: 333724/25

GETTING AROUND

ORIENTATION

The main arteries in Calcutta run parallel or perpendicular to the Hooghly. Chowringhee, Diamond Harbour Road, Red Road, Unitpore Road, Central Avenue, College Street, G.T. Road, run from south to north; Shakespeare Sarani, Ho Chi Minh Sarani, Hazra Road, Park Street, Dharantla Road, Mahatura Gandhi Road, Rashbahari Avenue runs east to west.

Calcuttans continue to call streets by their old pre-Independence names. Many simply are not aware of the new names.

New name	Old name
Albert Road	Uttam Kumar Road
Auckland Place	Benjamin Moloise Square
Bowbazar Street	Bepin Bihali Ganghuly Street
Camac Street	Abanindranath Tagore Street
Canning Street	Biplab Rash Behari Basun Road
Chitpore Road	Rabindra Sarani
Chowringhee	Jawaharlal Nehru Road
Clive Road	Netaji Subhas Road
Dalhousie Square	B.B.D. Bag
Dharamtola Street	Lenin Sarani
Free School Street	Mirza Ghalib Street
Grey Street	Sree Aurobindo Sarani
Harrington Street	Ho Chi Minh Sarani
Kyd Street	Dr Mohammed Ishaque Road
Landsdowne Road	Sarat Bose Road
Lower Circular Road	A.J.C. Bose Road
Moira Street	Rev. Martin Luther King Street
Red Road	Indira Gandhi Road
Ripon Street	Muzaffar Ahmed Street
Theatre Road	Shakespeare Savani
Tollygunge Road	Sadhu Tara Charan Road
Upper Lower Circular Road	Acharya Prafulla Chandra Road
Wellesley Street	Rafi Ahmed Kidwai Street
Wellington Square	Raja Subodh Mallick Square

MAPS

Book shops sell good road maps of India, Eastern India but no decent one of Calcutta. During *pujas*, the Dunlop company publishes schematic maps of areas where the best statues of Durga can be seen. The maps are reproduced in the *Telegraph*.

PUBLIC TRANSPORT

Bus: Calcutta has the largest concentration of buses in the world. They are operated by the Government (Calcutta Transport Corporation, West Bengal State Transport Corporation) or are private (mini-buses). Government buses are red, battered double-deckers or trailer-buses, a unique crossing between the bus and the trailer. Buses are ill-maintained, have all a defective carburettor and emit a dark, black cloud each time the driver accelerates. They are one of the chief polluters in Calcutta.

Most **taxis** are old Ambassador cars (the Austin Oxford still manufactured in India). They are black with a yellow top and fitted with a meter. Three-wheeler taxis, used to carry goods and called Matoder, are available at Barabazar.

Hackneys and Tongas: There are still fiacres in Calcutta. They ply on the Maridan, along the Strand and on Alipore. Their number has faded from 2,000 to 70. It is a popular mode of transportation for families and women in *purdah* during processions.

Rickshaws were introduced by Chinese businessmen in the 1920s. Calcutta is the only city in the world besides Hong Kong to have human-drawn rickshaws. Banned from the main arteries, they have their hour of glory during floods when they are the only possible means of transportation as the water level in the streets reaches 3 feet.

The Metro started running in 1984. There are services everyday from 8 a.m. to 9 p.m., between Esplanade and Tollygunge. Work is going on along the Esplanade, Shyambazar section.

The Circular Rail, opened in 1984 too, runs along the ghats from Prinsep Ghat to Sobhabazar.

Tramways started running in 1873. They are now often prevented from running by traffic or electricity cuts. In the morning there is still a ladies' tram to allow women to commute to work during office hours without being hassled by men. There are services between several ghats. The most active one, useful during jam hours, is the one between Howrah Station and the Chandpal Ghat.

PRIVATE TRANSPORT

Cars can be rented by visitors holding an international driving license. A third-party insurance is compulsory. The insurance must be paid with a company registered in India or with a foreign insurer who has a guarantor in India. The car-rental companies have updated lists of insurers.

Rent-a-Car Service, 1/5 Dover Lane, Tel: 467186, 423245
A & E Pte Ltd., 16B Gurusaday Road, Tel: 432317
Ashai International, 12/12 Hungerford Street, Tel: 441987
Car Rent Services, 233/4A, A.J.C. Bose Road, Tel: 441285
Durgapur Automobiles, 113, Park Street, Tel: 294044
Wheels on Road, 150 Lenin Sarani, Tel: 273081

One can also rent a small steamer launch to sail on the Hooghly at around INR 500 an hour at the following:
Hooghly Nadi Jalapath Paribohon Samabay Samity: 4/5 Rishi Bankim Chandra Road, Ganges Side, Howrah Station (Tel: 666080-250694)
Golden River Transport Corporation: 9/1A Bakery Road, Hastings (Tel: 458881)

WHERE TO STAY

HOTELS

There are in Calcutta 4- and 5-star hotels as well as YMCA's

First class hotels:

Oberoi Grand, 15 Jawaharlal Nehru Road (Chowringhee), Tel: 292323, 290181, Suite Rs. 3750; A.C. Double Rs. 1600; A.C. Single Rs. 1450.

Taj Bengal, 34B, Belvedere Road, Alipore, Calcutta 700 027. Tel: (033) 283939, Tlx: 021-4776/021-5998 TAJC IN; Fax: (033) 281766, 288805.

Intermediate hotels:

Carlton Hotel, 2 Chowringhee Place, Tel: 233009, 238853. Suite Rs. 265; Non A.C. Double Rs. 225; Non A.C. Single Rs. 140.

Fairlawn Hotel, 13/A, Sudder Street, Tel: 244460, 241835. A.C. Double Rs. 500; Non A.C. Double Rs. 450; A.C. Single Rs. 400.

Hotel Airport Ashok, near Dum Dum Airport, Tel: 575111, 31, 32. Suite Rs. 1350; A.C. Double Rs. 900; A.C. Single Rs. 800.

Hotel Hindustan International, 235/1, A.J. Bose Road, Tel: 442394, 287726. A.C. Suites Rs. 2000 to 3000; A.C. Superior Rs. 830 to 930, A.C. Standard Rs. 770 to 880.

Hotel Rutt-Deen, 21-B Dr. UN Brahmachari Street, Tel: 431691, 445210, 443884. Suite Rs. 1000; A.C. Double Rs. 550, A.C. Single Rs. 440.

Hotel Shalimar, 3, S N Banerjee Road, Tel: 285030. A.C. Double Rs. 350; A.C. Single Rs. 300.

Lytton Hotel, 14 Sudder Street, near Indian Museum, Tel: 291872. Suite Rs. 700; A.C. Double Rs. 500; A.C. Single Rs. 400.

New Kenilworth Hotel, 2 Little Russell Street, Tel: 448394/99, 443403/04. Suite Rs. 900; A.C. Double Rs. 650; A.C. Single Rs. 550; Deluxe Suite Rs. 1200.

Park Hotel, 17 Park Street, Tel: 297336. Suite Rs. 2500; A.C. Double Rs. 1100; A.C. Single Rs 1000; Business Suite Rs. 1600, Deluxe Suite Rs. 3500.

The Astor Hotel, 15 Shakespeare Sarani, Tel: 449950, 446215, 431931. A.C. Double Rs. 395; A.C. Single Rs. 375 to Rs. 395.

Cheap hotels:

Astoria Hotel, 6/2/3 Sudder Street, Tel: 241359, 242613. Tariff from Rs. 60 to 150;

A.C. Rs. 200.

Capital Guest House, 11 B Chowringhee Lane, Tel: 213844.

Great Eastern Hotel, 13 Old Court House, Tel: 282331/34. Suite Rs. 2000; A.C. Double Rs. 6000; A.C. Single Rs. 525.

Hotel Diplomat, 10 Sudder Street, Single Rs. 60; Double Rs. 70.

Salvation Army Red Shield Guest House, 2 Sudder Street, Tel: 242895. Single Rs. 35; Double Rs. 40 to 50.

Shilton Hotel, 5 A Sudder Street, Single Rs. 55; Double Rs. 80.

The Tourist Inn, 4/1 Sudder Street, Tel: 243732. Single Rs. 35; Double Rs. 70.

*Outside of Calcutta, visitors can stay at Government Circuit Bungalows and Rest Houses.

Bookings at Tourist Lodges in West Bengal: West Bengal Tourist Development Corporation (WBTDC), 3/2 B.B.D. Bagh (East), Tel: 285917

Bookings at Tourist Lodges outside West Bengal, Govt. of India Tourist Office, 4 Shakespeare Sarani, Tel: 441402, 443521.

Paying Guest Accommodation: Govt. of India Tourist Office, 4 Shakespeare Sarani.

Govt. of West Bengal Tourist Office, 2, Brabourne Road.

YOUTH HOSTELS

YMCA, 25 Chowringhee, Tel: 233504. Single Rs. 140; Double Rs. 170; inclusive of dinner and breakfast.
YMCA, 42 Surendra Nath Banerjee Road, Tel: 240260.
YWCA, 1 Middleton Road,
The Youth hostel, 10 J.B. Ananda Dutta Lane, Tel: 672869 Dormitory beds Rs. 10; each.

There are Youth Hostels at Darjeeling and Puri. The one at Darjeeling organises treks.
Darjeeling: 16 Dr Zakir Husain Road, Darjeeling 734101 West Bengal Tel: 2290
Puri: Sea Beach, Puri 752001 Orissa Tel: 424.

A complete list can be obtained from the Youth Hostels Association of India, S Nyaya Marg, Chanakyapuri, New Delhi 110021.

FOOD DIGEST

WHERE TO EAT

Since Bengali food is eaten traditionally at home, most restaurants serve Mughlai, Chinese, or more or less vaguely continental food. There are also some fast-food joints, a new phenomenon, and pastry shops, some of which existed since Independence.

MUGHLAI

Amber
11 Waterloo Street Cal-1
Near Coffee House; Tel: 286520/3477/6746
Bar facilities. Open 10 a.m – 11 p.m.
Thursdays closed.

Celebrity
17, Park Street Cal-16
In Park Hotel; Tel: 297336/7941
Open every day 12 p.m. – 3 p.m. & 8 p.m. – 11 p.m.

Gulnar
17 Park Street Cal-16.
Next to Park Hotel; Tel: 298947/7825
Open 10 a.m. – 12 a.m.
Thursdays closed.

Kebab-E-Que
15 Shakespeare Sarani Cal-71
In The Astor Hotel; Tel: 449950/57-59/6215/431931
Open every day 4 p.m. – 12 a.m.

Kwality
Off 2-A Gariahat Road Cal-19
At Ballygunge Phanri; Tel: 482982/477372
Open 10 a.m. – 10 p.m.
Wednesdays closed.

17, Park Street Cal-16
In Park Hotel Arcade; Tel: 247701/7865
Bar facilities. Open 10 a.m. – 11 p.m.
Thursdays closed.

Moghul Room
15 J.L. Nehru Road Cal-13
In Oberoi Grand; Tel: 292323/0181
Open 12.30 p.m. – 2.30 p.m. and
8 p.m. – 11.30 p.m.
Tuesdays closed.

Nizam's
22 & 25 Hogg Market

Peter Cat
18 Park Street Cal-16
Near Park St-Middleton Row crossing;
Tel: 298841
Bar facilities.
Open every day 10.30 a.m. – 11.30 p.m.

Rang Mahal
15, J.L. Nehru Road Cal-13
Opp. Roxy Talkies in Chowringhee Place;
Tel: 292323/0181

Royal Hotel
147, Rabindra Sarani Cal-73
Tel: 381073

Shenaz
2A Middleton Row Cal-16
Near Loreto House; Tel: 298383
Open 10 a.m. – 12 a.m.
Thursdays closed.

Shiraz
56 Park Street Cal-16
Near Park St-A.J.C. Bose Rd crossing;
Tel: 447702
Open every day 5 a.m. – 11 p.m.

Tandoor
25A Park Street Cal-16
Near Park Street-Free School Street crossing; Tel: 298006
Open 12 p.m. – 12 a.m.
Wednesdays closed.

BENGALI

J's Shop
123B Rashbehari Avenue.

Nari Seva Sangha Canteen
1/1 2A Gariahat Road.

Suruchi
89 Elliot Road Cal-16
Near A.G. School; Tel: 293292
Open every day 10 a.m. – 8 p.m.
Closed half day Sundays.

Sonar Gaon
In Taj Bengal, Tel: 283939

The Food Shop
2 Elgin Road, Calcutta 700020
Tel: 470152-472783

CONTINENTAL

Blue Fox
55 Park Street
Tel: 297948

Garden Cafe
15 J.L. Nehru Road Cal-13
In Oberoi Grand; Tel: 292323/0181
24-hour coffeeshop, poolside restaurant and patisserie.

Kathleen's
12 Mirza Ghalib Street Cal-87
Near Free School Street-Lindsay Street Crossing; Tel: 249293 or
1 A.J.C. Bose Road Cal-20
At Lord Sinha Road-Lower Circular Road crossing; Tel: 441205

La Rotisserie
15 J.L. Nehru Road Cal-13
In Oberoi Grand; Tel: 292323/0181
Open 7.30 p.m. – 12 a.m.
Sundays closed.

Magnolia
12 K&N Park Street Cal-16
Opposite Oxford Bookshop; Tel: 248997
Bar facilities. Open 11 a.m. – 11 p.m.
Thursdays closed.

Maple
15 Park St Cal-16
In Park Hotel, at Park St-Russell St crossing;
Tel: 299192
Bar facilities. Open 12 p.m. – 10 p.m.
Tuesdays closed.

Mocambo
25B Park Street
Near Free School St-Park St crossing;
Tel: 294152

Skyroom
57 Park Street Cal-16
Near Park St-Free School St crossing;
Tel: 249323.

Trinca's
The Other Room, 17B, Park Street;
Tel: 298947
Thursday closed.

VEGETARIAN

Gupta Brothers
18B Park Street, Tel: 299687.

Invader Centre
12 Dr U.N. Brahmachari Street Cal-1
Near Belle Vue Nursing Home; tel: 448552

Vineet
AC Market Shakespeare Sarani.
At Lord Sinha Road-Theatre Road crossing;
1st Basement Cal-17.

SOUTH INDIAN

Jyothi Vihar
3/A Ho Chi Minh Sarani, Tel: 449791.

FAST FOOD

Fast Food Centre
7/1 A.J.C. Bose Road Cal-17
Around the corner from Kala Mandir.

Fish for Dish
13A Shyamsquare Lane, Cal. 700003;
Tel: 555803

Invader Centre
12 Dr U.N. Brahmachari Street Cal-1
Near Belle Vue Nursing Home; Tel: 448552

Super Snack Bar
27A N.R. Sarkar Ave, Blk B, New Alipore
Near Southern end of Majerhat bridge Alipur Cal-53; Tel: 452764
Vegetarian. Beside Bidya Bharati School in New Alipur.

PASTRIES, ICE CREAMS & SWEETS

Flury's
18 Park Street Cal-71
At Park Street-Middleton Row crossing;
Tel: 297664

Ganguram
38 B.B. Ganguly Street, Cal-12

Kookie Jar
42A Shakespeare Sarani Cal-71
Next to Auckland Square.

La Patisserie
In Taj Bengal, Tel: 283939

Nahoum's
F-20, New Market, Lindsay Street Cal-13
Tel: 243033.

Kathleen's
12 Mirza Ghalib Street Cal-87
Near Free School Street-Lindsay Street crossing; Tel: 249293
or
1 A.J.C. Bose Road Cal-20
At Lord Sinha Road-Lower Circular Road crossing; Tel: 441205

Sub-Zero
1A Russell Street; Tel: 298359

CHINESE

China Bowl
122A Southern Ave Cal-29
On Southern Avenue opp. the Lakes;
Tel: 465042
Open 12 noon-11 p.m. Tuesdays closed.

Chinoiserie
In Taj Bengal,Tel: 283939

Ming Court
15, J.L. Nehru Road Cal-13
In Oberoi Grand; Tel: 292323/0181
Open 12.30 p.m. – 2.30 p.m. and
8 p.m. – 12 a.m.
Mondays closed.

COFFEE SHOPS

Cappuccino
17 Park Street Cal-16
In Park Hotel, 24-hour coffee shop;
Tel: 297336

Coffee Shop
Calcutta Airport Cal-52
In Hotel Airport Ashok; Tel: 575111
24 hour.

Four Seasons
235/1 A.J.C. Bose Road Cal-20
In Hotel Hindustan International;
Tel: 440061/2394 (20 lines).

Flury's
18 Park Street Cal-71
At Park Street-Middleton Row crossing;
Tel: 297664

Garden Cafe
In Oberoi Grand; Tel: 290181
24-hour coffeeshop, poolside restaurant and patisserie.

The Esplanade
In Taj Bengal; Tel: 283939
24-hour coffeeshop.

THINGS TO DO

CITY

Daily conducted excursions around Calcutta are organised by the Tourist Bureau of the Government of West Bengal (3/2 B.B.D. Bag East, Calcutta 700001, Tel: 288271). A permanent feature is the daily tour.

By Coach "in and around Calcutta", 7.30 a.m. to 11.40 a.m., Rs. 25; 12.40 p.m. to 5 p.m., Rs. 25

Daily

Dances of India
Academy of Oriental
6.30 p.m. at Hotel Oberoi Grand

Rabindra Sadan.
Cathedral Road, Calcutta-71
Tel: 28-9978

Academy of Fine Arts,
Cathedral Road, Calcutta-71
Tel: 28-4302

Sisir Mancha,
1/1 A.J.C. Bose Road, Calcutta-20
Tel: 28-1451/28-5645

Nandan, Behind Rabindra Sadan
Tel: 28-1210

Kala Mandir, 48,
Shakespeare Sarani, Calcutta-17
Tel: 44-9086/43-2197

Hotel Oberoi Grand,
15, J.L. Nehru Road, Calcutta-13
Tel: 29-0181

COUNTRY

The Tourist Bureau of the Government of West Bengal organizes tours all over the state to palces that are otherwise complicated to reach. "*Calcutta This Fortnight*" available at the Bureau (3/9 B.B.D. Bag East, Calcutta 700 001) or on major hotels lists tours being currently organized. Rates are cheap (INR 350. for two days, INR 500 for three; bus transport, accommodation, packed lunch included). The Tourist Bureau offers not only towns to specific sites, but also thematic ones such as the sacred *pithas* of Bengal or the Ganga Sagar Mela.

TOUR OPERATORS

Tourist Bureau, Govt. of West Bengal, 3/2 B.B.D. Bagh East, Tel: 288271 (for information & tours), 288272 (car, coach and launch rental).

TOUR GUIDES

Trained English speaking guides are available at fixed charges from the Government of West Bengal and the Government of India Tourist Offices

Unapproved guides are not permitted to enter protected monuments, and tourists, therefore, should actually ask for the services of guides who carry a certificate issued by the Department of Tourism.

CULTURE PLUS

MUSEUMS

Calcutta has a wealth of museums and permanent exhibition.

Academy of Fine Arts
Cathedral Road, Calcutta 700016, Tel: 44-4205
Timings: 3 p.m. - 6 p.m. Closed on Mondays.
Entry: Rs O.25
Collection: Rabindranath's paintings and personal belongings, letters, manuscripts, sculpture, old miniature paintings, lithographs, manuscripts, engravings.
Library, guide service, lectures, film shows once a month.

Asiatic Society
1 Park Street, Calcutta, Tel: 240539
Timings: 12 noon - 7 p.m. on working days; Saturdays: 12 noon - 3.30 p.m. Closed on Sundays.
Entry free.
Collection: Manuscripts, coins, paintings, sculpture.

Ashutosh Museum of Indian Art
Centenary Building (First Floor), Calcutta University, College Street, Calcutta 700073, Tel: 343014
Timings: 10.30 a.m. -15.30 p.m. Closed on Saturdays, Sundays, and university holidays
Entry free.
Collection: Stone, bronze, sculpture, paintings, coins, terracottas.

Birla Academy of Art and Culture Museum
108-109 Southern Avenue, Calcutta 700029, Tel: 469802
Timings: 3.30 p.m. - 6 p.m. Closed on Mondays.
Entry: Adult Rs 0.50, Child Rs. 0.25
Collection: Paintings of the medieval period, modern art, anthropology. Library.

Birla Industrial and Technological Museum
19A Gurusaday Road, Calcutta 700019, Tel: 447241 (3 lines) and 446102.
Timings: 10 a.m. - 5 p.m. Closed on Mondays, *Holi* and *Kali Puja* days.
Entry: Rs 1.00, free for organised student groups.
Collection: Models and exhibits on various branches of physical sciences, industry and technology including original objects.
Library, guide service, film shows from Tuesday to Friday at 3 p.m. Saturdays and Sundays at 12.30 p.m. and 3 p.m.

Birla Planetarium
96 Jawaharlal Nehru Road, Calcutta, Tel: 446619
Timings: 12 p.m. - 7.30 p.m. on weekdays; 10 a.m. - 9 p.m. on Sundays and holidays.
Entry: Rs. 2.50. Rs 1 per head for student groups; free for handicapped children, inmates from orphanages, defence personnel.
Collection: Exhibits pertaining to various fields of astronomy, astrophysics and celestial mechanics.

Indian Museum
27 Jawaharlal Nehru Road, Calcutta, Tel: 239855, 234584, PBX: 230742-43
Timings: March to November 10 a.m. - 5 p.m.; December to February 10 a.m. - 4.30 p.m. Closed on Mondays and important holidays.
Entry: Rs 0.50 Adults; Rs 0.10 Child; Friday free.
Collection: Ivory, bronze, jewellery, temple banners, costumes, masks, sculpture, terracottas, coins, manuscripts, mammals, reptiles, birds.

Marble Palace Art Gallery and Zoo
46 Muktaram Babu Street, Calcutta 700007, Tel: 343310
Timings: 10 a.m. - 4 p.m. Closed on Mondays and Thursdays.
Entry free.
Collection: Marble, bronze, woodwork, paint, glass, porcelain.

National Library
Alipore, Calcutta 700027, Tel: 455381
Timings: 10 a.m. - 5 p.m. on weekdays.
Collection: Rare books, manuscripts, original letters and notes of eminent personalities.

Nehru Children's Museum
94/1 Chowringhee Road, Calcutta 700020, Tel: 443516
Timings: 11 a.m. - 7 p.m. Closed on Mondays.
Entry: Adult Rs. 0.50
Collection: The Ramayana depicted in 1,500 miniature models; the Mahabharata depicted in 2,000 miniature models, dolls and toys, science gallery.

Netaji Museum
Netaji Research Bureau, Netaji Bhawan, 38/2 Lala Lajpat Rai Road, Calcutta 700020, Tel: 473745
Timings: 12 noon - 6 p.m. Closed on Mondays and declared holidays.
Entry: Rs 0.25
Collection: Original letters, manuscripts, paintings, sculpture, original documents and photostat copies of letters, documents concerning the life, activities and thoughts of Netaji Subhas Chandra Bose and Sarat Chandra Bose.

Rabindra Bharati Museum
6/4 Dwarkanath Tagore Lane, Calcutta 700007, Tel: 345241
Timings: 10 a.m. - 5 p.m., Saturdays 10 a.m. - 1.30 p.m. Closed on Sundays, government holidays and university holidays.
Entry free.
Collection: Paintings of Tagore, photographs, personal effects, books, journals, tapes and disc records.

State Archaeological Gallery
33, Chittaranjan Avenue (1st and 4th floors), Calcutta, Tel: 236631, 236635/6.
Timings: 12 noon - 4 p.m. Closed on Saturdays, Sundays, public and gazetted holidays.
Entry free.
Collection: Antiquities, sculpture, metal, ivory, paintings, manuscripts.

State Archaeological Museum
1 Satyendra Nath Roy Road, Behala, Calcutta 700034
Timings: 12 noon - 4 p.m. Closed on Sundays and government holidays.
Entry: Rs 0.25
Collection: Prehistory, stone artefacts, pottery, antiquities, metal, ivory, coins, manuscripts.

State Archives of West Bengal
6 Bhowani Dutta Lane, Calcutta 700034, Tel: 347182, 341133.
Timings: 10.30 a.m. - 5.30 p.m. Closed on Sundays and government holidays.
Entry free.
Collection: East India Company's administrative records from 1770-1858. Persian, Bengali, Dutch, Danish records.

Victoria Memorial Hall
1 Queen's Way, Calcutta 700071, Tel 445154
Timings: 1 March to 31 October 10 a.m. - 5 p.m.
1 November to 28 February 10 a.m. - 4 p.m. Closed on Mondays and gazetted holidays.
Entry: Adult Rs 0.30; Child Rs 0.15; Fridays: Adult Rs 0.50; Child Rs 0.25; Rs 0.15 for students and *jawans* in uniform.
Collection: Drawings, busts, statues, manuscripts, documents, stamps, coins

Museum and Art Gallery
Institute Chandernagore, The Residency, Chandernagore
Timings: Weekdays 4 p.m. - 6.30 p.m.; Sundays 11 a.m. - 5 p.m. Closed on Thursdays.
Collection: Relics of French in India and valuable documents; relics of local fighters, paintings, terracottas, antiques.

Central National Herbarium
Botanical Survey of India, India Botanic Garden, PO Botanic Garden, Howrah 711103, Tel: 67323
Timings: 10.15 a.m. - 5.15 p.m. Closed on

Sundays, 2nd Saturdays and central government holidays.
Entry free.
Collection: 1.5 million dried plant materials. Largest herbarium in South East Asia having rich collections of eminent botanists of the last 200 years. Main centre in India for taxonomic research.

ART GALLERIES

Calcutta has several art galleries, mostly private, that regularly organise exhibitions of contemporary artists:

The Calcutta Art Gallery: 10E, Ho Chi Minh Sarani. Private gallery of paintings by Indian contemporary artists – exhibition and sale. Tel 477668. Timings: 10 a.m. to 1 p.m. and 4 p.m. to 8 p.m.

Churakoot: Private art gallery, 55, Garihat Road.

Chitrabanu; Private art gallery, 162/2, Rashbehari Avenue, (Gariahat Junction).

Academy of Fine Arts; Cathedral Rd Cal-16
Beside Rabindra Sadan; Tel: 284302
Accessible by any bus going towards Rabindra Sadan

Calcutta Information Centre; 1/1 A.J.C. Bose Rd Cal-20
Beside Rabindra Sadan; Tel: 281210
Accessible by any bus going towards

Tollygunge Metro Station; permanent gallery organizing exhibitions by young painters.

Gallery 88; 28B Shakespeare Sarani, Calcutta 700017, A. Mondy.

CONCERTS

Calcutta has the largest concentration of concert halls of all Indian cities:

Rabindra Sadan, A.J.C. Bose Road, Tel: 449937

Kala Mandir, 48, Shakespeare Sarani, Tel: 449086

Biswaroopa, 2A, Raja Raj Kissen Street, Tel: 553210

Star Theatre, 79/34, Bidhan Sarani, Tel: 551139

Padatik, 6/7 Acharya Jugadish Bose Road, Calcutta 700017, Tel: 446087

Calcutta School of Music, 6B Sunny Park, Calcutta 700019 (opp Ballygunge Post Office), Tel: 471375

Namdan, behind Rabindra Sadan, Cathedral Road, Calcutta 700071, Tel: 281210

Sigir Mancha, 1/1 A.J.C. Bose Road, Calcutta 700020, Tel: 28145/285645/441451

Academy of Fine Arts, Cathedral Road, Calcutta 700071, Tel: 284302/444205

Rabindra Sadan, Cathedral Road, Calcutta 700071, Tel: 289978

Kala Mandir, 98 Shakespeare Sarani, Calcutta 700017, Tel: 449086/432197

Hotel Oberoi Grand, 15 Jahawarlal Nehru Road, Calcutta 700013, Tel: 290181

THEATRES

Most theatres are in Bangla or Hindi. Plays in English are usually staged downtown at Kala Mandir.

BENGALI PLAYS

Bijon Theatre; 5A Raja Raj Krishna Street Cal-6
Tel: 558402

Pratap Mancha; 84 A.P.C. Rd Cal-9

Tapan Theatre; 37A & 37B Sadananda Rd Cal-26
Tel: 425471

ENGLISH PLAYS

Kala Mandir; 48 Shakespeare Sarani Cal-17
Near A.J.C. Bose Road-Theatre Road crossing; Tel: 449086

HINDI PLAYS

Gyan Manch; 11 Pretoria St Cal-71

MOVIES

Newspapers publish daily the list of movie houses showing films in Calcutta. The Government of West Bengal has opened in 1988 a centre to screen Bengali movies and to arrange film festivals: Nandan (1/1 A.J.C. Bose Road, Calcutta 700020; Tel 281210). This comes in addition to the Calcutta Film Society (Mr. Borun Roy Tel 482940) the traditional organiser of film festivals in Calcutta in several halls in the city. Foreign consulates also have regular film festivals on their premises, at Nandan or at the Ice Skating Ring.

NIGHTLIFE

PUBS & BARS

There are few watering places in Calcutta: the **Esplanade** at the Taj Bengal, and the **Chowringhee Bar** at the Oberoi Grand. The Meccas for a sunset drink are the **Tippu Sultan Bar** at the Tollygunge Club and the **Verandah** at the Calcutta Club. The Tippu Sultan Bar serves the best pink gin (gin & Augustura) in town.

DISCOS

The only decent disco in town is the **Pink Elephant** at the Oberoi Grand. Admission is restricted to members, their guests and visitors staying at the hotel.

CABARETS

Calcutta had great cabarets and nightclubs. Only remain the Blue Fox, Trinca's and the Moklin Rouge on Park Street, the three of them pale reflections of what they used to be.

SHOPPING

WHAT TO BUY

Calcutta has many shopping areas. In the White Town, Government Emporium offers handicraft from Bengal, Eastern India and the rest of the country. There are also antique shops selling such items as Rajasthani jewellery, old prints and postcards, Tibetan handicraft (Chamba Lama at New Market), toys (Hobby Centre), linen (the Good Companion), ethnic chic clothes (Sacha's, Ritu's).

The bazaar area in North Calcutta spreads over a good third of the city. Many streets are specialised in one item (jewellery, sarees, musical instruments). There are shops, but also *gaddies*, (smaller shops with an elevated floor) where the owner and his staff sit on the floor, and street hawkers selling posters, bags, secondhand books or records, pets and animals (Natibagan), second-hand furniture (Mullick Bazar), firecrackers (Old China Bazar), electrical goods (Paddar Court), shoes (Bentinck Street), jewellery (P.B. Sarkar, P.C. Chandra at Bowbazar).

At Kidderpore, the Five Star Market on Circular Garden Beach Road is the largest smuggled goods market in town. In Winter, especially during the Puja festivals, melas, sorts of open-air commercial fair appear all over the city, selling keatiles, jewellery, handicraft and toys.

SILKS

Indian Silk House
Gangadeen Gupta, 1 Shakespeare Sarani, G/F Air-conditioned Market, Calcutta 700071.

BENGALI SAREES

Kundahar, 10, Sarat Banerjee Road, Tel: 481111
Meera Basu, 8, Dr. Sarat Bose Road
RMCA Basak, 48 Nandi Street (beside Ballygunge New Market)
Toontoni, 10, Satyen Datta Road, Tel: 461114

JEWELLERY

B. Sirkar, Johwree Pte Ltd, 166 B.B. Ganguli Street, Calcutta-12
P.B. Sarkar and **P.C. Chandra** on Dharamtola Street.
Saraj, 3A Camac Street (Silver jewellery from Rajasthan)

RECORDS

Second-hand records on Free School Street (Paradise Music Centre), Dharamtols Street, B.B. Ganguly Street (Chora Bazar)
Santosh Kumar Sarkar, Hg Chora Bazar.

ANTIQUES

Saroj: 3A Camac Street Calcutta 700016 Tel 291002
Oberoi Ground has an antique shop.

TEXTILES/CLOTHES

Ananda: 13, Russell Street.
A.W. Mondal: 13/3 Collins Lane, 2/F, Calcutta 700016 (table linen, bedspreads, handkerchief)
Burlington's of Calcutta Bootery: Park Mansions, 43, Park Street
Guys N' Dolls: 14, Sudder Street
Jete: Park Centre, Park Street
Karma Kutir: 32, Ballygunge Place
Modern Hand Embroidery: Village Kadipara, P.O. Babnan. Dist. Hooghly (table linen. To be contacted by telegramme. Will come to your hotel).
Nekita: 650 Ballygunge Circular Road.
Ritu's Boutique: 46A Rafi Ahmed Kidwai Road.
The Good Companion: 13C Russell Street, Calcutta 700016
Women's Friendly Society: 29 Park Lane, Calcutta 700016
Victoria Terminus: Hindusthan Road

BOOKS

Oxford Book and Stationery: 17 Park Street, Calcutta 70001, Tel: 240831/240832
Modern Book Depot: 78 Chowringhee Centre, opp. New Empire Cinema, Calcutta 700013, Tel: 290933/293102 (books on anthropology and the North-East)
Seagull Bookshop: 560 Mirza Ghalib Street (Free School Street), Calcutta 700016 (books on theatre, cinema, social sciences)
Day's Publishing: 13 Bankin Chatterjee Street, Calcutta 700073
The Sun Revolves Round the Earth once a Year: 22, Ganesh Majhi Lane, Howrah.
Chuckervertty, Chartterjee & Co.: 1st Floor, 15 College Square, Calcutta 700078
Punthi Pushtale: 136/4B Bidham Sarani POB 16602, Calcutta 700009 (old books)
Second hand books on Free School Street, on Sudder Street. Old National Geographic issues on the pavement next to the Oberoi Hotel in Chowringhee.
every year at the end of January the Calcutta Book Fair on Cathedral Road on the Meridan attracts over a million visitors.

TEA

Dolly's Tea Shop: CIT Complex, Dhakuria

HANDICRAFT

Airport Hotel Souvenir Shop (Krishnanager clay figurines of characters of the Raj period).
M.H. Rickshaw Co.: 44/1 Ratu Sirkar Lane, Calcutta 700001 (rickshaw!)
Bengal Home Industries: 57 Chowringhee
Government Emporia: open-air meaLs.

FLOWERS

Flower Range: New Market
Jute Box: 40H Free School Street, Calcutta 700016

GOVERNMENT EMPORIA

Central Cottage Industries Emporium, 7, J.L. Nehru Road
Handloom House, 2, Lindsay Street
Khadi Gramodyog Bhawan, 28, Chittaranjan Avenue
Assam Emporium, 8, Russell Street

Bihar Emporium, 145, Rashbehari Avenue
Kashmir Art Emporium, 12, J.L. Nehru Road
Cauvery, Karnataka State Arts and Crafts Emporium, 7, J.L. Nehru Road
Manjusha, West Bengal Handicrafts Development Corpn., 7/1D, Lindsay Street
Meghalaya Emporium, 9, Russell Street
Phulkari, (Punjab), 26B, Camac Street
Rajasthali, 30E, J.L. Nehru Road
Refugee Handicrafts, 2A & 3A, Gariahat Road
Uttar Pradesh Govt. Handicrafts, 12B, Lindsay Street
New Shopping Complex in South Calcutta – Dhakhinapan, C.I.T. Complex, Dhakuria. State Government Sales Emporia under one roof.

SPORTS

CLUBS

If the night life of Calcutta is of limited interest, there is an active social and sports life revolving around clubs. There are lunch clubs, country clubs and sports clubs:

The Bengal Club; 1/1, Russell Street, Tel: 299233. Affliations: Royal Overseas League – London Travellers' Club – London, St. James' Club – London, Sind Club - Karachi, Hong Kong Club, Welington Club - New Zealand.
The Calcutta Club; 241, Acharya Jagadish Chandra Bose Road, Tel: 443318. Affilations: National Liberal Club - London.
Tollygunge Club; 120 Deshpran Sasmal Road, Tel: 463141. Affilations: The Royal Overseas League – London, Royal Bangkok Club, Dubai Country Club, Qatar Doha Club.
Saturday Club; 7 Wood Street, Tel: 445411. Affliations: The American Club, Singapore; Chittagong Club; Columbia Club, Indianapolis; Dhaka Club; Doha Club, Qatar; Hong Kong Football Club; The National Liberal Club, London; United Oxford and Cambridge University Club, London.
Royal Calcutta Gold Club, 18 Golf Club Road, Tel: 421352.
Calcutta Polo Club, 51, J.L. Nehru Road, Tel: 442031
Calcutta Racquet Club, Maidan, near St. Paul's Cathedral, Tel: 441152
Royal Calcutta Turf Club, 1 Russell Street, Tel: 291103
Calcutta Swimming Club, 1 Strand Road, Tel: 282894
Calcutta Rowing Club, 15, Rabindra Sarobar, Tel: 463343
Mohan Bagan Athletic Club, Maidan, Tel: 281634
East Bengal Club (Football), Maidan, Tel: 284642
Calcutta Cricket-Football Club, 19/1, Gurusaday Road, Tel: 478721
Bengal Rowing Club, Rabindra Sarobar, Tel: 411751
Lake Club (Rowing), Rabindra Sarobar, Tel: 462538.
Conclave, Acharya Jagadish Chandra Bose Road
The South Club, Elgin Road

Other clubs:

Hotel Oberoi Grand, 15, J.L. Nehru Road, Tel: 290181
Castle Corner Yoga Centre, 3A Albert Road, Tel: 434801
Yoga Shakti Mission Trust, Gurusaday Road

Most clubs accept visitors as temporary members on proper introduction by a resident permanent member. Visitors without local acquaintances may also contact the Club Secretary. Members of clubs abroad with reciprocal agreements with clubs in Calcutta must get a letter of introduction from their club before leaving for India.

Parks & Reserves

PARKS & GARDENS

The main public park in Calcutta is the Maidan, over 1,000 acres (hectares) of green space in the middle of the White Town. At the northern end of the Maidan are the small Eden Gardens with a small lake for boating. South of the Maidan are the Belvedere, the Agro-Horticultural Society gardens, the Zoological Gardens, the Dhakuria Lakes and the Tollygunge Club.

The Belvedere is the estate on which stands the Vice-regal Lodge, now the National Library. The Agro-Horticultural Society gardens are famous for their flower-shows and open-air concerts. In the Zoological Gardens is a small lake where birds spend the winter, escaping the harsh climate of Siberia. The Dhakuria Lakes are surrounded by a public park and ??? clubs; the main activity there is rowing. A toy train for children runs around the lakes. The Tollygunge Club accepts temporary members. Its park is recommended for horse-rides in the early morning or at the end of the afternoons.

There is hardly any green space in North Calcutta. On the Howrah side are the Botanical Gardens, the main attractions are the largest banyan tree in the world, the Orchid and Palm House, as well as th eornamental avenue lined with palms. Most gardens and parks are crowded during the weekend and on holidays, but empty the rest of the week.

East of Calcutta, on the way to the airport, the Salt Lakes are now partly reclaimed but still constitute a unique environment with berries (fish-farms). A common bird there is the dowster, a variety of carmaran.

South of Calcutta, in the delta, the Sunderban Wildlife Reserve has the largest concentration of tigers in the world. Domestic tourists must obtain a permit from the Field Director, Sunderban Tiger Reserve, P.O. Canning, District 24 Parganas. Foreigners must apply to the Secretary, Dept of Forests, Government of West Bengal, at Writers' Building. Individual trips are difficult to organise. It is advisable to join two-day tours organised regularly in winter by the Tourist Bureau of the Government of West Bengal (3/2 B.B.D. Bag).

Special Information

DOING BUSINESS

Calcutta is the only large city in eastern India. Together with Bombay, it is also the city through which industrialisation entered India. A good third of India's top groups are based in Calcutta – Marwani families (Birla, Goenka, Jhawar, Bangur, Singhania, Khaitan, Bajoria), Khatris from the Punjab (Thappar). The Parsee Tata group of Bombay generates a good part of its turnover in Eastern India (Tata steel, Tata tea). Its management for the region is based in Calcutta, in the Tata Centre, one of the tallest buildings of Calcutta. The city is also the seat of many pakkha companies as firms formerly or still controlled by British companies are called: Indian Tobacco, Inchcape, McNeil Magur, Shaw Wallace. Contact with Calcutta's companies can be established by contacting the local Chamber of Commerce (Indian Chamber for Marwani Companies, Bengal Chamber of Commerce and Industry for pakkha companies) or foreign trade commission.

Although there are in the area many sunset industries (heavy machinery, steel, jute), some activities such as tea are still flourishing.

CHILDREN

The hot and sultry monsoon is not recommended for children. The right time is the mild Calcutta winter, much warmer than

Dehli's.

The main attraction is the Nehru Children's Museum. It exhibits toys from most states of India and from all over the world. The chief attractions are the Mahabharata and Ramayana galleries where both legends are told to children through dioramas with clay figurines. The museum operates a toy train going around the Dhakuria Lakes.

Finally, the Zoological Gardens deserve a good half-day. Shops but also open-air fairs sell wooden and metal toys that are found nowhere in developed countries. In the evening, children can go to the Children's Little Theatre, Aban Mahal (tel: 461200).

PILGRIMAGES

There are many pilgrimage places in and around Calcutta. Most of the 51 pithas or places where fell fragments of Shakti's body are in West Bengal. The best known one is the **Kali Temple** at Kalighat in Calcutta proper. **Dakshineshwar** and **Belur Marth** in the northern outskirts are frequented chiefly by devotees of Ramakrishna and Vivekananda. **Tarkeshwar**, 80 kilometres (50 miles) north-west, is a Tantric pilgrimage centre. **Mayapur** and **Nabadwip**, 170 kilometres (105 miles) north on the eastern side of the Hooghly, are places of Vaishnab worship.

The headquarters of the ISKON movement are in **Mayapur**. Bauls gather for three nights of devotional singing at **Balpur**, 180 kilometres (110 miles) northwest, from January 14 to 17. **Vishnupur**, 170 kilometres (105 miles) west, becomes on Jhapan in August, a centre of snake worship. Some 120 kilometres (75 miles) south of Calcutta, **Sagar Awip** is the venue of the *Ganga Sagar Mela* from January 13 to 15.

Bihar is another major pilgrimage area with the **Parasnath Hills** where 20 out of 25 Jain *tirthankara* (prophets) reached nirvana, the **Konhara ghat** near Patna, the venue of the *Sonepur Mela*, both a religious Sun festival and the largest cattle and animal fair in the world. Above all, Bihar is where the Buddha attained illumination and preached. Every year in winter, thousands of pilgrims visit **Nalanda**, **Rajghir**, **Gaya** and **Bodhgaya**, all places connected with the life of the Buddha. In Orissa, the main pilgrimage centre is **Puri** where the *Rath gatra* festival in late June - early July draws several hundreds of thousands of pilgrims.

PHOTOGRAPHY

Indians love to take photographs, to have their picture taken, but also to watch tourists take picture. Often several smiling faces will appear around the one you want to take a picture of. As a matter of courtesy, ask for permission before taking a photograph. In case of portrait, keep unwanted subjects at bay by compromising on a group shot afterwards. Avoid Polaroid photography if there are too many people around. Each one will insist on having his portrait taken.

There are several taboos: women at the bathing ghat, cremation ceremonies. Avoid political meetings. Photographying Howrah Station, Dum Dum Airport and the Hooghly Bridge could lead to trouble. Special permission of Archaeological Survey of India, New Dehli, is required for use of tripod and artificial light to take photographs of archaeological monuments.

Photography in the wildlife sanctuaries is allowed on payment of a prescribed fee which varies from one sanctuary to another. Full particulars can be obtained from the nearest Government of India Tourist Office.

The best season for taking photographs is winter. The sky is blue and the light in the early morning and after 4 p.m. has beautiful reddish and golden hues. Photographying during the monsoon is not easy. Because of the high humidity, details do not come out sharp and colours are bluish and flat. Opening by 1 f.stop does not help as the skylight is too luminous and white. Closing by 1 f.stop does not help either as details will then appear even less clearly.

It is advised to bring one own's films for slides or Polaroid pictues. For paper print locally produced Kodak gold films is available. Processing should be done preferably outside of India for paper prints; even more so for slides. There are few labs and photoshops. The main one is Bombay Photo Stores on Park Street.

LANGUAGE

Three languages are spoken in Calcutta - Bangla, English, and Hindustani. Both Bangla and Hindustani are Sanskritic languages. Bangla has declensions but no genders. Hindustani, the language of everyday life in Northern and Central India, from where artificially formed Hindi originated has genders, but no declensions. Fluency in English is high in Calcutta. Even if a visitor asks a question in Bangla or Hindustani, the reply will be in English.

A few words in Bangla or Hindustani will certainly help establish contact, but for the rest, the conversation will be in English, or rather in Indian English. Indeed, English, as spoken in India, has incorporated words from Asian languages enough for a specialised dictionary, the Hobson-Jobson, to be compiled.

Forms of address vary, depending on the sex, the age, the race, the religion. Sir, Madam, Miss can be used on all occasions.

Bengali gentlemen can be addressed by adding "Babu" to their first name. Mr Gangaprasad Mukherjee will be called Gangaprasad Babu. Europeans are called Mr, Madam, Miss but Sahib, Memsahib, Baba (or Master for boys, Missy for girls) are still used, even among the Indians, as a mark of humble respect that smacks in some cases of colonialism fossilised. Policemen, anybody in uniform can be called "Officer Sahib", Sikhs "Sardarji", Nepalis "Bahadur", old Muslims "Maulana", young man as "Brother, Bra or Bhai". To attract attention, say "accha" loudly.

There are several forms of greeting : "Hello" is widespread as well as "Salaam". You can also say "namaste" or "namaskar" in Hindi, or "nomoshkar" in Bangla, "assalam alekum" in Urdu. When leaving, use "Bye-bye", "Salaam", "huda hafez" in Urdu, "namaste" in Hindustani, "ashi" or "ashbo" (I am coming back) in Bangla.

Good language manuals to learn Bangla are difficult to find. For Hindustani, *Hindustani in three months* (Hugo Language System, Vikas Publishing House, Delhi) is perfect. It is always interesting to carry a Sanskrit manual along to understand names of temples places or persons. Michael Coulson's *Sanskrit* (Teach Yourself Books) is excellent. Both Hindi and Bangla are covered by *Languages of Asia, a Traveller's Phrasebook*, by Prof. Charles Hamblin (Toppan/Angus Robertson).

ashustho : untouchable
Anglo-Indian, or "AI" : Eurasian. Has replaced Eurasian found derogatory. First meaning before the shift : Creole, Indian born British
alpana : floor painting with symbols of fertility (fish, bangles, jewellery, footsteps of Lakshmi, the Goddess of Fortune), drawn with a paste made of rice-powder or flour mixed with water, usually round or square like a mandala, on such occasions as weddings, the Lakshmi festival or other functions.

Bangal : from Eastern Bengal
bungalow : house
betki, bekti : a variety of fish
basha : hut
Baul : Bengali bard
budgerow :
breast cutlet : braised cutlet
bearer : head-servant, waiter
bhang : marijuana-leaf pasted with milk. The traditional drink of all castes and classes during the Holy festival
burga : Muslim veil
Blighty : the U.K. (from willayet, the country in Persian)
Banya : trade caste
boli : sacrifice
Brahmin : priestly cast
bhadraloke : the Bengali Honest Man
Babu : the Bengali man
Bhangra Disco : modern dance, combination of Punjabi Bhangra and Disco Music. Born in London, has reached Calcutta.
Burra bun, Baro Din : Christmas (the Big Day)
box walla : entrepreneur

chokidar : watchman
chukka : time during a polo match

chokra : young kid
Cal : Calcutta (Affectionate name)

darwan : door-keeper, gate-keeper
dak : mail
Darj : Darjeeling (affectionate)
dhobi : clothe-washer
dhoti : the Bengali sarong

fakir : Muslim, sufi, holy man. Equivalent of Sadhu.
fresh : new (fresh passport, fresh copy of newspaper)
frisk : to search

Ganga Jhol : the water of the Ganges
gothi : from Western Bengal
gari, gharry : car, carriage
godown : warehouse
Goonda : "antisocial", "sea-urchin" are other Calcutta equivalents
garden house : house on the river
garden : plantation (tea-garden)
gur : date-palm sugar
gali, gully : lane

hartal : general strike
hath gori : hand-pulled goods cart. Pullers are called *Hath Gari Walla*
Hindi Belt, Hindustan : Northern, Central and Western India by opposition to the former Madras and Bombay Presidencies.
hackney : fiacre
hookah : water-pipe made with a dried coconut
hilsa, hilish : river fish, part saltwater. Eaten smoked. A Calcutta Specialty
hijra, or *hijra sara* : eunuch

jira, jeera : cumin
jaljeera, jhol jeera, jeera pani : cumin juice
jatra : street theatre
jaggery : date-palm sugar

kirtan : religious song
kaestho : the caste of doctors, writers, clerks, philosophers.
kshatriya : warrior caste. There are few kshatriyas in Bengal
Ko-hai : old Indra hand
kaccha : young, unripe, immature, too young
kobiraj : coverage. Egg covering a cutlet

lathi : Police bludgeon ("Police lathi-charged a demonstration today")
load-shedding, *lod* in Bangla : power cut

Madrasi : from the South (Tamil Nadu, Kerala, Andhra Pradesh)
mela : fair (Book Mela) or large religious festival (Ganga Sagar Mela)
munshi : teacher
maidah :
mordha :
murthi : image, statue
Mogh : Buddhist from Chittagong. Moghs are the best cooks in Calcutta
Mughlai : Moghul
machan : observation tower in a Game Reserve

neel kothi : indigo planter's bungalow
nullah : canal
nor'wester' : storm

pankawalla : servant in charge of producing wind with the *panka*, or *punkah*, a large swinging fan made of a piece of cloth stretched on a rectangular frame
peon : office boy
para : neighbourhood. Para boys; local youths
payal : ankle chain
purda, purda system : custom in which women are not exposed to public scrutiny. They have their private apartments the zenana, and, in the case of the Muslim women, wear a burga (veil). The custom is disappearing.
pen, paan : betel
paan paraag : betel granules
puchkha walla : food hawkers
Puja : Bengali festival
pandal : street structure erected to contain the murthi during *pujas*
pakka : good, solid, cooked

roko : blockade, in protest against an issue. During Rail-Roko, demonstrators sit on the rails, during Rasta-Roko or Road-Roko, on the pavement

Sradh : religious ceremony in the memory of a deceased
shamyana : tent, dais, used for outdoor functions
satyagraha : passive resistance through non-obedience, boycott, blockade
sadhu : Indian holy man (*Fakir* for Muslims)

syce : stable-lad
shroff : money-changer, cashier
sangeet : songs
Sahib : Brown Sahib, or Kala Sahib
Shakti : the female consort and Energy of a God. Shaktism : the cult of Shakti

taziya : model of the graves of Wassan and Wussein carried by Shiites at Ashoura
thela : hand-pulled goods cart. Pullers are called the *pawalla*
tonga : fiacre
thana : police station
trailer-bus : phenomenon unique in Calcutta
thali : metal plate

Vaishnab : Vishnu devotee
vomitory : exit

Walla : person. Delhi-walla, "Delhiite"

zamindar : tax-collector, land-lord after 1793

FURTHER READING

GENERAL

- Rai, Raghu, *Calcutta*, Singapore : Time Books, 1989.
- Lapierre, Dominique, *The City of Joy*.
- Racine, Jean, Calcutta; *La ville, sa crise, et le débat sur la planificatron et l'awénagement urbain*, Paris : Maison des Sciences de l'Homme. 1986
- J.P. Losty, *Calcutta, City of Palaces*, London : British Library - 1980
- Mitra, Ashok, *Calcutta Diary*, Calcutta Rupa 1983
- Singh, Raghubir, *Calcutta, the Home and the Street*, Thames & Hudson, 1988
- Singh, Raghubir, *Calcutta, photographs*, Hong Kong: The Perennial Press, 1975
- Moorehouse, Geoffrey, *Calcutta, the city revealed*, Harmondsworth, Middlesex : Penguin, 1971 (reprints)

PEOPLE

- Sealy I. Allan, *The Trotter Nama*, London : Viking, 1989 (Anglo-Indians)
- Timbery, Thomas, *The Marwaris, from Traders to Industrialists*, Delhi: Vikas 1978 (Marwaris)
- Wacziarg, Francis & North, Aman, *The Painted Walls of Shekhavati*, Delhi: Vikas, 1982 (Marwaris)
- Jenkins, Sir Owain, *Merchant Prince*, London : BACSA 1987 (British businesswomen during the Raj days)
- Seth, Mesroub Jacob, *Armenians in India*, Calcutta : Rupa 1937 reprinted 1984 (Armenians)
- Chopra, Dr P.N., *Religious and Communities of India*, Delhi:Vikas 1982

ARTS

- Porg Desmond, *Calcutta, an Artist's Impression*, Calcutta: The Statesman 1969
- *The Performing Arts*, Special issue, Bombay : Marg Publications 1984
- *Trends and Transitions in Indian Arts*, Vol XXXVI no.2, Bombay : Marg Publications
- Mukherjee, B.N., *Kalighat Patas, Album of Art Treasures*, Calcutta : Indian Museum, 1987
- Paul, Ashit, editor, *Woodcut Prints of Nineteenth Century Calcutta*, Calcutta : Seagull Books 1983
- Shellim, Maurice, *India and the Danniell's*, London: Spink, 1988
- Shellim, Maurice, *Oil paintings by Sir Charles d Ogly, 1781-1895*, London : Spink, 1989
- The Indian Museum, The Birla Academy of Art and Culture, the Academy of Fine Arts, Dunlop India, ITC (Indian Tobacco), the Rabindra Bharati Society regularly publish portfolios of reproduction of paintings by major Calcutta and Bengali artists.
- Archer, Mildred, *Company Drawings in the India Office Library*, London : Her Majesty's Stationery Office, 1972
- Archer, Mildred, *Indian Popular Painting in the India Office Library*, London: Her Majesty's Stationery Office, 1975

- Archer, William, *Kalighat Paintings*, London: Her Majesty's Stationery Office, 1971
- "The Art of Jamini Roy, *Calcutta*, Birla Academy of Art and Culture. 1987
- Gupta, R.P., *Visions, Modern Bengali Painting and Graphic Art*, Calcutta : Ladies Study Group and Indian Chamber of Commerce.1986
- *Arts of Bengal and Eastern India*, Calcutta: Crafts Council of West Bengal: 1986
- *Mahamaya, The Crafts and Craftsmen of Eastern India*, Calcutta : Crafts Council of West Bengal, 1986
- Godrey, Dheroza & Rohatgi, Pauline, *Scenic Splendous - India through the printed image*, London : British Library, 1989

CULTURE

- Col. Henry Yule & A.C. Burnell, *Hobson-Jobson, a glossary of collognial Anglo-Indian words and phrases, and of Kindred terms, etymological, historical, geographical and discursive*, New Delhi : Munshiram Manoharlal, 1984 (reprints)
- Tagore, Rabindranath, *Selected Works*, London, Delhi : Penguin. 1988 (reprint)
- Kipling, Rudyard, *Selected Verse*, London : Penguin Books 1977 (includes A Tale of Two Cities, The Overland Mail, One viceroys Resigns, The Song of the Cities).
- Dubois, Abbot J.A, *Hindu Manners, Customs and Ceremonies*, Delhi: Oxford University Press. 1983 reprint

HISTORY

- Basham, A.L., *The Wonder that was India*, Calcutta : Rupa 1954
- Cotton, W.E.A., *Calcutta Old and New*, Calcutta: General Printers and Publishers 1980
- Nayak, N.K., editor, *Calcutta, 200 years - A Tollygunge Club Perspective*, Calcutta : Tollygunge Club, 1981
- Davies, Philip, *Splendours of the Raj*, New Delhi : Dass Media in association with John Murray, London 1985
- Bose, S.K., *Netaji, a Pictorial Biography*, Calcutta : Ananda Publishers & Netaji Research Bureau 1984
- Perkins, Roger, *The Regiments of Empire*, Newton Abbott, Devon TQ12 1XV : published by author. 1990
- Edwards, Stuart, Ivor, *The Calcutta of Begum Johnson*, London : BACSA, 1990 (76.1/2 Chartfield Avenue, London SW15-6HQ)
- Das Gupta, Ashim and Pearson M.N., *India and the Indian Ocean 1500-1800*, Calcutta : Oxford University Press. 1987
- Barr, Pat, *The Dust in the Balance : British Women in India 1905-1945*, London: Hamish Hamilton. 1989
- Blechyuden, Kathleen, *Calcutta Past and Present*, Calcutta : General Printers and Publishers 1978 (reprint)
- Nair, P.Thankappan, *A History of Calcutta's Streets*, Calcutta : Firma KLM. 1986
- Ballhatchet, Kenneth, *Race, Sex and Class under the Raj*, Delhi, Vikas, 1979

RELIGIONS

- Wilkins, W.J., *Hindu Mythlogy*, Calcutta: Rupa, 1988
- Mookerjee, Ajit, *Tantra Art*, New York, New Delhi, Ravi Kumar, 1971
- Tagore Rabindranath, *The Religion of Man*, London : Unwin, latest reprint 1988
- Bhattacharya, Deben, *Songs of the Birds of Bengal*, Calcutta New York : Grove Press. 1969
- Anboyer Desnoyees, Jacqueline & Nou Jean-Louis, *Buddha, a Pictorial History of His Life and Legacy*, Delhi : Roli Roli Books 1983
- Bandyopadbyay, Pranab, *The Goddess of Tantra*, Calcutta : Pushti Pushtak. 1987
- Chopra, Dr P.N., *Religions and Communities of India*, Delhi:Vikas, 1982.

GUIDEBOOKS

- Israel, Samuel & Grewal, *Bikram, India-Insight Guide*, Hong Kong : APA Productions. 1985
- Mc Cutchion, David, *Brick Temples of Bengal*, Princeton : University Press 1983
- Shellim, Maurice, *The South Park*

Street Cemetary, London : BACSA 1986
- Labonchardiere, Basil, *The French Cementary, Calcutta*, London : BACSA 1983
- Michell, George, *The Islamic Heritage of Bengal*, Paris : UNESCO 1984
- Woodcock, Martin, *Birds of the Indian Subcontinent*, London : Collins 1980
- Israel, Samuel, Sinclair, Toby; Grewal, Bikram, *Indian Wildlife*, Hong Kong : APA Productions. 1987
- Nicholson, Louise, *India in Luxury. A Pratctical Guide for the Discerning Traveller*, London : Century Publishing. 1985.

OUTSIDE CALCUTTA

- Van Strydanck, Gary; Imaeda Yoshio & Françoise, *Bhutan, a Kingdom of the Eastern Himalayas*, Boston : Shambhala, 1985
- Berwick, Dennison, *A Walk along th Ganges*, London : Century Hutchinson, 1986
- Carralho, S.A., *The Bandel Church*, Krishnanagar, West Bengal : South Joseph's Press - (For sale at the Bandel Church)
- Singh, Raghubir, *Ganga, Sacred River of India*, Hong Kong : The Perenial Press. 1984

USEFUL ADDRESSES

TOURIST INFORMATION

Government of India Tourist Office, 4 Shakespeare Sarani, Tel: 443521.
India Tourism Development Corporation, 46C, Jawaharlal Nehru Road, Tel: 440922.
Calcutta Information Centre, 1/1 AJC Bose Road, Tel: 441451,
Tourist Bureau (Government of West Bengal),
3/2 B.B.D. Bagh, Tel: 238271.
West Bengal Tourist Information Counter Calcutta Airport (Domestic) Tel 572611 Extension 440
Howrah Station, Tel 663518.
Government of India Tourist Information Counter
Calcutta Airport, Tel 572611 Extension 444
ITDC, 46C Chowringhee Road Cal-71, Tel 440922

LOCAL OFFICES

Agra
191, The Mall, Tel: 72377

Aurangabad
Krishna Vilas,
Station road, Tel: 4817

Bangalore
K.F.C. Building
48, Church Street
Tel: 579517

Bhubaneshwar
B-21, Kalpana Area
Tel: 54203

Bombay
123-Maharishi
Karve Road
Opp. Churchgate
Tel: 291585/293144

Calcutta
'Embassy'
4-Shakespeare Sarani
Tel: 441475/443521/441402

Cochin
Willington Island
Tel: 6045

Guwahati
B.K. Kakati Road
Ulubari, Tel: 31381

Hyderabad
3-6-369/A/25&26
Sandozi Building
2nd Floor
26 Himayat Nagar
Tel: 66877

Imphal
Old Lambulane
Jail Road, Tel: 21131

Jalpur
State Hotel, Tel: 72280

Khajuraho
Near Western
Group of Temples
Tel: 47

Madras
154-Anna Salai Road
Tel: 88686/88685

Nahariagun
Sector 'C', Tel: 328

New Delhi
88-Janpath
Tel: 3320008/3320005/
3320342/3320109/
3320266

Panajl
Communidade Building
Church Square
Tel: 3412

Patna
Paryatan Bhavan
Bir Chand, Patel Marg
Tel: 26721

Port Blair
VIP Road;
Junglighat P.O.
Port Blair
(Andaman & Nicobar Islands),
Tel: 21006

Shillong
G.S. road;
Police Bazar
Tel: 25632

Trivandrum
Trivandrum Airport

Varanasi
15-B, The Mall
Tel: 43744

OVERSEAS OFFICES

AUSTRALIA
Sydney
Level 5,
65 Elizabeth Street
Sydney NSW 2000
Tel: (02) 232-1600/1796
Fax: (02) 2233003

CANADA
Toronto
60 Bloor Street
West Suite No. 1003
Toronto
Ontario M4 W3 B8
Tel: 416-962-3787/88
Fax: 416-962-6279

FRANCE
Paris
8 Boulevard de la
Madeleine
75009 Paris
Tel: 42-65-83-86/77-06

HOLLAND
Amsterdam
Rokin 9-15
1012 Amsterdam
Tel: 020-208991

ITALY
Milan
Via Albricci 9
Milan 20122
Tel: 804952/8053506

JAPAN
Tokyo
Pearl Building
9-18 Chome Ginza
Chuo Ku, Tokyo 104
Tel: (03) 571-5062/3

MALAYSIA
Kuala Lumpur
Wisma Hlm
Jalan Raja Chulan
50200 Kuala Lumpur
Tel: (04-04) 2425285
Fax: 00603-2425301

SINGAPORE
Singapore
05-01 Podium Block
5th Floor
Ming Court Hotel
Tanglin Road
Singapore 1024
Tel: 2355737/2353804
Fax: 0065-7328820

SPAIN
Madrid
C/o Embassy of India
Avenida PIO XII 30-32,
28016-Madrid
Tel: 4570209/265

SWEDEN
Stockholm
Sveavagen 9-11
1st Floor, S-111 57
Stockholm, 11157
Tel: 08-215081/101187
Fax: 46-8-210186.

SWITZERLAND
Geneva
1-3 rue de Chantepoulet
1201 Geneva
Tel: 022-321813/315680
Fax: 0041-227315660

THAILAND
Bangkok
Singapore Airlines Building
3rd Floor
62/5 Thaniya road
Bangkok
Tel: 2352585

UAE
Dubai
PO Box 12856
NASA Building
Al Makhtoum Road
Deira, Dubai
Tel: 274848/274199

Bahrain
P.O. Box 11294, Bahrain
Tel: 715713

UNITED KINGDOM
London
7 Cork Street
London WIX 2AB
Tel: 01-437-3677/8
Direct Line: 01-434-6612
Fax: 01-494-1048

USA
New York
30 Rockefeller road
Suite 15
North Mezzanine
New York NY 10020
Tel: 212-586-4901/2/3
Fax: 001-212-582-3274

Chicago
230 North Michigan
Avenue, Chicago
Illinois 60601
Tel: 312-236-6899
312-236-7869
Fax: 001-312-236-7870

Los Angeles
3550 Wilshire Road
Room 204, Los Angeles
California 90010
Tel: (213) 380-8855
Fax: (213) 380-6111

WEST GERMANY
Frankfurt
77 (lll) Kaiserstrasse
D-6000 Frankfurt AM
MAIN-1
Tel: 235423/24
Fax: 069-234724

Art/Photo Credits

Photographs by

Page 186, 187	Birla Art Academy
3, 38, 49, 63, 84/85, 86, 87, 105, 110, 118, 119, 120/121, 126/127, 138, 141, 143, 151, 156, 157, 161, 163, 172, 188/189, 204, 228/229, 235	Das, Sujoy
220	Denzau, Getrud & Helmut
37, 40/41, 42, 46, 47L, 52, 53, 54/55, 56/57, 58/59, 62L, 62R, 64L, 64 R, 65L, 65R, 66L, 66R, 67L, 67R, 80L, 80R, 81, 82/83, 88, 89, 92/93, 94, 96, 98, 100, 102, 104, 107, 111L, 111R, 112, 113, 120/121, 122/123, 124/125, 140, 142, 145, 149, 150, 154, 158, 162, 164/165, 173, 174/175, 179, 180R, 181, 182, 183, 185, 190/191, 193, 194, 195, 196, 197, 198, 199, 200, 201, 202/203, 206L, 206R, 207L, 207R, 208, 209, 211, 212, 213, 215, 216, 217, 218, 219, 222/223, 224, 225, 226, 227, 232, 233, 234, 236, 237, 239	Gelenine, Michel
146, 147, 169	Höfer, Hans
39TL	House Of Birlas
36	Imperial War Museum, London
18/19, 22, 25, 101, 139, 159, 160, 176	Massot, Gilles
cover, 9, 14/15, 16/17, 20/21, 114/115, 133, 152/153, 171, 240	Naylor, Kim
90	Private Collection
26/27, 30, 31, 32, 33, 34, 35L, 35R, 39BL, 39TR, 43, 44, 47R, 48, 51, 60/61, 76R, 91, 95, 103, 108/109, 116, 134/135, 144, 166, 168, 170, 178, 230	Private Collection (M. Gelenine)
205	RIJKS Museum Amsterdam
221	Singh, Brijendra
99	Siniscal, Jeanine Vatin
68/69, 70/71, 73, 74L, 74R, 75L, 75R, 76L, 77, 79, 180L	Sen, Puritosh
72	Victoria Memorial Hall
Maps	Berndtson & Berndtson
Illustrations	Klaus Geisler
Visual Consulting	V. Barl

INDEX

A

Aldeen, 151
Academy of Fine Arts, 148
Achipur, 52, 53
Afghanistan, 36, 45, 48
Agri-Horticultural Society's Gardens, 177
Air-Conditioned Market, 110
Ajanta, 75
Albert Hall Coffee Shop, 162
Alipore, 47
Allahabad Bank, 142
Anandamath (Bankim Babu's poem), 36
American Independence War, 32
Amir, Shaik Mohammad, 73
Ananta Vasudeva Mandir, 197
Andrews, St., 33, 142
Anglo-Indian Food, 119
Anglo-Indians (formerly called Eurasians), 49
antarajali, 167
Arabian Nights (illustrations), 76
Arampur, 221
Archbishop's House, (residence of the Catholic archbishop), 148
Armenia, 50
Armenian Ghat, 169
Armenians, 29, 33, 49, 50
Arunchal Pradesh, 200
Aryans, 61, 199
Ashoka, (Emperor), 226, 227
ashram, 194, 208
Ashura, 49
Asian Games, (1962 India beat Korea in foot ball for gold medal), 88
Asiatic Society, 34
asvamedha jajna, (horse sacrifices), 215
Assam State Emporium, 112
Assam, 35, 36, 37, 52, 90, 98, 200
Assembly House, 144
Aurobindo, Sri (terrorist, then preacher), 35
Australia, 50, 52
Azad Hind, (provisional govt. of Chittarajam Das), 36

B

B.B.D. Bag (Binoy, Badal, Dinesh revolutionaries), 132, 140, 141
Babu, 34, 45, 46
    Bankim, 34, 36
    Culture, 46
bagda chingri (tiger prawns), 117
Baghbazar, 46, 171, 172

Baij Ramkinker (sculptor), 78
Bain Kunth Temple, 157
Bakhim, 233
Bakkhali, 216
Bakraid (festival), 49, 102, 139, 170
Ballygunge, 47, 132, 182
Band Stand, 168
Bande Mataram (Hail thee, Motherland), 36, 63
Bandel de Hooghly, 210
Bandel, 29, 151, 193
Banerjee, Shute (cricketer), 87
Banerjee, Surendranath (nationalist), 35
Bangal (usually refugees), 45
Bangal Food, 117
Bangladesh War, 38
Bangladesh, 45, 132
Bangurs, 47
Bankibazar, 29
Bankim, Chandra Chatterjee, 24, 34
Bansberia, 210
Baptists, 24, 34
    missionaries, 34
Barabazar, 48, 156
'Barefoot' Babus, 88
Barrackpore, 207, 210
    Park, 150
Barvalis, 218
bas-relief, 78, 147, 199, 205, 210, 216
Basul, Jyoti (Chief Minister, Murkerjee's deputy), 38
batis (bowls), 118
Battle of Plassey, 31
Baul Mela (festival), 67, 97
Baul, Purna Das, 67
Bauls, 67
Beggars, 50
Begum, Ghasiti, 30
Beliaghat Road (tower of silence is situated), 48
Belnos, Madam S.C.
Belur Math, 205
Belvedere (former Vice-Regal Lodge), 177
Benares, 47
Bengal Oils, 73
Bengal Secretariat, 143
Bengal, 30, 32, 33, 34, 35, 36, 45, 49, 50, 52, 61, 66, 74, 87
    Boy, 37
    Club, 105
    Renaissance, 34
    tiger, 220
    West, 193
    young, 34
Bengali Durga, 24, 31
Bengali, 24, 33, 35, 36, 37, 45, 46, 49, 97, 188
    festivals, 167
    foods, 117
    Nationalists, 30
    neighbourhoods, 82
    sports fan, 86
    Writers, 31
Bengali-Harijans (untouchables), 45
Bentinck, 155
Bepin Behari Ganguly Street, 156
bekti (sea-fish), 117
Bhadeshwar, 29`
Bhadreswar, 207
Bhagirat (son of Brahma), 215
Bhai Phonta, 101
bhang (paste made of cannabis indica leaves), 179

Bhanjaras, 50
bhapa doi (steamed yogurt), 118
Bharatnayam (form of dance), 103
bhel puri (*batata puri*), 120
Bho, 197
Bhoga Mandap, 196
Bhubaneshwar, 197
Bhutan (Eastern, Western, Central), 233, 234, 235
Bhutanese Monastery, 231
Bichitra Bhawan, 158
Bihar, 32, 35, 46, 47, 195, 225
   Sharif (capital of Bihar), 48
Biharis, 46, 47, 48
Birch Hill, 231
Birla Academy of Art and Culture, 132, 181, 186
Birla House (House of Birlas headquarters), 143
Birla Industrial and Technological Museum, 182
Birla Planetarium, 148
Birlas (Marwari family), 37, 47
biryani, 119
Black hole of Calcutta, 30, 141
Black Town, 131, 132
Bodhgaya, 196, 227
Bohras, 49
Boishnab Charan Seth, 167
Boitak Khana, 161
Bojaxhim, Agnes Gonzha (Mother Theresa), 67
boli (sacrifice of animals), 178, 179
Bombay, 24, 32, 35
Bomdila Pass, 200
Boro mosh, (festival), 97
Bose Nandalal, 76
   Netagi, 139
Bose, Rash Behari, 36
Bose, Subhas Chandra, 36, 46
Botanical Gardens, 231
Bowanipore, 48
Bowbazar, 162
Brabourne, Sir Michael, 143
Brahma (god of creation), 61, 215
Brahmins, 45
Brahmo, 34, 35
   Sabha, 65
   Samaj, 46, 65, 210
Braque (painter), 76
Britain, 36
British Artists in India (book), 71
British Colonies, 32, 37
British Tea Planters, 90
British, 35, 47
Buddha Jayanti, 99
Buddha, 225, 226, 227
Buddhist University of Nalanda, 225
Budge-Budge, 53
bumisparamudra, 227
Bumthangkha, 234
Burdwan, 193
Burma, 37, 50, 52
Burmese Pagoda, 167

C

Cachar, 90
Cairo, 24
Calcutta University, 24, 34, 161
Calligraphy, 81
Canada, 52

Carey, William, 34
camera obscura, 72
Carmichael Cup (polo), 91
Cassimbazar, 29
Central Municipal Offices, 155
Chandernagore, 31, 151, 193, 207, 208
Chandni Chowk, 48, 119
Charass, 46
Charnock, Job, 29, 45, 63, 143
Chartered Bank, 142
Chater, Paul, 50
   (became Governor of HongKong)
Chatterjee, Bankim Chandra, 24, 34
Chawan (form of polo), 90
Chaugan, 90
cheechees (half-cast women), 32
Cherrapunji (wettest place in the world), 200
chhana (curded milk), 118, 119
Chhatawala gully, 155
Chhor Bagan, 158
Chhotanagpur Plateau, 45, 196
China trade, 32, 33, 35, 38, 52
China, 38, 50, 52
   Chinese, 52
   Chinatown, 52, 53
   Chinese New Year, 98
Chinese Consulate, 184
Ching Ming, 98
Chinsurah, 29, 50, 151, 193, 209
Chintamoni, Kar, 78
Chittagong, 29, 35
chogyal, 232
Cholera, 23, 31
chorten, 238
Chowdhury, Sabarna Roy, 29
   Family, 178
Chowrasta, 231
Chowringhee, 48
Chowringhee, Lane, 49
Chowringhee Mansions (El Hadj Mansions), 146
Christians, 49, 61
Christmas, 101
Churches
   Church of England, 143
   Our Lady of Bandel, 210
   Our Lady of the Rosary Cathedral, 49, 156, 168
   Sacred Heart Church, 49
   St. Andrew's, 142
   St. John's, 30
   St. Paul's Cathedral, 146, 148
   The Armenian Holy Church of Nazareth, 50, 168
   United Church of North India, 49
Churchill, Sir Winston, 23
Cinema, 104
City Hall, 144
City of Palaces (Calcutta), 23, 33
Claudius, Leslie, 89
Clive, Robert, 31, 32, 45, 137, 159
Clubs
   300 Club, 37
   Bengal, 37
   Calcutta, 34, 37, 106
   Chambers, 106
   Conclave, 106
   Cricket, 34
   Dum Dum Golfing, 99
   Football, 87, 88, 182
   Fort William, 106

Ladies Golf, 106
Mohun Bangan Football club, 88
Polo, 99, 106, 138
Rowing, 106
Royal Calcutta Golf, 34, 89, 106, 151
Royal Calcutta Racing Club, 138
Saturday, 106
Silchar Kanjai, 90
Swimming, 106
Tollygunge, 37, 106
Turf, 34
Cockfight (painting by Zoffany), 72
Coco Islands, 37
Col. Polier and his friends (painting), 72
College Street, 161
Colony of Rats, 139
Company Servants ('writers'), 31, 32
Congress Party, 38
coolies, 46, 52
Copenhagen, 34
Cottage Industries Emporium, 113
crimes passionels, 74
cult of idols, 34
Curzon, Lord, 35, 147
  Park, 139
Cuttack, 199
Cuttackis, 48
cyclones, 23

D

Daiku (Japanese form of polo), 90
dakrunners, 215
Dakshinapan (shopping enclave), 111
Dakshineshwar, 205
dal (lentils), 118
Dalhousie Square, (name after Lord Dalhousie, first Governor of Bengal), 140
Damodar River, 52
Danes, 29
Daniell, 72
  Thomas
  William
Danish University, 34
Darijhals, 218
Darjeeling, 231
darshan, 217
darwanis (door-keepers), 46
Das, Chittaranjan (Mayor of Calcutta), 36, 46
dashabhuja, 62
de Rozio, Henry, 34
Dead Telephones (memorial), 23, 142
Deb, Raja Naba Kissen, 31, 46, 62, 131, 159
Deben Bhattacharga, 67
Dehli, 38
deities, 35
Delta of the Ganges, 195
demon, 31
Deorali, 232
Derozio, Louis Vivian, 34
Deul, 197, 199
Devanagari, 82
Dewani rights, 32
dewans, 45
Dhaka, 35
Dhauli Hill, 198
dhokra, 113

dhotis, 46, 111, 160
Diamond Harbour, 216
Didarganj Vakshi, 225
Digamber Jains, 48
dim sum, 156
Dimapur, 200
Diwali, 47, 101, 168
Dochula, 238
Dogs in a Landscape (painting), **73**
Dol Purnima, 98
dosa (rice flour pancake), 119
Doyly, Sir Charles, 72
Drake, Governor, 30
Druk Yul, 233
Drukpas, 234, 236
Dubdi, 233
duels, 31
Dum Dum
  airport, 36, 53
  golfing club, 89
Durga (symbol of prosperity and victory over evil), 61, 62
Durga Puja, 31, 62, 97, 100, 117, 159, 160, 178
durries, 111
Dusserah (festival), 48, 138
Dutch, 29, 30
Dutta, Michael Madhusudan, 24, 34, 151
Dzongs (fortresses), 237
Dzongkha, 234
Dzongri, 232, 233

E

East India Company, 29, 32, 46, 50, 62, 143, 167
Eastern Railways, 142
Eden Gardens, 167
  Cricket Stadium (Mecca of Indian Cricket), 168
Eden Hindu Hostel, 161
education, 24, 34
  English system, 24
Eglise du Sacré Coeur, 209
Emden (German cruiser), 37
Emporiums (shopping)
  Assam State, 112
  Cottage Industries Emporium, 113
  Gujarati Emporium, 110
  Gurjari, (Gujarati State), 111
  Manjusha, (Bengal State), 111
  Partridge, (Haryana), 111
  Phulkari (Punjab), 112
  Poompuhar, (Tamil Nadu), 111
  Pumposh (Kashmir State), 112
  Rajusthan, (Rajusthan State), 111
  Tantuja, (Bengal State), 111
  Tantushri, (Bengal State), 111
  Tripura State, 112
  Utkalika (Orissa State), 112
  Weaver, (Haryana), 111
Empress of India (Queen Victoria), 33, 148
  see Victoria, Queen
English Bazar, 29
eri (shawls), 112
Esplanade Mansions, 139
Establissements Français en Inde, 208
European, 23, 31, 32
  culture, 34
  population, 31

women, 32
Everest, Mount, 231
Evil Eye, 50
Ezra Cup (for polo), 91

F

Falta, 30, 38
fengshui, 184
firni, 119, 120
Five Star Market, 171
Five-Point Crossing, 160
Forest Lodge, 218
Fort St. George, 31
Fort William, 29, 30, 32, 137, 138
Fort William College, 24, 34
Foster, Sir William, 71
Fraser, James, 72
Frasergunge (fishing village), 216
free trade, 34
Fujianese, 52

G

galatea (British ship), 87
Gandhi,
    Indira, 101
    Rajiv, 38
    The Mahatma, 37, 47, 77, 78, 80
Gandhi Rajiv (former Prime Minister of India), 38
Gandhi, The Mahatma, 37, 47, 77, 78, 80
Ganesh (God of Wealth, son of Goddess Parvati), 62, 98
    Ganesh Charthurthi (festival), 100
Ganga Jhol (water from the ganges), 167
Ganga Sagar Mela, 97, 195
Gangtok (capital of Sikkim), 232
Ganin, 221
Gaur, 193
Gaya, 226
George V, (King), 36
Germany, 36
ghazal (classical music), 104
ghee (clarified butter), 118
Ghosh, Rasbihari (nationalist), 35
Gitinitya, 103
Glenary's (cafe), 231
Goanese, 49
Gobindapur, 29
Goenkas, 47
Gokhole, Gopal Krishna, 24
gomasthas, 46
Gopal Mandir, 180
Gosaba, 219, 220
Gothi Bengan (real Calcuttan), 45
Gothi food, 117
Government House (Raj Bhawan), 23, 33
Government of India, 33
Government of West Bengal, 30
Governor-General, 32, 33, 35
GPO, 141
graffitti art, 80, 82
Graham's Homes, Dr. (boarding school), 231
Grand Durbar, 33
Great Eastern Hotel (famous landmark), 140
Greeks, 29

Grey Town, 131, 132
Gridhrakuta, 226
Guangdong (province in South China), 53
Gujaratis, 33, 49, 111
Gupta, Prodosh Das, 78
Gurkhas, 98
Guru Nanak, 48
guru, 50, 64
Gurusaday Museum, 74, 184
Gyalwa Karmapa, 232
Gypsies, 50

H

Habeeb Mullick (curios), 231
Hakkas (tanners and shoemakers), 52, 53
Haldia, 38
Hamilton, Dr (surgeon), 30
Hare Krishna, 64
harems, 210
Haripura Posters (commissioned by Mahatma Ghandi), 77
Hastings House, 151, 177
Hati Bagan, 155
hawa ghar (covered shelter), 231
High Court, 33, 144
hijras (eunuchs), 47, 50
Himalayan Mountaineering Institute, 231
Himalayan Zoo, 231
Hindu, 24
    religion, 35
    values, 36
Hinduism (religion dominated by male gods), 61, 217, 235
Hindustan International Hotel, 184
Hindustan Motors (first car factory in India), 37
Hodges, William (painter), 71
Holi (festival), 48, 98
Holumba, 231
Halwell Monument (to the victims of the Black Hole), 143
Hooghly, 21, 30, 46, 49, 52, 131, 132, 150, 177, 205, 210
    Hooghly Heritage, 205
    Second Hooghly Bridge, 171
hookah (water pipe for opium smoking), 32, 46
Hore, Somenath (painter), 78
Hosie Alec, 87
Howrah, 30, 49
    Bridge, 169
Howrah Station, 169
Huen, Tsang, 52
Hussain (founder of the Shiite sect), 49

I

Idulfitr (festival), 49, 102, 139
illegal trade, 33
Imperial Capital, 33, 34
India trade, 32, 33
India, 23, 24, 34, 36, 52, 61
Indian
    Association, 24
    citizen, 67
    classical music, 102
    Congress, 24

Council Act, 33
groups, 37
Independence, 46
Museum, 33, 145, 146
Indo-China, 38
Indra Jayanti, 101
Institute of Tibetology, 232
International Society for Krishna Consciousness, 64
Ispahan, 50

J

Jaffar, Mir, 31
Jagamohana, 196, 199
Jagannath (festival), 65, 99
Temple, 198
jaggery (brown sugar), 119
Jain temples, 160
Jalkabar (mid-morning meal), 118
Jamshedpur, 196
Janmashtami, 99
Jaital Deul, 218
Japan, 36, 76
Jatadwip Island, 218
Jatra, 104
Jenkins, Sir Owen, 105
Jesuits, 34, 184
Jews Iraqi, 33, 50
Afghanistan, 33
Ashkenaz, 50
Jhapan (festival), 194
Jhogra Kothi, 157
John's, St. 33
joint-ventures, 33
Jones, Sir William, 34
Joransako, 157

K

Kabulis (money lenders), 50
Kobiraj (cutlet covered with egg), 119
Kabul, 45
Kaesthos (caste of scribes, doctors and professors), 45
Kagyet, 232
Kali Bari (Lake), 181
Kali Pujas, 24, 47, 63, 184
Kali, Rakshaya (Goddess Kali), 62, 63, 74, 97, 112, 179
temple, 132, 178
Kalighat, 30, 46, 74, 77, 132, 178, 179, 184
Market, 112
Kalika Puranas, 62
Kalimpong, 231
Kalishetra, 30
Kamakhya Mandir, 200
Kanchenjunga, 231, 232
kantha (quilts), 77, 113, 184
Kanto, Radha (son of Nobo Kissen), 160
Kapila (an incarnation of Vishnu), 215, 217
Kartitik Purnima, 225
Kashmir, 90
Kaziranga Game Reserve, 200
Kechiperi, 233
Kendulbilwa, 195

Kerala, 45
Kettle, Tilly (British painter), 71
Keventers (milk bar), 231
Khadi, 46
Khandagiri, 198
Khan Kublai, 90
Khan, Ali Vardi, 30, 31
Khan, Ghulam Ali, 73
Khana Buddos, 50
Khejuri, 215
Khols (waterways), 217, 218
Khorasan, 50
Khorgho, 63
Kiel, 34
Kipling, 23
Klikata Village, 30
Kohima, 200
Kolikata, 29
Konarak, 199
Kumartuli, 172
Kunming (port in China), 37
Kuomingtang (schools and clubs), 53
Kurtas, 111, 231
Kurtoekha, 234
Kushtia (a form of wrestling), 89
Kirtan,
Padabali, 103
Kyichu Lhakhang, 237

L

La Martiniere College, 183
La Martiniere School, 34
Laddu (sweetmeats), 157
Lake, Salt, 38
salt water, 31
Lakshmi (goddess of fortune), 61, 63, 98
narayan temple, 182
Lal Bazar, 155
Lalita Giri, 199
lamas, 232
Longfield, Tom, 87
Lascar War Memorial, 171
Les Hindous, 72
Liberti, Eaglite, Fraternite (motto of the French Republic), 207
lingam, 194
linguae francae (Persian, Portuguese), 32
Lissanevitch, Boris (a white Russian emigrant), 37
Literature and Poetry
Bengali, 24
Bangla, 34
Loktak Lake, 200
London, 29, 32, 33
London Cenotaph, 139
loochis (bread), 118
Loreto College, 151
Lucknow, 48

M

Ma Bono Bibi (Goddess of the Forest), 221
Macaulay, Thomas Bubington, 34
Macchuabazar, 157
Madras, 30, 32
Maghen David Synagogue, 50

Magnum Opus, (mural), 78
Maharaja of Cooch Behar, 66
Mahatma Jayanti (Ghandi's Anniversary), 100
Mahavira Jayanti, 48, 99
Mahavira, Lord, 48
Maidan, 31, 36, 48, 49, 86, 89, 119, 120, 137, 138
Maijhilpur, 217
Majumdar Nirode, 78
Makar Sankranti (festival), 97, 217
Mela
  Baul, 195
  Gangasagar, 217
  Hindu, 137
  Karashilpa, 158
  Kasta, 194
  Maidan, 137
  Pushkar, 196
  Sonepur, 196, 225
malaria, 31, 137
Malaya, 38
Malda, 193
Mall, 231
Mahisasura (demon), 62
mandir (Bengali temple), 180
Manipur, 103, 200
manipuri (dance), 103
  Martial Arts, 103
Manzil, Vijay, 177
Maratha Ditch, 30
Marathas, 30
Marble Palace, 158, 159
Markandeyesvara Mandir, 197
Markets (shopping)
  see Air-Conditioned Market, 110
  see Dakshinapan, 111
  see Kalighat, 112
  see Masala, 111
  see Treasure Island, 110
  see Vaibhan Shopping Complex, 110
  see Vardaan, 110
Marwaris, 33, 37, 47, 119
Murshidabad, 31, 32, 48, 193
Martin, Maj-Gen Claude, 34, 72
Marxism, 45
masala, 119
Masjid, Tippu Sultan, 145
Mahakal Mandir, 231
Mawphluang (barren plateau), 200
May Day, 99
Mayapur, 64, 193
  Sri (temple), 65
Meghalaya, 200
Metiaburuz (Shiite neighborhood), 49, 170
Military Burial ground, 151
Military Secretariat, 139
Minto, Lord (Viceroy), 159
Missionaries of Charity, 67
mishti doi (sweet yogurt), 118
Mitra, Ashoke, 24
Mizaram, 193
moccha (banana flower), 117
Modern dance, 104
Moghs (best cooks), 50
Moghul Emperor, 30
Mohun Bagan Football Club, 88
Mongolia, 90
monopoly, 32, 33, 37
Monsoon, 23

moori (puffed rice tossed with mustard oil), 118, 120
muga, 112
Mughal, 75
Mughlai Food, 119
Muharram, 49, 170
Mukhopadhyay, Binode Behari (famous for his murals), 78
Mukkerjee,
  Ajoy, 38
  Meera, 78
Munshees, 45
Murkande Yesvara Mandir, 197
Museums
  see Victoria and Albert Museum, (London), 74
  see Gurusaday Museum, 74
  see Indian, 132
mutiny, 33
Mymensigh, 35
Mysore Gardens, 180

N

"**Netaji**" (the leader), 36, 97, 102
  House, 184
nabe mil ke cha (strong tea), 120
Nagaland, 200
Nagis, 197
Nakhoda Masjid, 162
Nalanda, 196
Narayangunge, 37
Nata Mandir, 196
National Geographic, 145
Natyanatga, 103
nauch girls (usually courtesans), 32
Nawab Asaf-ud-Daula, 72
Nawab of Bengal, 29, 30, 50
Nawadip, 193
neel kothi, 132, 180
Nehru, Jawaharlal (a former Indian Prime Minister), 80, 145
Nepalese (usually door-keepers), 50
Netaji, Subhas Road (formerly Clive Road), 141
New Market (Sir Stuart Hogg Market), 110, 145, 155
New Testament, 207
New Year's Day, 97
New Zealand, 50
newspapers
  English Language, 34
Ngalong, 234
Nilhat House, 143
Nimtola Ghat, 171
Nirmal Hridoy Manzil (Mother Theresa's house for the poor and destitute), 179
Nizam Palace, 184
Nobel Prize, 35, 67
  Peace (*see* **Bojaxshim** Agnes Gonzha), 67
  Literature (*see* **Tagore**, Rabindranath), 35
Novoborsho, 101
North America, 32
North Point, 231
Numdas (shawls), 112

O

Oberoi Grand Hotel, 146
Oberon, Merle (movie actress, Anglo-Indian), 49
objet d'art, 46
Old China Bazar, 168
Omar Resort, 216
Oostende Company, 29
opium, 32, 35, 36, 46, 48, 156, 206, 208
    exports, 32
    trade, 32, 48
    ventures, 32
Order of British India, 34
Odissi (classical dance of Orissa), 103
Oriental
    languages, 34
    scenery (engravings), 72
Orissa, 32, 35, 50, 196
Oriyas, 50
Orthodox Hindu, 34, 47
    traditions, 34
Otcherlony Monument, 49
Oxford Bookshop, 231

P

"Partner in Empire", 32
paan (areca-nut), 118, 120
pabda kakkra (hardshelled crabs), 117
paladas (the one who conducts rituals), 179
palangtod paan, 120
Palki, 156
Pandim, 232
panch-ratna, 180
pantua, 119
papadum (crispy wafer), 118
Parasnath Hills, 47, 196
Parganas (rice growing area on the East Bank of Hooghly), 31
Park Street (named after Sir Elijah Impey's deer park), 148
Parliament, 32
Paro Valley, 237
Parsee, 33, 47, 48
Partridge (Haryana Emporia), 111
Parvati (consort of Shiva), 61, 62
Patna, 47, 195, 225, 227
patnas, 74
patola (vegetable dye-prints), 111
pats, 46, 74, 113, 179, 180, 184
Paul's St., 33
peekey putts (clay cups), 120
Pemayangtse, 232, 233
Persia, 50
Peshawar, 48
Phalut, 231
Philippines, 38
philosopher, *see* **Roy**, Ram Mohan, 34
phool (mango mousse), 119
Phodang, 232
Phulkari (embroidery on bed covers and cushions), 112
Picasso (Spanish painter), 76
pigtails, 52
pitha (pilgrimage shrine), 178, 179
political

figures, 24
life, 24
leadership, 24
Poompuhar (The Tamil Nadu Emporium), 111
Port Canning, 218
porte cochere, 158
Portuguese, 29
Prabhupada Swami, 64, 65
printing (Bibles, books), 34
Private Trade, 32
proclamation, 33
Prussians, 29
puchka, 120
puchkawallas (hawkers), 119
puja (offering to the presiding deity), 97, 132, 221
    Shitola, 99
    Charak, 98
    Chhat, 46, 101, 167
    Jagad hatri, 101
    Lakshmi, 97, 100, 167
    Manasha, 100, 167, 194
    pandal, 90, 100
    Kali, 100, 167
    Vishna Karma, 100
Punjab, 48
    Bhawan, 48
Puratani, 103
purdah, 167
Puri, 198

R

Rabindra, Jayanti, 99
    Sangeet, 103
    Bharati Museum, 158
    Bharati University, 158
    Mancha, 158
    Sadhan, 148
    Sarani, 155
Raja Basanta Roy (a play), 160
Rajasthali (The Rajasthan State Emporia), 111
Rajasthan, 33, 37, 47, 48
Rajghir, 196, 225
Rajput, 75
Raktaviya, 63
Ramakrishna Math, 24, 35, 66, 98,
Ramakrishna Mission Institute of Culture, 181
Ranji Trophy (for cricket), 87
Rath Yatra (festival), 99
Rathayatra (chariot festival), 65
Ravan, 48
refugees, 23, 30, 45
religion
    Brahmajism, 24
    Buddhism, 24, 48
    Christianity, 49, 61
    Hinduism, 61, 217, 235
Republic Day, 97
Rishra, 29
rituals, 24, 46
rossogolla (sweets), 118, 119, 172
Roy, Jamini, 77
Roy, Dr. B.C., 38
Roy, Raja Mun Mohun, 46
Roy, Ram Mohan, 34
Royal Bengal Tiger (main attraction), 177, 220
Royal Charter, 34

Royal Durbar, 36
Royal Stock Exchange, 142
rui maccher jhol (carp cooked in cummin and other spices), 118
Rumania, 50
Rumtek Monastery, 232

S

"sleeping dictionaries" (local mistresses), 32
Sagol Kangjei (*sagol*-horse) (*kang*-ball, *jei*-stick) (polo), 90
Saidabad, 29
Sajnakhali Bird Sanctuary, 219
  Tourist Lodge, 219
sal moori, 120
salpetre, 32, 35, 206
Salwar Kameez (cushion covers), 111
Samadhi, 180
Sandakphu, 231
sandesh (pastry moulds), 118, 119, 184
Sandheads, 215
Sanskrit, 46 college, 161
Santiniketan, 77, 194, 195
Saravasti (goddess of learning), 62, 63
Sargardwip Island, 215
sati, 210
Scots, 32, 33
Sechuan, 32
Sen, P. (son of Santosh), 38, 78
Serampore, 29, 151, 193, 206
  Press, 34
servant, civil, 34
Sewerage system, 34
Shabdrung, 236, 238
Shah, Hezat Wajid Ali, 170
Shahbani Begum Mosque, 184
Shaheed Minar (Ochterlony Monument), 139
Shaktism, 61
Shaktis, 61, 63, 100
Shanghai, 24
Shanghainese, 52
Sharchops, 235
Shibpur Botanical Gardens, 170
Shiites (muslim sect), 49
shillong, 200
Shitola, (the 'cooling one' – goddess of the monsoon and small-pox), 63
Shiva (the destroyer), 61, 62, 63, 64
Shivalingam (shrine), 178
Shivarati, 98
Shobha Bazar, 159
Shova Jatra, 65
Shyambazar, 160
Sibsagar, 200
Sikh *dhaba*, 120
Sikhs, 48
Sikkim, 231
silk, 32, 112
Silk Road, 50, 52
Silver, 32, 46
Singapore, 36, 50
Singhanias, 47
Singhara, 118
Singla Bazar, 231
Siraj-ud-Daula, 30, 31, 62
Siyar, Farruck (Moghul Emperor), 30

Skinner, C.H., 87
slums, 23
Societies (learned), 34
  see Asiatic Society, 34
Solvyns, Balthazar (Belgian painter), 72
Son et lumiere, 158, 199
Sonaguchi, 160
Sonapatti, 157
Sondesh, 119
South American, 32
South Eastern Railways, 170
South Lodge, 151
South Park Street Cemetery, (the oldest one the remains), 148, 150
  Scottish Cemetery, 151
South-East Asia, 50
Spain, 32
Sports, 86
  cricket
  equestrian
  golf
  hockey
  polo
  rugby
  soccer
  squash
  tennis
Sqraffito (Italian style), 142
St. Paul's (London), 141
Stephen, Arathoon (owned the Grand Hotel in Calcutta; set up Raffles Hotel in Singapore and Eastern and Oriental in Penang), 50
Stephen's House, 143
Subramanyam, K.G. (disciple of Benode Behari), 78
Suez Canal, 35, 36
sukto (diced and fried vegetables), 118, 119
Sun Yat-Sen, 53
  street, 53
Sunderbans, 219, 220
Sunni (Muslims), 47, 48
Supreme and Unique God, 34, 44
Supreme Court, 33
Sutanuti, 29, 131, 172
Sydney Cricket Ground, 87
Svetamber (sect), 48

T

Tadzong, 237
Tagore
  Castle, 157
  Thakurbari, 157
  Villa, 205
Tagore
  Abanindranath (nephew), 76
  Gaganendranath (elder brother), 76
  Rabindranath, 24, 35, 66, 76, 77, 78
Taiwan, 36, 53
Taj Bengal, 177
takin, 238
Taksang, 237
taktaposh (low padded divans), 157
Tamils, 49
Tamralipti (now Tamluk), 52
Tan, Yun-Shan, 24
tandoor, 119

Tangra (Chinatown in Calcutta), 53
Tantuja, 111
Tantushri (Bengal State Emporia), 111
Taoist temple, 53, 184
tarka (*dal* fried with eggs), 120
Tarkeshwar, 194
Tashichhodzong, 238
Tashi View Point, 232
Tashiding, 233
Tata, Jameshed, 48
Tawang Monastery, 200
taxes, 32
Teesta Bazar, 231
tempera, 74
textiles, 29
Thakur (God of fertility), 64
thakur dalan, 158
thali (silver or aluminium plate), 117, 119
Thana House, 151
Tharpa Choling Monastery, 231
The Calcutta Group (young painters), 78
The Chinese Journal of India, 53
The Company School, 73
The Hong Kong and Shanghai Banking Corp, 141
The Last Supper (painting), 72
The Sanskrit, 207
Thimphu, 233, 238
Tibetan, 98
Tiger Hill, 231
Tippu Sultan, 151
Tiretta Bazar, 53, 155
Tolly's Nullah, 177
Tollygunge Club, 37, 180
Tongsa Penlop (Governor), 236
Tongsa, 238
trade, 30
   see China trade, 32
   see illegal trade, 33
   see India trade, 32, 33
   see Opium trade, 32
   see Private trade, 32
traders
   Armenian, 29
   European, 29
   Prussian, 29
trading rights, 32
tram way-line (horse-drawn), 34
Travels to the Moghul Empire (book by Bernier), 220
Treasure Island Market, 110
Tripura, 200
Tripura State Emporium, 112
Tsuklakhang, 232
Tulapatti, 157

U

U.S.A., 52
U.S.S.R. 36
Udayagiri, 198
Uluberia, 29
Union Francaise, 208
United Services Club (Geological Survey of India), 146
Universal Dictionary of Thirteen Indian Languages, 207
Universities
   see Calcutta University, 34
   see Danish University, 34

V

Vaibhan Shopping Complex, 110
Vardaan Market, 110
Varma, Ravi (Indias first painter), 75
verandahs, 33
viceroy, 33, 35
Victoria and Albert Museum, 74
Victoria Memorial Hall (Calcutta), 48, 71, 146, 147
Victoria, Queen, 33, 147
Views in the Himal Mountains (painting), 72
Viharas, 225
Virginia House, 148
Vishnu (the preserver), 61, 62
Vishnupur, 194
Vishvakarma Puja, 64
Vivekananda, 35, 97

W – X

wonton, 156
"writers" (Company Servants), 31, 32
   building, 33, 141
Western
   academician, 75
   classical dance, 103
   classical music, 102
   clothes, 46
   genres, 34
   ideas, 45, 46
   influences, 45
   liberal ideas, 45
   modern music, 102
   novels, 34
   pop music, 113
   style, 71
   technic, 74
   values, 35
Wallahs, 52
Wandiphodrang, 238
Waterfront, **132**
Watson, Admiral Charles, 31
Weaver (The Haryana Emporium), 111
Wellesley, Lord, 23
West Bengal Archaeological Museum, 184
White Town (formerly Kalikata), 131, 132
Xavier's College, St (Jesuit College), 184

Y – Z

Yang, Tai-Chew (tea-trader), 52, aka Ah-Chi
Yongle (Ming Emperor), 52
Yunnan, 32, 52, 90
Zoffany, John (painter of the 'Last Supper'), 71, 72, 143, 147
Zakaria Street, 162
Zamindari, 29, 32, 50
Zamindars, 45.
Zheng He, (Chinese admiral), 52
Zoological Gardens, 177